Honest Graft

Honest Graft

Big Money
and the
American
Political Process

Brooks Jackson

ALFRED A. KNOPF *New York* *1988*

THIS IS A BORZOI BOOK
PUBLISHED BY ALFRED A. KNOPF, INC.

Copyright © 1988 by Brooks Jackson

Library of Congress Cataloging-in-Publication Data
Jackson, Brooks.
Honest graft.
Includes index.
1. Campaign funds—United States. 2. Political
action committees—United States. 3. Coelho, Tony.
I. Title.
JK1991.J28 1988   324.7′8′0973   88-45323
ISBN 0-394-56452-9

Manufactured in the United States of America

FIRST EDITION

For Betty and Dean Jackson

Contents

Honest Graft

Introduction

Congressman Tony Coelho is looking me in the eye across the white tablecloth as we lunch in the "members only" dining room in the House of Representatives. "I'm going to treat you like staff," he says. "You'll see everything we do."

It is an odd bargain the congressman and I are making, and a risky one for him. He looks at me the way a mongoose might regard a cobra, confident but wary. We are natural enemies, by Washington's normal standards. I am an investigative reporter for the *Wall Street Journal,* specializing in covering money in politics. Coelho specializes in raising money, and spending it by the millions to elect Democrats to the House of Representatives. He is the Democratic representative from California's largely agricultural 15th District.

He runs a modern-day political machine, a sort of New Tammany Hall in which money and pork-barrel legislation have become the new patronage. It is the Democratic Congressional Campaign Committee, currently in the midst of early preparations for the 1986 House elections. As we talk, the congressman and I, it is the spring of the year and election day itself is still many months away. He is agreeing to give me regular access to the committee's inner workings. My part of the bargain is to hold off writing about what I learn until after the election is over and the information can't harm candidates.

I've reported on his committee before, but only from the outside. I know that much of his money comes from lobbyists and special-interest groups trying to sway public policy—bankers, the real-estate lobby, subsidy-hungry maritime unions, the American Medical Association, the trucking industry, auto and textile unions demanding protection from foreign imports. He gathers millions more in "soft money," which would be illegal if given directly to a candidate's campaign committee. It pours through a variety of loopholes in the federal laws that are supposed to regulate and restrict it, under the tolerant watch of election-law enforcers who serve the politicians, not the public. This soft money comes from labor unions using members' dues, from rich people who give more than the law allows in federal elections, and even from businesses making donations from their corporate treasuries. Much of it is given in secret, so voters won't know who is paying.

The congressman is proud of what he has built. He's managed to frustrate Republican hopes of capturing control of the House, despite the GOP's overwhelming financial superiority. Coelho is given much credit for that, yet he feels people don't understand him or the institution he has created from practically nothing. This will be his third and last election as chairman of the committee. He portrays himself as a sort of missionary, a political Robin Hood, taking campaign money from the rich and using it to build a financially secure party to help the poor. In the many conversations to follow, he will speak of his "burn" to help the needy. Although he pretends not to care, it obviously pains him that colleagues openly suspect he has compromised personal integrity to raise his millions in campaign donations. "They don't understand what I do," he says, more than once.

He once aspired to be a priest, but his critics now fear he's selling his party's soul to business interests. It isn't hard to see why. Coelho talks of politics itself as a "business." He fights to retain tax breaks for oil and gas drillers. Among his major financial backers, I will discover, are a multimillionaire grain merchant who was a central figure in the Koreagate scandal of the late 1970s, the boss of the crime-ridden Teamsters' union, a scandal-ridden Wall Street firm, and a Texas wheeler-dealer under federal grand-jury investigation.

He pressures business lobbyists for campaign money in ways that sometimes amount to intimidation. In the months to come I will watch as he takes a hand in killing a bill that would require public disclosure of his secret soft-money donors. While I won't see Coelho commit any clear, deliberate violations of law or regulations, he does things that will eventually cause him embarrassment. He is openly ambitious, and running hard for election to the post of Majority Whip, the number-three spot in the House leadership. One moment he is the kindly padre, the next moment a cold-blooded Machiavelli. What a delightful puzzle.

I find, as we finish our lunch, just what a paradoxical blend of idealism and tough practicality he is. He is being unbelievably open. Though I will later gain access to some sensitive meetings on the Republican side, Coelho's frankness and willingness to reveal himself and his political operation flabbergast me. He even grants my request to get copies of the written reports that his key aides give him each week. In fact, the copies I will receive will contain his own written comments and orders to his staff. This is more than I had dared to hope for. What I'll have is a documentary record of the committee's inner workings during the climactic months of the 1986 elections.

Then the contradiction: in exchange for such honesty, I must agree to a deception. The only ones who are to know

I'm getting the material are the committee's executive director, the press spokesman, and perhaps one or two assistants who do the copying. The congressman doesn't want his other aides to know that I'm reading their confidential memoranda.

"I don't want them writing the reports for you so they'll look good for the book," he says. "I want them to be writing for me. So if anyone asks you if you are seeing the weeklies, I want you to say no." Giving some wishy-washy evasion won't do. "I want you," he says, "to lie."

I hesitate. News reporters like to think they have a mission to *expose* lies. But I can't deny the logic of his demand. I don't want his aides grandstanding for my benefit any more than he does. To get the truth, I must lie, if necessary.

"O.K.," I say.

With that, we seal our bargain. I have the feeling I'm being let in on a conspiracy.

1

"Why Money Is Important"

I acknowledge that you can't keep an organiza-
tion together without patronage. Men ain't in
politics for nothin'. They want to get somethin'
out of it.
*   But there is more than one kind of patronage.*
                —GEORGE WASHINGTON PLUNKITT,
                    DEMOCRATIC LEADER OF THE
                        I5TH ASSEMBLY DISTRICT,
                    NEW YORK CITY, I905

Tony Coelho sat at the head of a conference table rimmed by his top staff aides in a glass-walled room in the Democratic party's new headquarters building, beginning a Monday morning strategy session. Outside, visible through the fan-shaped leaves of a ginkgo tree stirring in a warm June breeze, could be seen the twin smokestacks of a grimy heating plant. The stately Capitol was out of view, three blocks to the north.

Coelho was starting another week of chasing money. He pursued it not for personal gain, though he lived comfortably enough with the help of personal-appearance fees from lobbyists. He solicited money for the power it purchased, power for his party and for himself. Like the old machines that dominated big-city politics in the era before civil-service jobs and television, Coelho's machine ran on patronage. The old system used municipal jobs and contracts; Coelho's patronage was the federal government's array of

subsidies, entitlements, tax breaks, and commercial regulation. The machines were paid directly in votes or in electioneering labor by government employees. Coelho's operation reaped money, which he converted to votes through the
acquisition of what he called "political technology"—polling, television advertising, and computer-driven mail.

Like the Tammanys of old, Coelho's machine gave incumbents a firm grip on their jobs and reduced the political
opposition to frustrated impotence. It viewed attempts at
reform with suspicion. Meanwhile, the House remained a
soil where scandals sprang up like weeds. But where the old
bosses held sway in a single city or county, Coelho's machine straddled the entire nation.

Coelho had already read a thick sheaf of weekly reports
from his staff. His finance director, Terence McAuliffe, reported that now, barely midway through 1986, the committee had taken in nearly $2 million. Roughly two-thirds of
that was from rich donors, lobbyists, and political action
committees, or PACs, run mainly by labor unions, corporations, and business and professional groups. About one-
third had come through the mail from rank-and-file Democrats sending in small donations. That $2 million was only
the "hard money" raised according to the strictures of the
federal election law, which among its many intricate provisions limited party organizations to taking no more than
$20,000 per year from any one person, or $15,000 per year
from any PAC, and required that donations be fully disclosed. Coelho could use hard money, in amounts also limited by law, for donations to House candidates or for paying
their campaign bills, and for meeting the operating expenses of the campaign committee.

Besides the hard money, however, McAuliffe reported
that the committee also had received more than $600,000 in
soft money from union treasuries, rich backers, and some
corporations, sources that technically made it illegal to use
the money directly in connection with federal elections. But
the law was so full of loopholes and so poorly enforced that

Coelho easily used these additional funds to help elect Democrats to the House. Furthermore, much of the income and expenditure of soft money wouldn't have to be disclosed.

McAuliffe was projecting a good haul from a weekend trip during which Coelho planned to parade Speaker Thomas P. "Tip" O'Neill through a series of money-raising events in Los Angeles and San Francisco. O'Neill, the most powerful Democrat in Washington, was Coelho's best draw. Rich donors bought $1,000 tickets to have a drink with the big Irishman.

"We are in good shape in California," McAuliffe wrote in his report. "We should bring back $350,000–$400,000. I will be out there all week and I hope to get another $50,000–$75,000 next week."

"Great!" Coelho responded, scribbling on McAuliffe's report. His writing, like everything he did, was punctuated with underlinings and exclamation points.

Much of the California money was coming from the movie and real-estate industries, both of which wanted to preserve some lucrative loopholes in the tax code, which Congress was rewriting. Movie mogul Lew Wasserman, chairman of MCA Corp., and multimillionaire real-estate developer Walter Shorenstein were sponsoring events.

McAuliffe pushed Coelho to try for even more movie money. "Have you had an opportunity to call Jack Valenti?" McAuliffe reminded him. Valenti was president of the Motion Picture Association. "No, because we have Lew Wasserman on board," Coelho responded. "But I will!"

This week, as every week, Coelho would devote time to raising money, spending it, trying to cut off his enemy's supply of it. His quest for money never ceased, in both off years and election years. He understood, better than most of his colleagues, the simple reality that politics had become a capital-intensive enterprise. The campaign-money reforms of the 1970s, far from ending the days when lobbyists furtively passed around sacks of cash, had only brought the traffic in campaign money into the open, given it legal sanction, and turned lobbyists and commercial interests into regular collection agents for lawmakers. Favor seekers paid to gain the ear of members of Congress in the hope of influencing their votes. Understanding that reality, Coelho exploited it with the same exuberance with which he attacked everything else.

This morning Coelho was working, as always, to persuade business lobbyists not to give money to Republican candidates. Coelho's rival, the National Republican Congressional Committee, was planning to raise funds from business groups by exploiting the prestige of President Reagan. The Republican committee invited managers of hundreds of business-sponsored political action committees to a cocktail party with the President at a downtown hotel. For $5,000, two people would be admitted. And for $20,000, four PAC officials could enter an inner sanctum, the "President's Circle," where each could line up for a production-line, souvenir photo with the President. Republicans were figuring that the event could bring in $500,000 or more for twenty-four incumbents whom Coelho hoped to defeat.

Coelho was trying to find a way to scare timid corporate executives away from the event. He wanted to plant a news story suggesting that donors might be in legal trouble. Republicans were calling their event a "bundling party," because they would use a legal trick called bundling to get around donation limits in the federal election law. The law allows a PAC to give only $15,000 per year to party organizations such as the Republican campaign committee. But party officials planned to bundle up the checks and deliver them to the candidates, making sure that the PACs wrote the checks directly to the candidates. That way the money wouldn't pass through the party's bank account and wouldn't count against its limits. This was one of the mildest forms of evasion, but such tricks had become so common that limits on donations and spending had become nearly a dead letter and even the President himself aided the process. Still, some potential Republican donors were nervous.

The GOP committee included a three-page legal opinion with its invitation.

Coelho saw an opening. "I think we have a real PR opportunity here," wrote his press secretary, Mark Johnson. "At the very least, our good friend Fred Wertheimer should not let this one slide by."

Wertheimer was president of Common Cause, a reform group that pushed for limiting PAC donations. Democrats, however, were far more reliant on the special-interest money than Republicans and got their share of criticism from Wertheimer. Coelho didn't really view him as a "good friend"; Johnson's reference was ironic. Johnson also suggested that, rather than arouse Common Cause, the Democrats might throw a bundling party of their own. "We could just copy the idea," he said. Democrats had lifted many Republican fund-raising ideas before. But no Democrat could match Reagan's drawing power with business PACs, and Coelho decided this time to attack rather than imitate.

At first he proposed a press release denouncing the Republicans directly, but was quickly reminded that Democrats lacked the moral standing from which to criticize.

"Should we mention that it's being questioned legally?" he asked his staff.

"But some of our candidates take bundled checks," warned an aide.

Indeed, bundling was invented by a PAC that gave almost exclusively to Democrats, the anti-nuclear Council for a Livable World. A women's group also bundled donations to female Democratic candidates for the Senate. The name of the group was EMILY, which stood for "Early Money Is Like Yeast": it raises the dough. A direct attack on the legality of bundling would backfire, or just be laughed off.

"One party accusing the other of violating the spirit of the law is like the pot calling the kettle," said Martin Franks, Coelho's chief of staff.

Coelho tried it anyway, indirectly. He wrote to Common Cause and to another public-interest group, the Center for Responsive Politics, saying, "I am sure you will agree" that the GOP event "is indeed a violation of the spirit if not the letter of the law." He added, "I hope you also agree that this matter is worthy of your public denunciation."

But Franks was right. Neither reform group would carry Coelho's water. Common Cause simply kept quiet. The Center for Responsive Politics sent a letter to the Republican committee saying that their bundling event seemed to be a violation, but it also questioned Coelho about his own use of soft money. "We would enjoy an opportunity to meet with you and share our insights on this issue," wrote Ellen Miller, the group's executive director. Coelho was collecting soft-money donations as large as $100,000 each to subsidize a television studio to produce campaign commercials. He dropped the matter and the Republican bundling party went off smoothly.

After the Monday strategy session Coelho spent much of the week, as he did every week, at money-raising events for Democratic House candidates. He agreed to be listed as a "co-sponsor" of many of these events. His name was a valuable commodity. At Coelho's insistence, House Democrats had made the chairman of the campaign committee officially part of the "leadership," the powerful circle that included the Speaker, the Majority Leader, the Majority Whip, and the chairman of the Democratic Caucus, to which all House Democrats belonged. The campaign committee chairmanship formerly carried no official rank. That Democrats would elevate it to such lofty official status showed how tightly special-interest money had become intertwined in the process of government. It also helped make Coelho's name a magnet for the dollars of lobbyists; they tended to treat invitations from high-ranking lawmakers as assessments.

In trying to move one rung up the leadership ladder, to the post of Majority Whip, the number-three spot, Coelho handed out money, night after night, courting the support of his Democratic colleagues. Monday he swung by a hotel near the Capitol to drop off a check for $1,000 for Ralph Hall of Texas. It was drawn on Coelho's personal political action committee, the Valley Education Fund, named for California's Central Valley, which contained his congressional district. It wasn't just corporations, unions, trade groups, and ideological crusaders who maintained PACs; ambitious politicians had their own. Sometimes Coelho carried half a dozen white envelopes in his inside jacket pocket, each containing a Valley Education Fund check for $1,000 or more for a colleague or a struggling newcomer.

Tuesday morning Coelho was receiving money. He spoke to a breakfast meeting of the California Cable Television Association, part of an industry that wanted Congress to restrain the power of local governments to regulate rates charged to subscribers. Coelho nailed down a donation of $1,000 to the Valley Education Fund from the group's president, Spencer R. Kalitz of Castro Valley, California. The congressman's personal PAC was filled with such special-interest money.

A few hours later Coelho co-sponsored a fund-raising luncheon for Rep. Edward Feighan of Ohio at a large home near the Supreme Court building, owned by a wealthy liberal, Stewart Mott, heir to a General Motors fortune. Coelho gave another $1,000 from his PAC. Several blocks away at the Democratic Club, a lobbyists' lair next door to party headquarters, Coelho was simultaneously sponsoring another fund-raiser, this one for David Price, a Duke University political science professor running for the House in North Carolina. Coelho gave Price $1,000 too.

On Tuesday evening four different fund-raising events were scheduled between six and eight o'clock. Coelho co-sponsored three: one for Rep. Larry Smith of Florida on the rooftop of the Hotel Washington, another for Rep. Paul Kanjorski of Pennsylvania, and a third for Rep. Frank McCloskey of Indiana at party headquarters. These functions were such everyday occurrences that Democrats built catering facilities into their new building to accommodate them.

One event wasn't sponsored by Coelho. Rep. Beryl Anthony of Arkansas was a senior member of the tax-writing

Ways and Means Committee and hardly needed Coelho's help to attract lobbyists' money. His committee had the power to raise or lower the taxes of specific industries by tens of billions of dollars.

On this busy Tuesday night Coelho gave $1,000 from his PAC to Anthony and $1,000 to Smith. He had donated $1,000 to Kanjorski a few months earlier. He skipped giving to McCloskey, who owed his seat to Coelho anyway. Coelho resurrected McCloskey after Indiana state officials declared him the loser in the 1984 election. He engineered a recount in the House, where Democrats transformed McCloskey into the winner by a party-line vote, leaving Republicans sputtering in impotent rage. In revenge, GOP congressmen refused to allow taxpayers' money to be used to pay legal bills arising from the recount, as had been the custom. Coelho had to divert campaign money into an undisclosed recount fund. McCloskey was supposed to raise labor-union money to replenish the fund but fell short, leaving Coelho stuck for tens of thousands of dollars. So McCloskey got nothing from Coelho's PAC.

On Wednesday Coelho was feeling high; his financial advisers had just told him that dollars were cascading into the campaign committee coffers. "All of our money stuff is doing better than I had expected," he said.

"The only negative has been the media center."

The new television studio in the basement of party headquarters was Coelho's pride, but it had been hemorrhaging money since it opened for business a few months earlier. Coelho had been counting on getting substantial business from his labor-union allies, liberal not-for-profit groups, and political consultants with commercial clients. His budget called for them to throw enough business his way to pay the staff salaries and the mortgage on the elaborate new facility, but that had turned out to be a miscalculation. Of the $630,000 worth of work he had expected by now, only a little better than one-third had actually materialized, and payment had been made for only a fraction of that. Coelho was so upset he had taken to dunning deadbeats personally, even threatening to sue a House colleague who wouldn't pay. The financial troubles of the studio were becoming a serious preoccupation, but Franks and McAuliffe assured him that the losses could be more than offset by the better than expected flow of money from donors. Franks was projecting, among other things, that he'd take in at least $1 million in soft money from several large labor unions, each pledged to give $100,000. "I'm not worried as much," Coelho said.

On Wednesday evening Coelho stopped by yet another fund-raising event, a reception for Rep. Jim Chapman of Texas aboard the yacht *High Spirits,* docked on the Potomac near a row of waterfront restaurants. The 112-foot craft—a small ship, really—was built in the Roaring Twenties and reflected that reckless era's preoccupation with conspicuous display of wealth. A promenade encircled the main salon, which was furnished with plump sofas, oriental rugs, and potted palms. It was launched in 1928, barely a year before the stock-market crash that ushered in the Depression. Now the *High Spirits* was once again maintained in gleaming condition by a full-time crew. It was financed by Donald Dixon, a man with a taste for four-star restaurants and real-estate gambles.

Coelho himself made frequent use of the yacht to entertain donors and lobbyists. He didn't ask how the bills were being paid, an oversight he would later regret. Chapman was also getting free use of the yacht. The normal charter fee was $2,000 per half-day, plus the cost of fuel and food, which came to $1,234 for Chapman's reception. The entire cost was being absorbed, apparently illegally, by Dixon's federally insured savings and loan, Vernon Savings and Loan Association of Texas, to which the yacht skipper remitted the bills. Vernon was in the process of collapsing into insolvency; it would soon be taken over by federal regulators accusing Dixon of plundering and wasting its assets through high living and mismanagement and driving it $350 million into the red. But as the liquor and money flowed at Wednesday night's dockside fund-raiser, Coelho and Chapman were oblivious to their host's legal problems.

When Chapman was later criticized for his free use of the yacht, he insisted that he had never met Dixon or done any favors for him. But he didn't reimburse Vernon. Instead, he amended his campaign finance reports to reflect the reception as a $234 personal contribution from a lobbyist for the Texas savings and loan industry, Durward Curlee, who lived aboard the *High Spirits* when in Washington. Chapman's staff claimed his use of the yacht was authorized under an election-law provision allowing volunteers to donate use of their personal residences.

Chapman, like McCloskey, owed a debt to Coelho. The Texan won it a year earlier in a special election that became a nationally watched showdown. GOP party strategists, hoping to demonstrate that conservative Southern Democrats were ready to defect in big numbers following Reagan's crushing defeat of the liberal Walter Mondale in 1984, tried to snatch a solidly Democratic district around Texarkana. Reagan made a federal judge of the Democratic incumbent, opening up the seat for a free-for-all election in 1985. The Republican candidate, Edd Hargett, spent $1.2 million but lost narrowly to Chapman, who spent $540,000. The defeat so demoralized Texas Republicans that now, only a year later, they were giving Chapman a free ride to re-election, having failed to field a candidate.

PACs were donating money to Chapman's campaign fund anyway, to help retire his debts from the special election and to get acquainted with a new House member who was likely to remain for many years. During 1986 Chapman reaped nearly $119,000 from PACs and paid off $130,000 in personal indebtedness, either money he had lent directly to his 1985 campaign or bank loans for which he had guaranteed repayment. Coelho considered giving $1,000 too, but saved the money for campaigns that needed it.

Later on Wednesday Coelho dropped off $1,000 for Rep. Dale Kildee of Michigan. Kildee raised about $19,000 in PAC money at a Coelho-sponsored party at the Democratic Club, including $2,000 each from the Teamsters and the civil-service pensioners' lobby.

At the same time, a couple of blocks away, lobbyists were attending a fund-raiser for Benjamin Cardin of Baltimore. Normally they shy away from non-incumbents, but Cardin, who was speaker of the Maryland House of Delegates, was looking like a winner for a vacant seat in a safely Democratic district. His event got $17,000 in PAC money, including $5,000 from the Teamsters and $2,500 from the United Auto Workers. Coelho dispensed another $1,000 check from his Valley PAC.

For Cardin's event the American Trucking Associations provided free use of their building near the Capitol, which they opened routinely for fund-raising receptions. It's illegal for corporations to subsidize congressional campaigns with company funds, but this corporate hospitality wasn't counted as a gift. The truckers said their facility was available free for non-campaign activities as well, such as retirement parties for lawmakers or Capitol staff members and events for credit unions and conservation groups favored by legislators. This exploited a provision allowing campaigns to use corporate facilities open to the general public. It was one of the many loopholes that were being stretched to allow lobbyists to deploy their money more freely.

On Thursday Coelho gave $1,000 for Chicago congressman Frank Annunzio at the Democratic Club. He also signed $1,000 checks to be sent off to two women candidates running in upstate New York districts, Louise Slaughter and Rosemary Pooler, and to Mike Espy, a black candidate running in Mississippi. That made a total of $11,000 given by the Valley Education Fund during the week. It was about average; his one-man PAC provided $513,600 to candidates in 1986.

Friday morning at eight Coelho left National Airport aboard a private plane supplied by the Philip Morris tobacco company, bound for California. The committee got the plane for much less than it cost the company to operate, using yet another loophole in the campaign-finance laws.

Philip Morris had millions riding on what Congress would do about the federal tax on cigarettes, so it was happy to pay. How much was it worth for the company's lobbyist to spend four uninterrupted hours with the Speaker of the House?

But Speaker O'Neill didn't make the trip after all. He begged off, saying his wife wasn't feeling well. Later, to his irritation, Coelho heard that O'Neill went golfing. It was the third time in four years that O'Neill had ducked out of a major money-raising tour at the last minute. The Speaker didn't enjoy the big-dollar circuit.

O'Neill's sudden withdrawal left Coelho personally embarrassed. Among the several events that weekend, he had arranged for a group of Taiwanese-Americans to meet O'Neill in a private room at the Beverly Hilton Hotel. The audience with the Speaker was their reward for raising $25,000 for the campaign committee. Finance director McAuliffe was upset because O'Neill canceled a meeting with the same group a year earlier, deeply offending their ethnic pride. "For them, that's an insult," McAuliffe said. "You just can't explain it to them." He tried for hours to telephone the event's main organizer, but couldn't connect. Finally, sixty-five Taiwanese donors arrived at the large suite, where a mortified Coelho broke the news that O'Neill wouldn't show. "It was just a heart-wrenching experience," McAuliffe said later. "They were very, very, very disappointed."

Without O'Neill the weekend events brought in $100,000 less than Coelho had hoped. McAuliffe knew he could have cashed in the Speaker's prestige for more money. "The Speaker never made a money call for us," he said wistfully. But the California weekend still produced about $300,000.

Coelho's detractors saw only a political opportunist, scooping up special-interest money to perpetuate Democratic power in the House. Years earlier a newspaper quoted an unnamed colleague as saying of Coelho that he had "one foot in the fast lane and one foot on a banana peel."

And yet Coelho saw his job in grand terms, like a bishop

raising money for a cathedral. He barely was able to contain his enthusiasm, bursting to explain the sense of mission that he felt.

"Unless you believe that the Democratic party can really help people change their lives and provide some hope, you don't understand what I'm doing," Coelho said one day. "You don't understand my drive, you don't understand why I want to change things. You don't understand why money is important." He radiated a sense of innocence.

Coelho believed he had turned aside a right-wing Republican revolution, fighting money with money. The way he saw it, his new political machine allowed Democrats to stymie GOP designs on the pensions of the elderly and to frustrate plans of hard-line militarists to finance a war in Central America. When Democrats spent money for such noble ends, who cared where it came from. "I have inner peace," he said.

Except for a twist of fate, Coelho would have entered the Roman Catholic priesthood. It wasn't hard to imagine him rising in a totally different hierarchy. For him, the Democratic House was a surrogate church. George Washington Plunkitt, the garrulous Tammany Hall chieftain, said more than eighty years ago that his own political machine "does missionary work like a church." Plunkitt added, "It's got big expenses and it's got to be supported by the faithful. If a corporation sends in a check to help the good work, why shouldn't we take it like other missionary societies?" Coelho's attitude was exactly the same.

In truth, only a stupid accident kept Coelho from the priesthood and set his course for political power instead. It happened on the struggling dairy farm of his parents, near the tiny town of Dos Palos, California.

The hired man at the wheel of the pickup truck was speeding far too fast down the slippery gravel road that summer day, but young Anthony Lee Coelho, just past his sixteenth birthday, hung on and said nothing.

The road curved along one of the irrigation canals that make the Central Valley of California a lush agricultural factory. Suddenly the speeding truck was flipping violently over into the canal. As it plowed into the water Coelho's head pitched forward and cracked painfully against the windshield, leaving him dazed. The truck sank, but Coelho floated up through the open window on his side. Family members came running from the nearby farmhouse as he and the uninjured driver pulled themselves onto the canal bank.

Coelho's head hurt, but he didn't tell anybody. He worried more that his father would be angry about the wrecked truck. The headache subsided, with no ill effects. Or so it seemed, until a year later when he suddenly blacked out while milking cows. He collapsed, his body shook, spittle bubbled up on his lips.

"The next thing I remember is that I was on the bed in my room," he recalled. "The doctor was there. . . . All I remember was waking up, being extremely tired, . . . and sleeping. And everybody panicking, and everybody concerned."

In the days and weeks that followed, there were more blackouts. Coelho saw one doctor after another. "I remember . . . they put me on all kinds of medication, and it never being right, for some reason. It didn't work. And I never questioned; I didn't think of questioning my parents as to why it wasn't working."

As the mysterious blackouts continued, he read Nevil Shute's best-selling novel *On the Beach,* about the doomed survivors of a nuclear war. "I got extremely depressed. I didn't say much to my parents, because they didn't understand that." His grandparents had come from a village in the Azores, islands that belong to Portugal. His father was suspicious of books and formal schooling, constantly drumming into him the idea that "your hands are more important than your head." But the teenager mastered school lessons by taping pages of notes on the metal partitions of the milking stalls, tending to the cows and reading as he went from one to the other. He hungered for a taste of the world beyond. Yet he was being struck down by a malady without a name. "I felt all alone," he said. It was his junior year in high school.

His parents sought out faith healers, to his great embarrassment. "I remember a black lady in Merced who I went to in the poor section of town. And she did a lot of hocus-pocus and praying and communicating with my grandfather." Another healer, a Portuguese man, poured oils on his head and brewed herbal teas for him to drink. "All I knew was that I supposedly was possessed by the devil," he recalled. Coelho finally told his parents he had no faith in the healers, and stopped seeing them.

He learned to live with the blackouts, which grew milder. He was alert to the warning signs—a sudden flush, a feeling of the walls closing in. He could avoid danger well enough to drive a car.

University life was liberation. Mentally quick, accustomed to long hours of work and little sleep, blessed with boundless energy and an easy way with people, Coelho became a standout at Loyola University in Los Angeles. He was the first of his family to attend college.

"It was absolutely a vacation for four years," Coelho said. He joined a "jock" fraternity, Phi Sigma Kappa. He partied. He drank. "I got good grades, I got very involved in activities, I got very involved in student government." He ran for sophomore class president, and won. "I loved it. . . . When I ran for student body president it was a foregone conclusion I would be student body president. It wasn't much of a race."

As he was beginning his freshman year in 1960, John F. Kennedy won election as the first Catholic President. Coelho was swept up in the aura of the youthful President's administration, his high-sounding speeches, his appeal to duty, and his call for self-sacrifice. Kennedy launched the Peace Corps. He ordered America to put men on the moon. Young people felt good about their government. Government was a force for good; it could do anything.

Coelho was captivated. "It's a Catholic university. They're

all excited, of course. His presidency is a happening for me. Anytime he's on TV, I'm there. I don't give a damn if it's in the middle of a final exam, I'm there watching him. . . . I read everything about him."

Then came the shock of Kennedy's murder in 1963. "I remember we got the bells going, the chapel filled up. It's a huge chapel at the campus. And people were out on the steps going into the chapel, and out on the street, all the way into the sunken garden in front of the chapel, just a mass group of teachers and students and priests and everybody praying for him. And then during the prayers we heard that he died.

"And it was very emotional, it was the first loss that I had that I felt something about. For the next four days I didn't do anything. I didn't shave. I didn't really eat. I just sat in front of the TV and watched it." In that state, Coelho pondered what to do with his own life. "I didn't feel committed to anything. All of a sudden the time that I had on my hands, to me became a sin. I wasn't doing anything worthwhile with my time." Making money didn't excite him. Neither did the idea of becoming a teacher. "I decided what I really wanted to do was get involved with people, and I decided . . . what I really wanted to do was become a priest."

The idea was no passing whim. His parents disapproved. His hometown girlfriend, after five years of waiting for a marriage, was bitter and angry. His fraternity brothers, he recalls, "were a little surprised, because I was a hellion." But he pressed ahead. "It burned with me, it became all-encompassing," he recalled. Jesuit mentors at the university sent him on a religious retreat to test his sincerity, and he emerged more convinced than ever that the priesthood was his calling. His friends gave him rosaries and Bibles and other religious books as graduation presents. His mother still worried, as she would tell a newspaper reporter years later, that as a clergyman her spirited son would be "one of those fooling-around priests." But in his mind, the course of his life was set.

His plans changed abruptly on his twenty-second birthday, June 15, 1964, in the office of Dr. John Doyle. It was there that Coelho finally learned the name of the affliction that haunted him: epilepsy. The blow to his head in that truck accident years earlier caused more than a temporary headache. His early blackouts and convulsions had been grand mal seizures. His later, milder attacks were petit mal seizures. Cruelly, the diagnosis handicapped him far more than the accident or the blackouts. Dr. Doyle broke the news to his patient that, under church law, epileptics couldn't be priests.

Coelho felt wronged, outraged, confused. "I functioned. I played sports. I drove a car. I screwed around. I drank. I got good grades. I was student body president. I was outstanding senior at Loyola. God, I'd lived a full life, and all of a sudden somebody is saying I'm handicapped, that I'm crippled, that I can't do certain things." California revoked his driver's license, no minor inconvenience in a society built around freeways. "I sent in my driver's license, because I had to. But I kept driving. . . . It was wrong, but I did. But I knew I was doing something illegal." Now he felt like an outlaw.

He told his parents of the diagnosis, thinking they would at least be pleased that he wasn't destined for the priesthood after all. He wasn't prepared for what they said.

"I barely got it out of my mouth, and my parents reacted very strongly. 'No son of ours has epilepsy.' "

Now it began to dawn on him. Folklore in the Azores, his grandparents' birthplace, regarded epilepsy as a disgrace, a punishment for some sin in the family. His parents had probably been denying the obvious for years. Surely the doctors who examined him early, when he was being struck down by grand mal seizures, correctly diagnosed what was wrong.

The gulf between Coelho and his parents widened even more. They insisted he come home to the farm, away from his "crazy friends in Los Angeles." He refused. "I resented their attitude, and I resented their comments," he said. "I was just devastated that they would have this attitude. And it built up on me."

He found it hard to get even a menial job. "The word 'epilepsy' was on every job application that I saw. I had never seen the damn word before, or I had never seen it as predominantly as I was seeing it now. And I of course marked 'Yes.' Well, that didn't get me anywhere." He landed a job behind the counter at a liquor store, but it lasted only two weeks. "I couldn't stand cashing Social Security checks for old ladies and then having them turn around and buy half-pints of liquor. . . . I didn't want to be a part of the downfall of these women." He blew up when a young couple, loading up with beer and snacks for a party, refused their child's request for candy. "The father said, 'Shut up, we can't afford candy bars.' It just hit me like a ton of bricks, the priorities that this guy had. . . . I said to the kid, 'What do you want? Take it. It's on me.' And I took the guy's money, walked in the back, and quit."

Jobless, living apart from his family in a nearly deserted fraternity house, his college friends mostly gone off to summer jobs or new careers, he sank into a bitter depression. He walked on a beach outside the house, drinking heavily while he watched waves rolling in from the Pacific. "Every night I ended up passing out, drunk." Sometimes he went to a nearby park, drinking and watching children riding a merry-go-round. Years later the carousel music still played in his head when he recalled those days.

He flirted with the idea of taking his own life. "I had gone downhill very fast. And I woke up one morning, and I was hung over, I was dirty, couldn't really recall where I had been. And I started thinking that there wasn't any hope. What was I going to do? There was no hope whatever for the future. Everywhere I turned there was rejection. And then I started thinking, the best way to resolve this, the easiest way to resolve this, was suicide."

The pain he experienced from feeling rejected as "handicapped" made Coelho uncommonly attuned to the pain and emotions of others. But he also emerged feeling a self-confident ambition that bordered on recklessness. His sensitivity would win him a wide circle of devoted and influential friends, helping propel him upward. His bold nonchalance would allow him to take on tasks and plunge into alliances from which more cautious men would recoil.

Even years later he hungered for physical contact, gripping an elbow, throwing an arm around someone's shoulder. On the floor of the House he looked like an amoeba, going from one colleague to another, trying to absorb each one in turn. "He isn't one of these guys who is always looking over your shoulder to see who just came into the room," said a friend, Rep. Ike Skelton of Missouri. "When he's listening to you, he really hears what you're saying."

Though his epileptic seizures were in time controlled completely through small daily doses of phenobarbital, he devoted himself to the handicapped. At a public benefit for the National Rehabilitation Hospital in 1986, he appeared on a stage of the Kennedy Center with Jim Brady, the press secretary to President Reagan whose brain was ripped open in 1981 by a bullet intended for his boss. Brady had planned to deliver a few words from the safety of his wheelchair, but Coelho helped him find the courage to rise and walk. Leaning on the slightly built Coelho to support his weak left side, Brady forced his uncooperating body to plod across the stage to a podium. "Coelho," the big Republican cracked, "you'll *always* be on my left!" The audience rose, applauding.

Surviving the black summer of 1964 caused Coelho to feel he could come through the worst that life might deal out. That is what he meant by "inner peace." He wasn't talking about tranquillity, but about self-assurance. "When you're in the gutter and you want to kill yourself because . . . you think that God's turned against you, you think your family's turned against you, you think your government's turned against you . . . and then you pull yourself out because you reoriented yourself, you've re-established yourself. Nobody else has done that for you; you've done it. And if you do that,

there's a certain amount of freedom there. A kind that nobody can ever take away from you."

He kept a sort of spiritual diary during his depression. A
close friend, Jack Kane, a former seminarian, gave him a
book and insisted that he read it. It was a curious little novel
published twenty years earlier. The novel was *Mr. Blue,* by
Myles Connolly, a story of an eccentric visionary named J.
Blue who squandered an inherited fortune living lavishly
and giving money away in an attempt to spread happiness.
In the book, Blue espoused a saintly philosophy of self-mor-
tification, and died penniless but content among Boston's
derelicts.

Coelho read it and reread it, underlining passages, writing in the margins, and sometimes commenting about his
own earlier notations. His thoughts of suicide faded as he
concluded that Blue's untimely death was a waste. Coelho
jotted, "God didn't intend for us to suffer or waste our talents
as he."

Young Coelho saw the fictional saintly Blue as a kind of
alter ego. The book described Blue as "a sort of gay, young
and gallant monk without an Order." That came close to
describing the carousing college hellion who wanted to be
a priest. Blue lived for a time alone in a wildly painted
packing crate on the roof of a thirty-story Manhattan building; Coelho lived in a half-empty fraternity house on the
beach. From his rooftop Blue flew kites, balloons, and a
pennant bearing the word "Courage." Years later, climbing
upward in the leadership of the House, Coelho still sent
cheerful bouquets of helium-filled balloons to friends on
special occasions.

Coelho seemed then to be genuinely moved by spirituality
and repulsed by the commercial world. He underlined a
passage in which Blue said, "Through suffering only can
one attain wisdom. Through suffering only can one attain
the greatest understanding. And without suffering it is hard
to attain the kingdom of heaven." Coelho wrote in the margin, *"Truly beautiful."* At another point the book's narrator
said of himself, "Business, I believe, is the backbone of our

civilization. . . . I want to make a great deal of money. I like the good things of life." Coelho wrote, *"Selfish."* This is the same Coelho who would later devote himself to raising tens of millions of dollars, courting the favor of the wealthy, and speaking of politics as a business.

Coelho emerged from his depression with help from a Jesuit friend, Father Ed Markey, who brought him a surprising opportunity. He said, "I have a job for you. . . . It's a good one. You'll be working for Bob Hope." The famous comedian and his wife, Dolores, who was active in Catholic charities, were looking for a bright young man to employ in their Palm Springs home. Father Markey told him the Hopes had already agreed to hire him.

"And he basically said, 'You're killing yourself.'

"I said, 'I know.'

"He said, 'You've got to come out of it.'

"And so I got excited, the first time in months that I got excited about anything in life. I was still drinking a lot. But all of a sudden, I saw some light. There was a flicker."

Living in the Hope household, he became almost part of the family. Here was a life of glamour, far from the drudgery of the dairy farm. He helped critique the comedian's new jokes, attended recording sessions of his television programs, and enjoyed VIP treatment at movie premieres. He arrived at the ballyhooed premiere of *My Fair Lady* in a Rolls-Royce loaned to him by a houseguest of his new employer. "I remember renting a tux and driving up and all the cameras flashing and the people wondering who I was, and who was the person I was with. It was fun. All of a sudden life took a different twist."

Hope took his young employee for midnight drives on the freeway after television recording sessions. "We'd talk. And he'd say, 'You know, what do you want to do with your life?' It's pretty obvious to me that he knew my troubles. And he finally said to me, 'It's obvious you have this burn to help people. It's just killing you that you want to help people.' "

Hope suggested an alternative—politics. "He said, 'If

you're really serious about helping people, if that's your bag, why don't you go to work for a member of Congress? You can satisfy your priestly needs and desires, you're working with people, you're helping people, you're correcting problems for groups of people.' " The idea of Congress as a substitute for the Church didn't seem at all outlandish to Coelho. Congress was passing laws to wipe out racial segregation and guarantee the vote to blacks. Elected in a landslide, President Johnson was laying plans for a grandiose "War on Poverty." Government seemed even more a force for good, a tool for helping people, than it had under Kennedy. Coelho seized Hope's suggestion.

Through a politically active uncle he got an interview with his local congressman, B. F. Sisk, during a Democratic party function in Los Angeles. Sisk offered a ninety-day internship and Coelho headed across the continent in his old Chevrolet jalopy—driver's license or no driver's license—to begin work in April 1965. Hope co-signed a note to help Coelho get a bank loan to resettle in Washington.

"That was the beginning of a whole new life," Coelho said. "I fell in love with the work, absolutely fell in love with the work, the fact that you could really help out people and you could change people's lives . . . I could do much more in this job than I could as a priest. And all of a sudden I wasn't bitter at the Church anymore. I knew that God had a different plan for me, and that I could be much more helpful in this way."

2

"An Iron Triangle"

*There's only one way to hold a district: you must
study human nature and act accordin'.*
—GEORGE WASHINGTON PLUNKITT

Tony Coelho studied political science at Loyola, but his
real education occurred while he was working for Sisk. His
apprenticeship included the offer of a $500 cash bribe on
his second day as the congressman's administrative assistant in 1970.

A representative of a Southern textile mill came into the
office to discuss a pending bill, in which he had an interest.
The lobbyist wanted to move the measure to the floor of the
House and asked for Sisk's support to get it out of the Rules
Committee, where it was stuck. The lobbyist—Coelho diplo-
matically forgot his name later—handed the young aide an
envelope as he was leaving. Inside Coelho found a business
card and five $100 bills.

That jolted him. "Here I was, the youngest AA on the hill,
young, impressionable. I didn't know whether it was for me
or for my boss. But I knew what it was. I knew it was illegal.
I fussed and fumed all day."

What worried Coelho was that his boss might be on the take, secretly accepting bribes. There were members of the House, he knew, who routinely demanded cash payments from lobbyists visiting their offices. It was a straightforward business deal: if you wanted to talk, first you paid. Perhaps, Coelho feared, Sisk was among these cash-and-carry lawmakers. Perhaps Sisk expected his chief aide to be the conduit for payoffs. "I believed in him and I believed in the system," Coelho said, "and I didn't want to be disappointed."

Uncertain what to expect, he showed the money to Sisk.

"You're the AA," said Sisk. "What are you going to do with it?"

"I want to send it back," Coelho said.

"Well, why don't you," Sisk said. "That's your job, you know. I expect you to handle it."

Delighted and relieved, Coelho quickly bought a cashier's check and put it in an envelope addressed to the cotton-mill lobbyist, with a covering letter perpetrating a polite lie. "It would be inappropriate for us to accept a campaign contribution at this time," Coelho wrote. He said Sisk didn't accept political contributions in cash. Actually, the lobbyist hadn't called the cash a campaign contribution or anything. Coelho could have put it in Sisk's campaign or in Sisk's personal bank account, or even taken it himself. There would be no record of it, no paper trail that any inquiring investigator could later follow. Only Coelho and the lobbyist would know what was in the envelope and neither would be likely to inform on the other; paying bribes is just as illegal as receiving them. Cash in politics can be what you want it to be.

The cotton-mill lobbyist handed Coelho those bills two years before Richard Nixon's burglars were caught with campaign cash in their pockets inside Democratic party headquarters in the Watergate complex. Later they were paid with leftover campaign cash to keep quiet. In the Koreagate scandals that followed, Tong Sun Park, the Korean-born playboy, rice broker, and confidence man, testi-

fied that he spread cash gifts all over Capitol Hill, mostly to
Democratic House members. Political campaigns at all levels—presidential, Senate, and House—ran on cash, unreported, untraceable, easily diverted from political use to
personal use. Only the most fastidious politicians insisted
on checks, or made anything like a full disclosure to the
voters. And a lot of the cash—nobody will ever know how
much—was simply pocketed by the lawmakers. In following the Koreagate trail, House investigators found unex-
plained deposits of $200,000 in the bank account of Rep.
Charles Wilson of California, for example. The source of
the money remained a mystery long after he was censured
by the House for unrelated financial misdeeds.

Coelho might have called the federal prosecutor's office to
report the $500 bribe attempt. The money could have been
a political donation, but Coelho said, "I knew what it was."
Still, he thought of the money less as evidence than as an
embarrassing burden. He didn't want to stir a scandal, and
he took the most diplomatic way out. That is the way on
Capitol Hill. Even so, the lobbyist hardly appreciated the
favor Coelho was doing him. He became indignant at the
rejection of his gift. "He absolutely resented it," Coelho
said. "He tried to get me fired." Laws had gone unenforced
for so long, and the cash culture so permeated Capitol Hill,
that accepting envelopes full of $100 bills was not just com-
mon practice, it was almost an obligation.

He had risen quickly on Sisk's staff; the initial ninety-day
internship became a full-time job, then a career. He had
always attacked nearly every task with abandon, even his
courtship in 1965 of a pretty and shy young Indiana farm
girl named Phyllis Butler. He showed then at the age of
twenty-two the same swashbuckling style he would later
bring to the wooing of campaign donors.

They met on a blind date. She also had just arrived in
Washington, to work in the office of a freshman congressman, Rep. Andrew Jacobs of Indiana, for whom she had
worked earlier in his father's Indianapolis law practice.
Coelho took Phyllis out two or three nights a week, calling

nearly every evening they weren't together, sending flowers once a month. He cut down his drinking to practically nothing in deference to her distaste for alcohol.

The courtship seemed to fizzle one night. During a long talk about marriage, Coelho said he wanted to remain single for five more years to attend law school. "I'm not going to wait five years for the guy," she later wrote to her sister. "I'll finish out the year and come home." She wept in her apartment that night. But the next evening, at a party given by Sisk at his home, she was astonished to hear her host say, "I have an announcement to make. I'd like to announce the engagement of Tony and Phyllis."

"Tony loves surprises," she said. She accepted on the spot. They married a year later.

In 1970 he became administrative assistant, or chief of staff. Of all the 435 top aides in the House, he was then, at the age of twenty-eight, the youngest. Archie Nahigian, who joined Sisk's staff as a congressional page the same year, recalled Coelho as "very demanding, on himself and on his staff . . . a perfectionist . . . always the first one in." But the would-be priest in him still showed. He remembered birthdays and wedding anniversaries, and developed a widening circle of friendships in Washington and, especially, back in the congressional district in California. "He is person-driven," Nahigian said.

Coelho and Sisk grew particularly close; Sisk's wife, Reta, was so fond of Phyllis that she treated her practically as an adopted daughter. The young couple would dine at Sisk's home three or four nights a week. The Sisks and Coelhos took in baseball games together before the Washington Senators moved to Texas in 1971. Sisk loved baseball; he was a good enough left-handed pitcher to have played some sandlot ball in his youth. Reta taught the younger couple to keep score. The Sisks were "Grandpa" and "Grandma" to the Coelhos' two daughters.

Sisk was a member of the powerful Rules Committee, which controlled the flow of legislation to the floor, and was widely respected by his colleagues. So much so, in fact, that shortly after Coelho became his top aide he ran for the post of Majority Leader. Sisk lost, partly because he had counted on support from members of his own California delegation who ended up voting for someone else, a lesson Coelho wouldn't forget.

Campaigns didn't cost a fortune in those days. House members didn't hire poll takers, media consultants, or television debate coaches. Getting elected and re-elected was a matter of traveling back to the home district whenever possible, addressing Kiwanis Club luncheons and company picnics and remembering precinct captains' birthdays. For many Democrats, re-election was practically guaranteed by patronage-driven local political machines, either of Northern big-city mayors or Southern rural sheriffs. For others, in swing districts, survival depended on the national economy and the way the electorate judged whether the party in power was doing a good job. House members could ride into office on the coattails of the President. The modest campaign budgets of House members went to pay for campaign buttons, billboards, or novelties such as pasteboard fans printed with the incumbent's name. At worst, House members were expected to contribute to the local political machine's election-day "walking-around money," which was used to buy citizens' votes outright in the poor rural backwaters or big-city wards where that ancient abuse persisted.

Campaign costs were low enough so that a House seat was within the grasp of ordinary people. Candidates could run without paying special court to commercial, moneyed interests. Sisk himself was a child of the Dust Bowl, driven from Texas to California by the Depression and the drought of the 1930s. He had been a truck driver, fruit picker, winery worker, union organizer, and, when he first ran for the House in 1954, a tire salesman. Sisk recalled that his first election campaign, in which he upset incumbent Republican Oakley Hunter to take over a seat that had been in GOP hands for twenty-eight of the preceding thirty years, cost him a total of $12,000.

Sisk's biggest donation was $500, from a farmer who liked his support for federal irrigation projects in the Central Valley. Sisk raised his election stake partly by selling a vacation cabin and a building lot owned by him and Reta.

Costs were rising by 1972. That was the first year candidates had to make a more or less full disclosure of their spending and donations under a new law that replaced an unenforced disclosure statute from 1925. The average House Democrat in 1972 outspent Republican challengers by $49,249 to $32,450. For competitive open seats, Democrats and Republicans spent about evenly, but still averaged less than $100,000. Those costs were low compared to what came later.

That was also the year that Richard Nixon's presidential campaign raised and spent $60 million to run a poll-driven, Madison Avenue campaign. At the presidential level at least, candidates were relying on polling to tell them what the voters wanted to hear and on television advertising to present a carefully edited version of themselves to the citizens. But those expensive techniques weren't yet widely used in House campaigns.

House Democrats were especially slow to recognize the changes that money was bringing to election campaigns. Few incumbents thought they had any real worries about re-election. Since World War II, the House had become a seemingly safe harbor from the national political storms; coattails were becoming as rare in politics as in the garment trade. Armed with large and growing personal staffs and the ability to flood their districts with free, self-promoting mailings, the typical House member felt all but invulnerable. In 1968 only thirteen House members were defeated, although the Democratic party was so deeply divided by the Vietnam War that its convention in Chicago provoked riots in the streets outside. Two years later, during Coelho's first year as Sisk's top aide, 95 percent of all House members who sought re-election won. In the following election the rate was 94 percent despite the crushing defeat of the Democratic party's presidential candidate, George McGovern. Nixon's massive, forty-nine-state victory was so remarkable for its failure to pull Republican House and Senate candidates to victory that Walter Mears, the chief political correspondent of the Associated Press, wrote an election-night report calling it a "lonely landslide."

The eighteenth-century gentlemen who composed the Constitution feared the House would be a body ruled by the passions of the mob. But in the late twentieth century the House had become for incumbents a political redoubt. More and more members of the House enjoyed, like Sisk, something close to life tenure. It was a proletarian House of Lords.

The House was evolving into a gigantic bureaucracy, a re-election machine designed principally to return incumbents to office. When Coelho first came to town in 1965, the pace of life on Capitol Hill was relatively easy. Sisk's office usually closed at 6 p.m., even though that was only midafternoon back in the Central Valley. The office shut down completely in the summer when Congress recessed and there wasn't any legislative business to attend to.

House staffs were still small in those early days; Coelho was one of only five employees in Sisk's Washington office. He and Phyllis, who kept her House job, could drive to Capitol Hill together in the morning around eight-thirty or nine. The House was ruled by the seniority system and a few powerful men, mostly Southern Democrats. Sisk recalled that Carl Vinson of Georgia was such a "total dictator" as chairman of the Armed Services Committee that he normally allowed freshman members to ask only one question per year at committee hearings. It wasn't very democratic, but everybody got to go home on time.

The pace picked up in the years that followed. Coelho thrived on the work. He began leaving home each morning earlier than Phyllis. "His theory was, if you got in there before nine, the phones weren't so busy and you could get things done," she recalled. He convinced Sisk to extend office hours so constituents back in California could still call Washington as late as 5 p.m. local time, which was 8 p.m. in the capital.

During Coelho's time as a staff aide Congress was increasing the federal government's power over the everyday lives of citizens and businessmen, enacting laws covering civil rights, consumer protection, and pollution, as well as Medicare, Medicaid, and other spending programs. As the federal bureaucracy dispensed more and more money and grew larger and more bewildering, more and more people came to Washington asking their congressman for help or relief.

Before World War II, House members got along with only two staff aides each, a secretary and a clerk. The budget for congressional staff is still called "Clerk Hire." By the time Coelho arrived the average staff numbered nine. When he became a congressman himself more than 7,000 persons were working directly on personal staffs, an average of sixteen per member.

Most of those aides worked on what House members like to call "constituent service." That means pursuing lost Social Security checks, wrangling with the Veterans Administration over disability benefits for a constituent, guiding a local mayor to a federal grant for a sewer system or hospital, or helping a county float a tax-exempt bond to provide a low-rate mortgage for a local manufacturer threatening to move his plant elsewhere. House members prefer this work to legislating: voting on a controversial issue is guaranteed to make somebody unhappy, but dispensing sympathy, assistance, and federal dollars is all pleasure. Deciding difficult issues loses votes; "constituent service" gains them. House members act accordingly.

Congressmen were lawmakers second, ombudsmen first. Asked to name the most important measure of a congressman, Sisk replied after his retirement, "There is nothing more important than communication with his constituents: keeping them informed, answering letters and telephone calls, talking to them and making himself available. Failure here is one of the reasons new members don't get elected a second or third time." One of Coelho's most important jobs was to draft answers to letters that poured into Sisk's office, often at the rate of more than 1,000 per week. The young staff aide was an apprentice in the re-election trade.

By the time Coelho ran for election himself, more than one-third of all House members' personal staff employees were working in their districts rather than in Washington. Sisk's California staff occupied not just one but three separate offices scattered about the district, in Modesto, Fresno, and Merced. It was no accident that Coelho, as a prelude to running, chose to give up the top staff job in Washington in favor of running the California offices. It put him directly in charge of the constituent-service apparatus, which performed many of the same functions that a campaign committee would.

Coelho, the would-be priest, loved congressional casework. The head of Sisk's Fresno operation once estimated that more than 10,000 persons a year received some sort of aid through the congressman's staff. A U.S. couple needed passports to visit their daughter who was dying in a Spanish hospital after an accident. A taxpayer's refund check was sent to the wrong person. The common-law wife of a veteran couldn't get a pension when he died. A Mexican woman needed proof that her father was born in the United States to establish her own claim to citizenship. Sisk's office paved over these and countless other difficulties for voters (or, in the case of the Mexican woman, potential voters). The payoff wasn't always gratitude; Sisk got more than one death threat from veterans who thought he hadn't done enough to help. But by and large, it was emotionally satisfying work, and politically rewarding.

There were grander ways to dispense federal aid. Sisk's career was built in no small part on his ability to deliver federal water projects, which looked like classic pork-barrel legislation to Easterners but without which the naturally arid Central Valley might literally have dried up and

blown away, as the Texas panhandle did in the congressman's Dust Bowl youth. In his first election campaign Sisk
attacked the incumbent Republican for opposing a federal
dam. Once elected, Sisk spent years pushing through what
became the San Luis Reservoir, which held enough water
to flood more than two million acres to the depth of one foot.
The first dam in the project was completed about the time
Coelho joined the staff, and is located not far from the farm
where he grew up. It finally began to fill in 1968, and by 1972
Sisk was pushing $1.6 billion in additional canals and reser-
voirs. His last term in the House was occupied partly in
defeating the attempts of a Democratic President, Jimmy
Carter, to cut back on such expensive federal water projects.

Coelho had been in junior high school in 1954, the year
that Sisk was first elected to the House. That was also the
last year Republicans held control of the House. When Coelho finally took Sisk's seat Democrats had enjoyed uninterrupted control of the House for an entire generation. Sisk
himself would serve twenty-four years without ever being
seriously challenged for re-election.

For his entire adult life, Coelho was steeped in the pecu-
liar culture of the House and the Depression-era attitudes
of the senior Democrats who ran it. He was no idea man. He
didn't come to politics with any agenda to accomplish.
When he joined Sisk's staff he was just a lonely young man
groping for structure in his life and an outlet for his extraordinary talent and energy. He wasn't aching to end a
war, build a dam, stop abortion, promote rights for women
or blacks or even Hispanics (though he would later claim
membership in the House's "Hispanic Caucus" by virtue of
his Portuguese ancestry). Coelho's urge to "help people"
was as vague as it was forceful. He accepted the political
and ideological agenda of the ruling House Democrats
pretty much as he found it.

The Democratic party's allies became his friends. He was
naturally inclined to support government subsidies for
farmers, of course, and especially small, struggling dairy

farmers like his father, who eventually was forced to sell the family spread and retire. But working for Sisk he learned to be pro-union, pro-Israel, and pro-oil.

Coelho developed a liking for the Teamsters' union. Dining at Sisk's table night after night, he heard the congressman tell of his days as a truck driver during the Depression, when he earned $15 a week making overnight runs between Wichita Falls and Amarillo. Once, when Sisk fell ill, his wife put their infant daughter in the cab and drove a load of glass 125 miles, then helped unload it. Later Sisk had been an organizer of the winery workers' union. He won his first election to the House with strong help from labor locals.

Coelho learned the importance of oil. The Central Valley contains the Coalinga oil field, making oil and gas production a major part of the local economy. He also understood the impact of oilmen's money in Democratic politics and what was required to keep it flowing. Sisk, recalling his first election, said a contribution of $2,000 had been promised to the local Democratic party for his campaign, but evaporated when he gave a speech backing reduced tax benefits for drillers. Later Sisk favored continued government controls on the price of natural gas. He recalled that a lobbyist for the Superior Oil Company, who had given $400 to his campaign, became "nasty and insulting."

"I blew up and escorted him out of my office," Sisk said in his memoir. "He seemed to think that he had bought me for $400." Despite such shows of independence, however, Sisk eventually became one of the staunchest defenders on the Rules Committee of tax breaks for independent oil and gas producers, and Coelho followed in his footsteps.

Few in the district cared one way or another about the fate of Israel, except for local raisin producers who had to compete against Israeli raisins in the world market. In Sisk's day the California Democratic party was fueled largely with donations from Jews who had deep feelings about the struggling Jewish state. Later, Coelho, the Catholic Portuguese-American, would meet and befriend wealthy Jewish political donors from New York while traveling to Israel. Israel would have no stronger ally in the U.S. Congress than Coelho.

The agenda of the Democratic party suited Coelho's instinctively compassionate nature. During his years with Sisk the party pushed through federal laws strengthening voting rights for blacks, expanding health insurance for the elderly and establishing it for the poor, regulating polluters of the air and water, requiring businesses to provide safer products and workplaces. When Lyndon Johnson's War on Poverty flopped, Democrats turned to an idea that was only slightly less grand: guaranteed jobs for practically everybody, embodied in various "full employment" proposals. This was helping people on a grand scale.

But even the U.S. Treasury wasn't inexhaustible. Democrats, seized by pacifism and isolationism after the Vietnam trauma, cannibalized the armed forces to pay for social programs. They enacted increases in payroll taxes on the young to fund rising Social Security benefits for the old, and allowed inflation to push their working-class constituents ever higher in the graduated scale of income-tax rates until factory hands began paying rates once reserved for millionaires. But still it wasn't enough: federal budget deficits soared; price inflation wiped out pay increases and made it foolish to save money, which only decreased in value at an ever-quicker rate.

By the time Sisk was nearing retirement Americans were disillusioned with the Democrats' approach and were demanding changes. A "tax revolt" swept the country. Democratic voters were abandoning the economic agenda of the party's liberal wing; they nominated for President in 1976 a Southerner whose views on taxation, inflationary budgets, and federal intrusion into the marketplace were closer to Dwight Eisenhower's than to Hubert Humphrey's or Edward Kennedy's. Meanwhile, more and more mainstream voters were abandoning Democrats altogether: Republicans might have won the White House that year if Gerald Ford hadn't pardoned Richard Nixon.

During the Carter presidency the national Democratic party itself began disintegrating. Carter's relations with Democrats in Congress were a disaster; they viewed him as an alien invader. Socially, Washington's Democratic establishment saw the man from Plains, Georgia, as a small-town clod. Politically, they viewed him as naïve, clumsy, and ignorant at best, and at worst a threat to their own re-election. Early in 1977 he proposed cutting money for nineteen public-works projects, without much taking into account how many votes those federal projects meant to House and Senate members. Carter had won election with only 50.1 percent of the popular vote. Many lawmakers had been elected with 70 or 80 percent or were so entrenched they faced no opposition at all. They raised such a furor over Carter's "hit list" of water projects that the President, after months of wrangling, had to accept a compromise, killing off only about half the projects he wanted to eliminate. Congressional Democrats never forgave Carter for threatening their pork.

The second-biggest project on Carter's original hit list was the Auburn-Folsom South Unit, part of the Central Valley Project serving Sisk's district. The 700-foot dam, being built on the American River north of Sacramento, had already cost $230 million and would require an estimated $900 million more to complete. Interior Secretary Cecil Andrus opposed it because it was in an earthquake-prone area like that of Idaho's Teton Dam, which had given way two years earlier. "I've been there when a dam collapsed," he said. But pressure from Sisk got the money restored. "Never in the history of this country," Sisk said years later, "have we elected a man who was more naïve and had less understanding of the relationship between the Congress and the President."

Carter also wanted to reorganize the jungle of federal departments, agencies, and bureaus into a streamlined system of government. A major campaign promise was to fold 2,000 federal agencies into 200. But congressmen stayed in office by providing a guide service for constituents lost in that very jungle. In May 1978 Carter railed, "There is in Washington an iron triangle of bureaucracy, congressional committees, and well-organized special interests who can mobilize strong opposition to the reforms we need." Indeed, Congress happily adopted Carter's proposals to create two new bureaucracies, the Departments of Energy and Education.

Among Carter's strongest campaign promises was a pledge to reform the loophole-ridden federal income-tax system, which he called "a disgrace to the human race." But he found no stomach among his Democratic colleagues in Congress for making good on such a promise. Congressional Democrats stayed in office by creating tax breaks. The money to run political campaigns didn't come from working-class taxpayers. Carter quickly set aside any notion of tax reform, and in 1978 Congress enacted and Carter signed yet another round of loopholes. Nestled among the special-interest provisions was one enacted specifically for the wealthy Gallo wine-making family, who would become constituents and financial supporters of congressman-to-be Tony Coelho.

Democratic lawmakers won re-election with Nixon or Ford in the White House. They could vote for popular spending programs and devote their time to non-controversial ombudsman chores, then blame the Republican President for inflation, unemployment, poverty, pollution, and racial injustice. Nobody had to be responsible; Democrats could continue to please the labor unions and liberal interest groups by agitating for expensive new programs like national health insurance, knowing the Republican President would take the rap for pointing out that the government was already spending more than taxpayers were willing to pay. But having a Democrat in the White House was turning out to be trouble. Now the Democrats had to govern as well as reign. The strains of that unaccustomed responsibility were fracturing the party.

Perhaps a more adroit, Washington-wise President could have coaxed Congress to enact more of his ideas or proposed fewer and less sweeping actions. Washington journalists, however, echoed the views of their long-established friends in Congress, blaming Carter's legislative failures on Carter. That judgment stuck. But congressional Democrats were equally at fault. They didn't heed the message the voters had sent by electing the fiscally conservative, efficiency-minded Carter in the first place. The message was: "Clean up government. Stop waste and dishonesty. Cut my taxes and make them simple and fair."

The rulers of Capitol Hill would pay dearly for failing to listen to that message. But in 1978 it was easy for them to ignore it. It was Carter's popularity that was plunging to below 40 percent, not theirs. Anyway, just in time for the midterm elections, he scored a dazzling accomplishment at Camp David by bringing the leaders of Egypt and Israel together in a peace agreement that seemed like a miracle. Republicans gained only thirteen seats in the House and three in the Senate, leaving Democrats in unquestioned control of Congress. The incumbency system was still working, re-electing lawmakers regularly no matter how angry voters had become at what they were doing in Washington. Few Democrats felt any need to change direction. Some, privately gloating over Carter's failures, dreamed of dumping him in 1980 and running a "real" Democrat, Edward Kennedy.

But it was Indian summer for Democrats. In 1978 a new factor was threatening to upset the comfortable arrangements that had kept one party in power since 1954: money.

A new day was dawning in House and Senate races. By 1978 more and more campaigns were employing modern polling and radio and TV ads crafted by consultants schooled more in the ways of Madison Avenue than Capitol Hill. Tony Coelho was alert to the change. Though he was privately certain that he would win, he outspent his Republican opponent by $266,000 to $104,000 in that first race. He may have been an adopted son of the old ruling class in the House, but he was young enough at thirty-six to see the need for using modern tools to shore up the ancient regime.

The cost of staying in office was rising rapidly. The incumbents of 1978 had spent on the average only $87,000 to win their seats two years earlier. But the average cost of winning rose by 46 percent, to nearly $128,000, in the 1978 campaigns. That included modest sums spent by many old-time incumbents who still got re-elected buying little more than some billboards and bumper strips. For newcomers like Coelho, the cost was much higher. Anyone running for a seat opened by the retirement or death of an incumbent, as Coelho was doing, needed to push his or her name into the consciousness of the voters. And those taking on the toughest of all campaigns, opposing an entrenched incumbent, simply could not hope to win without spending sums that had seemed extravagant, even sinister, only a few years earlier.

Politics was becoming a business, but the business was going to be good for Tony Coelho.

3

"Father Confessor"

Some people say they can't understand what becomes of all the money that's collected for campaigns. They would understand fast enough if they were district leaders.
—GEORGE WASHINGTON PLUNKITT

Coelho's talent for raising money set him apart almost from the day he became a member of the House on January 3, 1979. He was looking for a way to make a mark. Phyllis Coelho said, "I remember him telling me, 'There are some vacuums. There's a person; they could do so much with that job.' " The void Coelho set out to fill required cash.

Coelho had been functioning almost as Sisk's alter ego even before he was formally elected. Sisk had slowed down after losing the race for Majority Leader, allowing Coelho to fill in for him more and more at public functions. Coelho traveled to California at least once a month. "Little by little, we started going to more receptions," Phyllis recalled. One day Sisk said, "I'm going to be retiring soon. You ought to think about running for the office." In October 1977, Coelho left Washington and became head of Sisk's California operation, allowing him to live in the home district full-time.

By the time Sisk said publicly he wouldn't run again Coelho was his obvious and unbeatable heir.

"I knew the day I announced I was running that I would be elected," he recalled. Nevertheless, he waged a strenuous campaign, breakfasting with farmers in small-town restaurants and attending evening events with Phyllis at least five nights a week. She remembered, "I said, 'Tony, can't we slow down a little bit?' He said, 'We're going to be doing this for ten months. We're going to do it right the first time.' " Outspending his opponent by better than two-and-a-half to one, Coelho scored 60 percent of the vote, winning so convincingly that Republicans fielded only a token opponent against him two years later.

Normally, freshmen House members count for little in Washington. They're lost in the crowd of 434 other members. Freshmen spend their first two years building their staff, tuning up their constituent-service operation, flooding their district with newsletters and press releases, paying off campaign debts, raising a stake for the next election, and generally attending to the job of becoming sophomores. A Democratic member might hope to become a subcommittee chairman after two or three terms, merging into one of the scores of iron triangles in Washington, exerting power over an entire industry, perhaps even building a national reputation as a legislative expert. Many were treading that route, heading for the Senate, maybe dreaming of the White House.

Coelho, however, had learned during his nearly fourteen years as a staff employee that power in the House flowed not from legislative expertise or command of facts and issues, but from friendships built on small favors and courtesies. He had seen men fall out over so small a thing as the location of a parking space.

Sisk had been chairman of a three-man House committee that assigned parking places on the streets and plazas around the Capitol and in the underground garages of the House office buildings. Coelho handled the staff work. One day a particularly coveted space came open, next to an elevator. Nobody had requested the space, so Coelho checked to make sure that the Speaker, then Carl Albert of Oklahoma, didn't want it for himself. Then he assigned it to Sisk. Two months later Speaker Albert's chief aide called to say, "You've got a big problem."

Olin Teague of Texas, one of Sisk's personal friends and a fellow member of the Church of Christ, was fuming over the assignment. Teague, a much-decorated combat veteran, had lost a foot in World War II. He was also considerably senior to Sisk, having been elected in 1946. As a handicapped veteran with seniority, he felt the space should be his. "Teague has been in here practically every day," the Speaker's aide said. Coelho was astonished; Teague already had a space only a few feet away from Sisk's. He was going all the way to the Speaker of the House over a matter of no more than half a dozen steps. It was such a frivolous thing that Teague's own staff was too embarrassed to raise it with Coelho. But Sisk understood the seriousness of the seemingly petty tantrum.

"You don't understand," he told his aide. "Parking spaces are important." He gave the spot to Teague.

So Coelho knew that a small favor or an imagined slight counted for more than ideology or the merits of a specific House resolution. "The lesson is, it isn't H.R. 26 that divides friends," he said. "It's these little perks."

As a freshman member, Coelho set out to make a name for himself by delivering large quantities of an increasingly desired perk, campaign money. Raising funds was regarded in Congress as an odious necessity, which lawmakers usually were relieved to turn over to others. But Coelho attacked the task almost as though he enjoyed it.

He wasn't embarrassed about hearing donors turn him down. He lacked the fear of rejection that makes most people, especially lawmakers, hate to ask for money. Congressmen dislike being spurned more than most simply because they aren't used to it; they are surrounded by aides and lobbyists who make their living saying "Yes." Asking for contributions is one of the few times when they are likely to hear "No" for an answer.

Coelho found it easy to ask for money. He has a naturally ebullient personality. But more importantly, after enduring his crushing disappointment in the summer of 1964, he found it was nothing to be rejected by a potential political donor.

"A lot of people don't understand inner peace," Coelho said. "You've got to have inner peace. You've got to feel good about yourself. And particularly if you're dealing with money."

Some lawmakers dislike asking for funds because they know not all givers are altruistic: people expect something for their money, and it isn't always good government. "I've got guys coming into my office who are felonies waiting to happen," said Rep. Pete Stark of California. "I've got dip-shits talking about tax amendments, and in the same breath talking about raising money. You could put them in jail for that."

Stark, for one, saw the chairmanship of the Democratic Congressional Campaign Committee as a position demanding ethical compromise. "You can't be in that job and not sell part of your soul," Stark said. "There is no way"; money has too many strings attached.

Coelho, however, simply denied any strings existed. "I tell donors, 'I want you to help out the party and I want you to do something, but don't think you're buying anything. Don't think that you're making a deal with me,'" he insisted. It was hard to imagine him actually using those words to woo a contribution, of course. But that's the way he thought.

With that attitude he plunged ahead, raising money and making friends. He hustled tickets to the annual $500-a-plate fund-raising dinner at which the Democratic Congressional Campaign Committee realized most of its funds. The campaign committee staff kept a large chart on a wall in its cramped office, listing the names of House members and the amounts of money they had brought in. Coelho's name was second from the top.

Coelho raised about $50,000 his first year, and $50,000 more the next. It was a remarkable feat for a freshman with no particular influence to cash in with lobbyists.

But as the 1980 elections approached, Coelho got $80,000 for Jim Wright of Texas, the Majority Leader, who faced a strong Republican challenge. He raised $100,000 for James Corman of California, a twenty-year veteran of the House and chairman of the campaign committee. He staged a fund-raising event in Modesto for the Carter-Mondale campaign, getting $100,000 for the President's re-election effort from Central Valley oilmen and growers.

The money that Coelho raised in 1980 marked him as a comer in the eyes of the leaders of the House, especially Wright. But Coelho's big opportunity opened up on election night. Ronald Reagan, underrated by most Democrats and Washington journalists, who considered him a political and intellectual lightweight, seized the White House in an astonishing victory over Jimmy Carter, who managed but 41 percent of the vote and carried only six states and the District of Columbia. Republicans scored a rout in the Senate that was beyond their most optimistic hopes, defeating nine Democratic incumbents and picking up a net gain of twelve seats, thus taking control from the Democrats for the first time since 1954. Among the fallen were some of the best-known liberals: George McGovern of South Dakota, Birch Bayh of Indiana, John Culver of Iowa, Frank Church of Idaho, Warren Magnuson of Washington, and Gaylord Nelson of Wisconsin.

The House remained the last bastion of Democratic control and a relatively safe haven for incumbents, 91 percent of whom were re-elected. But even there Democrats were shocked by the unexpected Republican success. The GOP scored a net gain of thirty-three seats, their best pickup since 1966 and the second-best showing in thirty-four years. In all, twenty-eight Democratic incumbents were defeated for re-election, half of them veterans of at least ten years in the House.

The Democratic leadership was decimated: the fallen included the Democratic Whip, John Brademas of Indiana, the third-ranking member of the leadership; Al Ullman of Oregon, chairman of the Ways and Means Committee; and Harold "Bizz" Johnson of California, chairman of the Public Works Committee. In all, four committee chairman and fourteen subcommittee chairmen were defeated. Majority Leader Wright survived comfortably, winning 60 percent of the vote, but not before spending $1.2 million—a phenomenal amount at the time. It was a closer call than it seemed: a Fort Worth journalist wrote near the end of the campaign that he "wouldn't be stunned" if Wright lost. Ten other Democrats who survived saw their winning margins drop by ten percentage points or more from the previous election. Rep. Thomas Foley of Washington, who was chosen the new Whip, had himself survived a near-miss, winning with only 52 percent. The survivors still had a healthy majority, but for the first time in a generation the Democratic grip on the House seemed to be loosening.

Most humiliating in a way was the defeat in California of Corman. The campaign committee had proven so impotent that it couldn't save its own chairman. With Coelho's help, Corman raised $905,000, far more than the $560,000 spent by his opponent, an anti-busing activist. Corman refused to temper his support for racial school busing even though his Los Angeles constituents were outraged by a court-ordered scheme that forced some children to attend schools fifty miles from home. Coelho took over the management of Corman's campaign personally, filling in for an ailing administrative aide. The power of incumbency was so great that Corman might still have won if Carter hadn't conceded defeat to Reagan before the West Coast polls closed, causing some voters to stay home. But Corman was too far out of touch with his constituents and lost by 752 votes.

Corman's defeat opened a vacancy at the helm of the campaign committee. He had been a great favorite of Tip

O'Neill; they are both white-haired Irish liberals. Impressed by Coelho's ability to raise money, Corman recommended to the Speaker that the young man from the Central Valley be chosen to head the committee for the 1981–82 election cycle. To sound out Coelho, the Speaker dispatched his son, Christopher "Kip" O'Neill, a Washington lobbyist. Coelho made a surprising declaration.

"I said I could raise $5 million," he recalled.

He was promising to more than double the 1980 total. Under Corman, the campaign committee had come up with a little more than $2 million during the 1980 campaign, and ended up $200,000 in debt. Most of the money was produced at the annual dinner, from a thin stratum of wealthy liberals, union officials, and lobbyists for commercial interests. O'Neill, who had been chairman of the committee himself years earlier, didn't believe Coelho could possibly increase receipts so dramatically. But Kip O'Neill and Coelho, not far apart in age, had become personal friends during Coelho's years as Sisk's aide. O'Neill also, perhaps, saw more clearly than his father the potential for extracting money from Washington's network of PACs and business interests. He argued on Coelho's behalf, and the Speaker listened.

Technically, the chairman is elected by the Democratic Caucus, made up of all the Democrats in the House. As a practical matter, the leadership's wishes are seldom overridden in such matters. Coelho had a rival for the job, Tom Harkin of Iowa, a liberal who was two years senior to him. But Coelho got what he thought was a promise that the Speaker himself would nominate him for the job. Wright, the Majority Leader, would second the nomination. Victory seemed assured.

Something happened the night before the election, however, that sent Coelho scrambling. Without explanation, O'Neill sent word he wouldn't nominate Coelho after all.

"So I had to go to Jim Wright," Coelho recalled. "I told him Tip wouldn't. I didn't know why. Still don't. Would he? He said, 'Absolutely.' " So Wright nominated Coelho as the Speaker sat silently. Coelho still rolled over Harkin by a 2–1 margin. It was the start of a warm relationship with Wright, and a rocky one with the Speaker. While introducing Coelho at a formal meeting afterward, O'Neill mispronounced Coelho's name, saying it "KWAY-lo" instead of "KWELL-o." "Now, Tip mispronounces most names," Coelho said. "But I knew it was deliberate."

To O'Neill, Coelho represented the new generation of college-boy congressmen who were trying to take over. The Speaker was a big-city pol who would rather play golf than read a book. As the man at the top of the ladder, he didn't like sophomores shaking it. Coelho was small, quick, Portuguese, a former campus hotshot from across the continent. Worse, he was eternally in motion, always whispering to colleagues. O'Neill didn't like whisperers. Coelho was no bookworm either, but he read news articles and staff reports constantly, absorbing every word written about Congress and its politics, scouring his material for clues to the enemy's strategy or signs of weakness. He slept only a few hours a night, and would grind away in his basement study long after his wife and daughters had gone to bed. He made O'Neill nervous; eventually the Speaker came to believe that Coelho was plotting against him.

Still, House Democrats were desperate for money. "When they saw someone willing to raise all that money, without any agenda, but just wanting to be a player, they decided to take a chance," Coelho explained.

The 1980 election not only opened Corman's job for Coelho, it created an atmosphere of fear that would drive Democrats for the next six years. The reason that Coelho would court the wealthy so assiduously, badger business PACs so openly, and sell access to senior lawmakers so systematically was that he feared the Republicans' money and their political "technology." Democrats were afraid that with the polling, television, and mail that money could buy, Republicans might topple them from power at last. For the first time in a generation, complete control of the federal government seemed within the GOP's grasp. Conservative Republicans were claiming that a major political realignment was at hand, like the election of Franklin Roosevelt in 1932 that established Democrats as the majority party.

Previously the Democratic leadership had resisted the idea of building a well-financed, modern party apparatus. They had been able to win re-election easily enough without the help of any party organization. House members controlled the new forms of patronage directly, through the casework of their growing office staffs and through the federal grants and tax breaks they could secure for constituents. Besides, if a powerful organization controlled the flow of campaign money and other election resources, party leaders might demand greater discipline. National goals might have to take precedence over the local, parochial concerns on which House members preferred to concentrate. What was the point in passing tax reform or balancing the budget if it meant angering some voters and donors?

But while Democrats had been complacent, lulled by the ease with which they could win using the resources of their offices, the GOP was constructing a political juggernaut that threatened to change the balance of power. It was a remarkable comeback; only a few years earlier the Republican party had been flattened by Watergate. Donations had declined and talented candidates were reluctant to run as Republicans. In that political atmosphere Republicans had suffered a net loss of forty-nine House seats in the 1974 elections. But in the six years since then they had recovered miraculously, riding the crest of an anti-Washington, anti-tax wave. Tens of millions of dollars were tumbling in from a fast-growing list of middle-class donors furious at the excesses of big government and a permissive society.

Unlike the Democratic Congressional Campaign Committee, which stuck to its narrow base of affluent liberals and lobbyists, the National Republican Congressional Committee was forced to develop a new financial base by necessity. Using techniques borrowed from catalogue merchants and mail-order sellers, it was systematically sending millions of letters to people whose names appeared on likely-looking lists: lapsed Republican donors, registered Republicans in prosperous zip codes, subscribers to conservative magazines. And people were responding. The NRCC had so much money its biggest problem was figuring out how to spend it.

In the two-year election cycle leading up to the 1980 elections the NRCC raised $26.8 million, more than double what it had achieved two years earlier. Its income was thirteen times as great as the DCCC's. The Democratic committee considered itself successful if it could afford to donate $5,000 to the campaigns of its most threatened incumbents and influential committee chairmen, who viewed the contributions as entitlements of office. For non-incumbents, whether they were running for a vacant seat or challenging an incumbent Republican, there was little help. The Democratic committee was part of the engine of incumbency, designed to preserve the status quo, not to stir up change.

Republicans, however, were finding ways to spend tens of thousands of dollars in races where money could make a difference. They were recruiting candidates, giving them training in modern campaign techniques, steering them to the best political consultants, supplying them with free research on their opponents, "kick-starting" their campaigns with early infusions of cash, aggressively marketing candidates to the growing number of business PAC donors with money to give, and generally making life a good bit less comfortable for incumbent Democrats. The NRCC even spent millions on a national advertising campaign, sending the message: "Vote Republican, for a change." And disgruntled voters responded.

Before 1980 Democrats hadn't seen much need to match what Republicans were doing. The House leadership resisted suggestions that Democrats also try to raise money from small donors. William Sweeney, who had been executive director of the DCCC under Corman, had tried to institute a direct-mail program. But by 1980 the list of donors to the DCCC still numbered only 13,000, a small fraction of the size of the list on the GOP's computers. Sweeney got little encouragement for his efforts to build a donor file and occasionally had some roadblocks put in his way.

In fact, Speaker O'Neill once angrily demanded that Sweeney give back a $50 donation from a House employee. "Tip had an absolute rule that we could not solicit House staff people," Sweeney recalled. But a worker named Tommy Iorio, who had been a fixture in the House for twenty-five years or so, inadvertently received a solicitation. "He was on some Maryland Democratic party donor list, which we mailed," Sweeney said. "So he sent in all of $50. And we had a standard thank-you, approved by the Speaker, which went out. And he's walking around the House floor showing off his thank-you letter. I get a call over to the Speaker's office. He is furious. 'How could you let such a thing happen?' I'm wandering over there trying to figure out what in God's name we're talking about. I go walking in and the Speaker, who I think is a great man, *chews me out* for this thank-you letter for a $50 contribution from some Maryland Democrat who happens to work for the House. *Insists* I return the money. Says he's got a long-standing policy, and I know that policy, and how could I let that happen?"

Sheepishly, Sweeney tracked down Iorio and tried to give his $50 back. Iorio had fallen ill. "This man is in his hospital bed, saying, 'Keep the money. I love the Speaker. I'm a Democrat!'"

House leaders became more interested in raising money from small donors—and from all other sources, too—after the Reagan landslide. "All of those boys went through a whole life change in the 1980 election," Sweeney said. Coelho thus gained a free hand to build a new party machine.

He was no innovator; he stole his blueprints from the Republicans. He was keenly aware of the corporationlike party bureaucracy that the Republicans were constructing. The way he saw it, Republican money was turning politics into a business, and Democrats had to become businesslike themselves or give up their hold on the House. He began

laying plans for a new building, a television studio, computers. Whatever the Republicans had, Coelho wanted.

The DCCC had a long and checkered history before 1980,
and nobody had ever described it as a businesslike proposition. For generations it had been little more than a bank
account, and a thin one at that. In 1913, for example, each
member of the House was asked to contribute $100 to the
fund. In those days, party bosses made assessments on the
salaries of public officials. This was among the evils of the
spoils system, and led to federal laws prohibiting solicitation of campaign money from federal employees, or even
soliciting campaign funds on federal property. It was this
old-fashioned kind of abuse to which Speaker O'Neill was
still reacting when he forced Sweeney to return Iorio's $50.

Republican congressional committees, too, once raised
most of their money this way. A Senate investigation into
election fraud found that in 1878 a GOP congressional campaign committee took in $106,000, of which $80,000 came
from appointed officials. They were expected to kick in anywhere from 1 percent to 3 percent of their salaries.

The campaign committee also had been a notorious
money laundry, a discreet pipeline through which incumbent Democratic members of the House passed campaign
contributions they would have been embarrassed to accept
openly.

"If you were from a conservative state and couldn't show
labor money, it went through the Democratic Congressional Campaign Committee," said Sweeney. "If you were the
chairman of the Agriculture Committee, and . . . you didn't
want the sugarcane people showing up in your beet-sugar
district, it went through the campaign committee. That was
prior to my tenure, but that's what it was."

Sweeney joined the committee in 1974, but the laundry
business was still flourishing as recently as the 1972 elections, when the DCCC and other campaign committees
were used to circumvent new disclosure laws that took effect in April of that year.

In the 1972 elections, for example, labor-union money was

filtered through the DCCC's sister committee, the Democratic Senatorial Campaign Committee, for Sam Nunn of Georgia, who won election to the Senate that year, and for Sen. Thomas J. McIntyre of New Hampshire, who won re-election.

McIntyre had special reason to hide his union money; it was forbidden by state law. Although the law was rather clearly unconstitutional and was later nullified, McIntyre's handlers found it more convenient to conceal the money by directing it through the campaign committee than to confront the law head-on. He received $88,520 through the committee, almost half of it laundered donations from labor-union political action committees.

In another such case from 1972, Democrat Sen. John Sparkman of Alabama, then chairman of the Banking Committee, received $24,000 through the Senate committee from bankers, stockbrokers, and others, including the chairman of Lockheed Corp. The Lockheed money could have caused political embarrassment; Sparkman had urged passage of a controversial $250 million federal loan guarantee for Lockheed, which had passed the Senate by a single vote in 1971. Taking money openly from Lockheed would raise questions Sparkman preferred not to answer, so the donation was simply routed through the campaign committee and hidden safely from view. Only long after the election, when the public-interest group Common Cause brought a lawsuit and forced the campaign committee to open its books, did the subterfuge become known.

The House campaign committee also had been a patronage mechanism for the ambitious. When the young congressman Lyndon Johnson effectively took over the committee in the 1940 elections, he used it to dispense political funds to needy candidates from his wealthy Texas patrons, advancing a political career that eventually led to the White House. He was aided at the campaign committee by a young staff man named John Connally, who later became governor of Texas, Secretary of the Treasury, and, after switching parties and winning acquittal of a federal bribery indictment, a contender for the Republican presidential nomination.

A past chairman of the campaign committee, Wayne Hays of Ohio, used his control of donations to cement his formidable influence in the House, until his own career ended in a celebrated sex scandal. The committee's chairmanship also was a stepping-stone on the way to becoming Speaker of the House for Tip O'Neill.

Those were the days when political cash came in brown paper bags. "Tip tells the story that in the old days he would go around the country and play gin at parties," Coelho said. "On the bed would be a bag, and people would just throw in thousands, or whatever it was, and at the end of the evening he would just grab the bag and take off, and that's how he raised his money. . . . And people talk about *our* system being corrupt."

It was cash-and-carry politics; checks weren't required then. "There are members of Congress who used to charge people when they came in the office to lobby," Coelho said. "And it would be in cash."

History won't reflect all that went on at the DCCC in those days. Sweeney saw to that shortly after he was elevated from research director to executive director of the committee in July 1977. He rented a document shredder and spent two days destroying records of the DCCC going back thirty years.

At the time, investigators from several agencies and the House Committee on Standards of Official Conduct, better known as the "ethics committee," were pursuing claims of influence purchasing being made by a Korean playboy and confidence man, Tong Sun Park. It came to be known as the Koreagate affair, the Democratic equivalent of Watergate.

"One of the first things I did—I had been there since '74 and took it over in '77—is to say, 'What are all those file cabinets that have been locked in the back?' " Sweeney said. "Those are the committee's financial records going back to the 1940s. I called our general counsel and said, 'What is the federal law as far as keeping records?' They said, 'Five years.' . . . I said, 'Gentlemen, I am shredding the fishing hole.' "

Within months, investigators asked for access to the old records. "They had heard this rumor and that rumor." If he hadn't destroyed the records, Sweeney said, "I would have spent my entire tenure unearthing stuff that was done before I was born."

When Coelho took over the campaign committee his only worry about the past was how to pay off the $200,000 debt he inherited from Corman. The committee had borrowed from a bank to finance its last round of contributions in 1980. Even going into debt was an accomplishment; the committee previously didn't have a credit rating, and Sweeney took some pride in establishing the ability to borrow. But while the Democratic committee was in the red, the Republican congressional committee finished 1980 with a cash surplus of $4 million. It had in the bank twice as much money as the Democratic committee had been able to raise in two years.

In 1977 the committee was doing business from room B353 of the Rayburn House Office Building, on public property. Rent, utilities, furniture, and office equipment were paid for by the taxpayers. House Democrats thought of the campaign committee as akin to a legislative committee, like Armed Services or Ways and Means. The staff consisted of Sweeney, a secretary, and a bookkeeper. While Republicans were installing computers and a television studio, Sweeney was stuck with government-issue typewriters.

The committee soon lost its public subsidy. In a fit of reform, Congress evicted both Republican and Democratic fund-raising committees from the government quarters they had enjoyed for years. The same thing was happening to the two Senate campaign committees. By the time Coelho took over, the DCCC was in rented space. The staff had increased to eleven persons and a tiny direct-mail program had begun.

From that nucleus, Coelho started to build. He set up a dozen little committees of House members, stacked with his personal friends, each assigned to push some special project. He began laying plans for his own television studio, his own direct-mail fund-raising, his own public-opinion polling.

"He said, 'These are all the things the Republicans have. These are the things that we're going to have,' " recalled Marta David, the committee's research director.

Soon after Coelho took charge he hired his own man as executive director, Martin Franks, a money-wise veteran of years of Democratic political campaigns, whose previous job had been with the Carter-Mondale campaign. Sweeney moved on to become executive director of the Democratic National Committee. David was retained and promoted to political director. Franks and David constituted the entire senior staff of the committee in those early days.

"We had just taken this horrible loss, and Tony was the cheerleader," David said. "Tony was the one who was out there selling the committee to his peers, giving it credibility."

Corman had seldom visited the campaign committee's offices, but Coelho scheduled meeting after meeting, one hour apart, for three or four days on end. David learned early to set up meetings so the offices to be visited were as close together as possible. Working at the DCCC before and after 1980, she recalled, "was like working in two different places."

It was a scary time for the demoralized Democrats. "We were on the ropes in '81," Franks said. In a few short months President Reagan, flush with victory, pushed through a program of cuts in federal programs, cuts in taxes, and increases in military spending. Democrats were in such disarray that a celebrated "bidding war" broke out over the tax cut, with Democrats actually proposing deep cuts in business taxes as the price for winning a legislative "victory" that, in the end, eluded them anyway. Southern "boll weevil" Democrats were siding with the Republican President on vote after crucial vote.

Republicans figured it was possible to win enough seats

in 1982 to take control of the House. After their thirty-three-seat pickup in 1980, they needed to gain only twenty-six more to achieve a majority. They thought they would be helped by the constitutionally mandated redistricting that would follow from the 1980 census; the Democratic Northeast was certain to lose seats, and the more conservative Sunbelt states would gain them. Furthermore, Republicans thought they didn't need to win all twenty-six seats outright. If they could take something close to that number, a few Democratic turncoats could complete the job. There were enough conservative Democrats, in districts where Ronald Reagan was overwhelmingly popular, who might be convinced to switch parties. Many were already voting regularly with the Republicans anyway on important legislation.

Republican Rep. Guy Vander Jagt of Michigan, the Republican campaign committee chair, recalled that in 1981 "the House Democrats were nicer to House Republicans than at any time I have been there. It was *real* to them that they might be a minority."

Vander Jagt believed that a net pickup of twenty seats, perhaps as few as a dozen, would be enough to tip the balance of control and, with the help of a few party switchers, at last elect a Republican Speaker of the House. Nobody was certain exactly where the psychological tipping point lay. Hardly any Democrat, no matter how conservative or fearful of the Reagan tide, would defect to the Republicans at the cost of giving up a committee or subcommittee chairmanship. "There is absolutely no incentive to switch parties to be part of a bigger minority," Vander Jagt observed. But if the gap were closed enough, then Republicans could gain control by inducing only a handful to defect, promising them chairmanships in a GOP-controlled House.

Campaign contributors also felt the momentum toward the Republicans. "Lobbyists, PACs, the feeling was everywhere," Vander Jagt said. Money was flowing to the GOP even more rapidly than before, as were business PACs and conservative, ideological PACs. Money, always a necessity in politics, was now being viewed by Democrats as a decisive weapon.

Coelho got the campaign committee job because the party was desperate for money and he was good at raising it. There was still something of the would-be priest in him; twice, troubled couples asked him to be their marriage counselor, and one patched up their differences with his help. The House of Representatives became his parish. Colleagues came to him for political help, to find a good poll taker or a mailing list of political action committees.

"I became father confessor," he said. "People came to me with sexual problems, marital problems, financial problems, you name it. . . . I found out more about people than I ever wanted to know or hear about. I knew everything about a lot of my colleagues: the financial condition that they were in. How they were struggling with certain things."

Often, the balm he administered was money. He brokered campaign contributions for colleagues facing tough re-election campaigns. He arranged for colleagues who needed personal money to get appearance fees, typically $1,000, from friendly lobbyists.

Priestly compassion and friendship were so strong in Coelho that they sometimes outweighed his judgment. In 1981, to aid a friend whose nineteen-year-old son was in trouble, he wrote a letter that posed a threat to his political career. The son, David Weidert, had been convicted of a particularly brutal murder; the victim had been kidnapped, bludgeoned, stabbed, choked, and then buried alive. Weidert faced a probable sentence of life in prison without parole, but Coelho wrote to Weidert's probation officer arguing that a lesser sentence would save taxpayers $15,000 for each year taken off the life term.

Coelho's administrative assistant Archie Nahigian urged him not to write the letter. "I told him, 'Tony, it's a mistake. It's a political mistake,' " Nahigian recalled. "He said, 'I know, but he's a friend.' "

Coelho's gesture turned out to be useless; the judge said he couldn't give the letter any weight because the law made a life sentence mandatory in Weidert's case. But Coelho's action drew an outcry from the victim's mother and others.

He was accused of being influenced by campaign donations; Weidert's father, John, was executive director of California Westside Farmers, a group that had contributed $1,000 to Coelho's 1980 campaign and $1,000 more during 1981. "This case is an example of how politicians differentiate among their clientele," said retired sheriff Ed Bates. "I don't think he would have written a letter for some unknown person out there."

Bates, a celebrity because of his role in solving a 1976 case in which twenty-six schoolchildren and their bus driver were kidnapped, became the Republican nominee and campaigned against Coelho on a law-and-order platform. Former President Gerald Ford appeared on his behalf. President Reagan's political director, Ed Rollins, said Coelho was on a White House "hit list" of Democratic lawmakers; "I think that he created an issue when he wrote his letter of support for a convicted murderer," Rollins said. While he was under attack at home, Coelho also was being attacked by colleagues in Washington who were unhappy with the way he was rationing campaign donations from the Democratic Congressional Campaign Committee. "It was the worst couple of months I have ever spent in my life," Coelho said. During a flight between California and Washington he suffered an epileptic seizure, something he hadn't experienced in many years.

Fortunately for Coelho, Bates turned out to be a lackluster campaigner who couldn't raise much money. Coelho also had editorial support from the Fresno *Bee,* which praised his "political courage" for writing the letter. Coelho outspent Bates $768,000 to $108,000, and survived with 64 percent of the vote.

"Probably the one fault Tony has is, he believes the best in everybody," said Nahigian. "If somebody comes to him with a down-and-out, hard-luck story, he wants to help. He errs too much on the side of trying to help."

During 1986 Coelho took time to fulfill a deathbed promise to an old friend, the late Rep. Gillis Long of Louisiana, by helping his widow, Cathy, deal with a staggering debt she had run up winning election to her late husband's House seat. In this case the combination of priestly compassion and money-driven politics resulted in the narrowest of special-interest legislation, a bill to benefit one person.

"Gillis was one of my mentors," Coelho said. "And when he was dying he told me one day that he would like to make sure that I kept an eye out for Cathy. She really had never been on her own, had never done things by herself, and he'd appreciate it if I would keep an eye out. And I said yes, obviously." Long died in January 1985. In the Southern political tradition, his widow won a special election to succeed him. But to finance her victory she borrowed more than $400,000 and ran up unpaid campaign bills for thousands more. The same donors who had been happy to give to her husband, the third-ranking member of the Rules Committee, weren't inclined to give to her, the most junior member of the House, with no important committee assignments.

"People just took advantage of her," Coelho said. "She spent money to get elected that she didn't need to spend. And she thought that after she got elected she'd be able to pay it off. Gillis always did. And after she got elected she realized that nobody cared. And she called the same people that she had called for Gillis, and instead of giving her $1,000 they'd give her $50. PACs that Gillis had been close to, instead of giving her $5,000 they'd give her $200."

Saddled by debt and still feeling the pain of her husband's death, Long soon decided to retire without seeking a second term. But that only compounded her money problems. Donors found even less reason to give to a lame duck.

Coelho saw a solution in the campaign money that Gillis Long had left behind when he died. It was gathering interest at the rate of more than $2,000 per month. As of mid-1986 his fund contained $464,113.33, more than enough to pay off his widow's campaign debts. A loophole in the federal election law would have allowed Gillis Long to keep the money for personal use had he retired, and so it had become part of his estate. Still, there was a hitch; the money would be considered personal income to his widow and thus subject to a substantial federal tax.

"So she came to me," Coelho said. They sat together in the House chamber during official business one day, and Cathy Long quietly wept, overwhelmed by her burdens. "There's got to be a way to do this," Coelho said to her. He worked on the problem for months. The campaign committee's lawyer could find no way to accomplish a tax-free transfer. Neither could Ways and Means chairman Dan Rostenkowski, or even Sen. Russell Long of Louisiana, a distant cousin to Gillis and, more importantly, a power on the tax-writing Finance Committee. "This is a priority," Coelho wrote to an aide, Robert Chlopak. Chlopak brought back word that only an act of Congress could prevent Cathy Long from having to pay tax on her late husband's campaign money. Coelho sent her to appeal directly to Speaker O'Neill. "Cathy did speak with Tip yesterday and he said he would help; however, nothing specific came of it," Chlopak reported afterward. Coelho personally asked Rostenkowski to slip a special provision in the tax-reform bill that the Ways and Means Committee was drafting, and was furious when Rostenkowski refused. Coelho appealed to the Speaker. "I went to Tip and I said, 'This is very, very unfortunate. And I feel very strongly about it. There has got to be a way we can turn this around,'" Coelho recalled. "He said, 'O.K., we'll take care of it.'" A provision was tucked away in a budget bill. At last, on October 10, Chlopak reported, "The language is in the [budget] reconciliation conference report. There are no problems that we know about. When the conference report passes, the deed will be done." The bill passed without any debate on the few lines dealing with Cathy Long. Soon after, she cleaned out her late husband's leftover campaign fund, tax-free, and retired her personal debts.

Pushing through a special measure for Cathy Long was

an act of altruism for Coelho. She couldn't repay him for his help by voting for him to be Majority Whip in the next Congress, because she was retiring. Coelho acted for the pure satisfaction of helping a friend. But by doing so he only widened a loophole in the laws that are supposed to distinguish campaign contributions from bribes. It is illegal for members of Congress to convert their campaign funds to personal use, except for those who were already in Congress when the law took effect in 1980. Under a "grandfather clause," the more senior members can keep their political funds when they retire. Campaign funds are given mainly on account of official actions and thus would be illegal gratuities—a form of bribery—if put initially into the congressman's personal bank account instead of a campaign fund. The "grandfather clause" permitting post-retirement conversion of political funds is one of the most widely criticized features of the campaign laws, yet Coelho gladly exploited and exacerbated it, out of friendship.

As part of his ministry, Coelho dispensed money and advice as well as legislation. "There were some members who were in serious trouble, and we would help them with campaign contributions, honorariums, and DCCC money. And you know, as I used to laugh and joke about it, we were a one-shop service. They could come and tell me their sins and their problems, and confess 'em, and I'd deal with them as a counseling service. I've arranged for medical help for certain people, psychiatric. I've arranged for help from priests for certain people. I've arranged for attorneys for certain people. You name it. I'm a one-shop service. And I love it."

4

"Meat Market"

*A political organization has to have money for
its business . . . and who has more right to put up
than the men who get the good things that are
goin'?*

—GEORGE WASHINGTON PLUNKITT

If Democrats were to retain their control, the stream of
business money to Republican challengers simply had to be
stopped, or at least slowed. Coelho at first used friendly
persuasion and threats that were decently veiled.

In early 1981 the newly elected campaign committee
chairman began making the rounds of business groups,
seeking endorsements for Democrats from the U.S. Chamber of Commerce, the National Federation of Independent
Businesses, and others. He called this a "visitation program" to "keep the PACs honest." He tried to convince those
who controlled the money that some Democrats were pro-
business.

Democrats were frightened by business PACs. In the 1980
elections, challengers—almost all Republicans—received
$5.9 million from corporate PACs, $3.7 million from trade
and professional groups, and $2.5 million from freestand-
ing ideological PACs. Incumbent Democrats, who until

then had enjoyed a near-monopoly on PAC money, thought far too much was going to their rivals.

Democrats had been accustomed to business PACs that were pleasantly domesticated; now they saw yellow eyes burning in the night just beyond the campfire. Much of the business money in 1980 had come to Republican challengers in last-minute surges in races where Democrats were already hard pressed. Corporate and other business-related PACs were clearly growing more numerous, wealthier, and bolder, especially where they sensed political weakness.

The Houston-based Tenneco Employees Good Government Fund, for example, increased its donations more than fourfold in the 1980 elections. The PAC gave $191,550 to Republicans, but only $12,050 to Democrats. Its donations would double again in the next election. The Honeywell Employees PAC of Minneapolis nearly doubled its donations in 1980, giving $54,991 to Republicans and $9,225 to Democrats. Dow Chemical Co. maintained a network of six different PACs whose combined total donations nearly doubled in the 1980 campaign to just under $240,000, of which 82 percent went to Republicans.

Some trade-association PACs were becoming real giants, and tilting increasingly toward the GOP. The American Bankers Association PAC more than doubled its donations in the 1980 campaign, to $592,960. Republicans got 55 percent of the money, up from 48 percent in 1978. The National Association of Home Builders increased its donations sevenfold to nearly $380,000, of which Republicans received 52 percent, up from 42 percent in the previous election. The PAC of the National Association of Realtors, representing real-estate brokers and developers, gave more than $1 million to Republican candidates in the 1980 elections, more than double the amount it donated to Democrats. The Realtors were becoming even more partisan; in the 1982 elections they would provide more than $3 to Republicans for every $1 to Democrats.

Business PACs not only were growing at a much faster clip than labor and liberal PACs; they were thought to have much greater potential for future growth. At the end of 1980 corporate PACs already accounted for 47 percent of the 2,551 existing political action committees. And corporations were starting up new PACs at the rate of one every three days.

Coelho banked on the idea that the business PACs would respond to appeals to reason, that they weren't simply an arm of the Republican party. He would later write, in a confidential report to key House Democrats, that business PAC directors often insisted that they would give to pro-business Democrats if only the party could identify some. The PAC managers told him "the problem was not partisanship, but our failure to adequately market candidates," Coelho wrote.

So he set out to market Democratic House candidates in the increasingly crowded bazaar of special-interest money managers. He created a new post at the DCCC, PAC director, a staff aide who would devote full time to getting more PAC money for Democratic House candidates.

His staff made sales calls, pushing candidates who could claim business credentials. "We would try very, very hard to promote people who were more moderate," recalls Marta David. "We would go there with biographies and say, 'Well, look, he's owned his own Pizza Hut.'"

Coelho set up candidate forums at which PAC directors could look over the party's prospects. Lobbyists and candidates all milled around in a big room wearing name tags. Remembering his days as a class social chairman at Loyola University, Coelho said the PAC forums were "somewhat reminiscent of a freshman college mixer." Lobbyists called such events "cattle calls" and "meat markets."

Coelho didn't rely wholly on the supposed business credentials of his candidates, however. He announced he would record names of those who didn't support candidates he deemed worthy. It was as though a traffic cop were stopping cars to sell tickets to the police-union ball.

When the campaign committee set up the first of these mixers in October 1981, Coelho told a reporter, "In the past, this committee hasn't actively sought business PAC contributions. Now we do intend to go after them, so they won't have an excuse that we didn't try."

Then he added, "And we're going to keep a record."

At some of the meetings he held with PACs in those days, Coelho included two powerful House Democrats whose wrath no sensible businessman would want to incur, Dan Rostenkowski of Illinois, chairman of the Ways and Means Committee, and James Jones of Oklahoma, chairman of the Budget Committee. Rostenkowski presided over the taxes businessmen paid, Jones over the federal subsidies and contracts many of them relied on.

The threat was clear. Business would withhold money from Democrats at its peril.

The response was disappointing. "It was still very difficult for us to sell candidates to business people," Marta David said. She tried to promote a Democratic candidate from Roanoke, Virginia, James Olin, who had a seemingly flawless business résumé. He was retiring from a thirty-six-year career as an executive with General Electric Co., where he had been a plant manager and later general manager of the industrial electronics division. Who could be more attractive to corporate PACs? Still, David says, "they wouldn't give him any money."

That sort of thing happened time and again. Coelho, who after all was only a sophomore congressman from California, didn't move business groups to endorse many Democrats. In fact, the money continued to shift in the Republicans' favor. By the end of the 1982 campaigns corporate-sponsored PACs had actually cut the share of their money to Democrats to 34 percent, from 35 percent in 1980. The ratio for trade groups fell to under 43 percent, from 44 percent. It seemed that the long-held goal of Guy Vander Jagt was finally within his grasp.

Guy Vander Jagt did as much as anyone in Washington to promote the formation and growth of business-oriented political action committees. PACs had been invented by the union movement; the original Political Action Committee was formed by Sidney Hillman of the old Congress of Industrial Organizations when direct contributions from union treasuries to congressional candidates were outlawed in 1943. Unions, rather than using their own funds directly, organized separate bank accounts for the collection of voluntary donations from members. Union officials then financed the campaigns of friendly candidates, almost always Democrats. Labor PACs predominated for the next three decades, functioning almost as a financial arm of the Democratic party. Vander Jagt's dream, and that of other Republicans, was that business PAC money would stream to GOP candidates in the way that labor-union money flowed to Democrats.

He had been pursuing that design for six years, since taking over the National Republican Congressional Committee in 1975, after the Republicans had lost forty-three House seats in the 1974 midterm election following Richard Nixon's resignation as President.

Vander Jagt himself, though from a solidly GOP district, had been briefly projected as the loser by a news report on election night. He eventually won comfortably, but he recalled, "I was very discouraged, and very down." He fell to brooding and briefly considered retiring from politics. As he left for a post-election vacation in Jamaica, his top staff aide remarked that he would have to begin planning for the next election when he returned. "I don't know if there will be a next time," he said.

Vander Jagt's mood had improved when he returned from his Caribbean trip, however. Rather than retiring, he jumped impulsively into a contest for chairman of the campaign committee. The post was being sought by a member of the John Birch Society, John Rousselot of California, and by an heir to one of America's great industrial fortunes, Pete du Pont of Delaware, at the time a more liberal Republican. Vander Jagt reasoned that between two such ideological opposites there was some room in the middle. He won, eliminating Rousselot by a single vote on the first round and easily dispatching du Pont in the final runoff.

He took over an organization struggling to survive in a

radically new political and legal atmosphere brought on by the Watergate scandal. In a series of Senate hearings, trials, and news stories, the public learned what Washington politicians had known for decades: campaign-spending laws weren't being enforced, huge sums of money were being raised and spent in secret, and much of it was coming from illegal sources, including business corporations. When new campaign-finance laws were drawn up, they dictated that Republicans revolutionize their operations.

The new law put limits on the amounts the party could realize from wealthy donors, a traditional source of GOP money. But the law also firmly established the legal right of corporations and trade associations to set up political action committees. So the GOP began energetically to attract small donations to finance the party and to promote an increase in business PAC money to fund their candidates.

Although some trade groups and business corporations had sponsored political funds, PAC money came mainly from labor through the 1950s and 1960s. What business money there was often flowed through different channels. Company employees might be detailed to work on a friendly congressman's campaign at company expense. In many corporations, as the Watergate investigations made clear, business executives made "personal" donations that were quietly, though illegally, reimbursed through bogus expense accounts or bonuses. Some companies doled out cash directly, and quite illegally, through secret slush funds. But few businesses set up PACs.

A few statistics demonstrate labor's dominance of PAC money in those days. In the 1972 elections, labor PACs gave $3.6 million to congressional candidates, while business-related PACs gave $2.7 million. In the 1974 elections, labor PACs widened the gap, giving $6.3 million against $4.4 million for business PACs. Furthermore, the business PAC money tended to flow overwhelmingly to incumbents. Democratic incumbents didn't have to worry much about business donations financing their opponents.

At the end of 1974, a total of only 608 PACs were in existence, including 201 sponsored by unions and 89 set up by corporations, with the remainder a mixed bag of trade groups, professional associations, agricultural cooperatives, and freestanding political groups.

Vander Jagt set out to alter the balance. He gave speeches to hundreds of business groups, at conventions and in corporate boardrooms, promoting the creation of business PACs.

"They were still reluctant as hell," he said. "I spent a good deal of '75 and '76 going around beating them over the head."

Speeches were Vander Jagt's specialty. He was an old-fashioned orator, an anachronism in an age when television news editors favored politicians who boil their points down to one-line "sound bites." He believed people could still be moved by the spoken word. He wrote his own speeches, practiced them endlessly, and delivered them from memory in a resonant baritone. He was, besides being an attorney and a former television announcer, a graduate of the Yale Divinity School and an ordained Presbyterian minister. He was a preacher in the temple of free enterprise.

He was a believer, too. He told and retold the story of his immigrant father arriving in the United States nearly penniless from Holland and working his way to prosperity. The standard speech he gave to business groups, over and over again, was a plea for corporate managers to take a hand in government. "Into Washington have moved the Ralph Naders, the consumers, the environmentalists, the labor unions, and all of the rest," he said in an early version, given to two hundred executives of Dow Chemical Co. in Midland, Michigan. "And they really can't do anything except impact on political decisions. They don't have any achievements to their credit. That's all they do, but boy, they do that very, very well. And they've moved into the vacuum that you have left for them because you've been doing more important things."

To the congressman's way of thinking, followers of

Nader, the consumer advocate, were striving to smash a business system that, whatever its flaws, had produced a standard of living for the American public that was the envy of the rest of the world. Washington had grown angry toward business, he said, and much of that hostility was coming from tax-supported colleges and universities, creating a generation of business-haters. An alarming number of college students told poll takers they favored the nationalization of all basic industry, Vander Jagt said. Business executives and especially corporate managers should "move into the arena" of politics and "restore some balance."

In later versions of his speech Vander Jagt seemed to question the patriotism of any business executive who resisted the idea of setting up a PAC. He told his business audiences that a former colleague on the Michigan congressional delegation, Neil Staebler, had been denied reappointment as a Democratic member of the Federal Election Commission because he voted with Republicans in a landmark decision permitting the Sun Oil Co. to establish a PAC. That decision removed whatever legal ambiguity might have remained about the right of corporations to sponsor political funds and dashed the hopes of Democrats and union officials that a corporate PAC movement could be hobbled by regulatory decree. The vote naturally angered many Democrats, and President Carter appointed someone else when Commissioner Staebler's term expired. "This Democrat gave his political life to open the door for you," Vander Jagt would tell his business audiences. "And if you then don't have the gumption to walk through that open door, to take advantage of the chance he gave you, you have no right to call yourself Americans."

That was pretty strong stuff, but such was Vander Jagt's zeal. Patriotism, capitalism, Republicanism, and business PAC money were all mixed together in his mind.

He was part of an effort pushed by the National Association of Manufacturers and the U.S. Chamber of Commerce to draw businessmen into politics. In 1975 and 1976 the num-

ber of corporate-sponsored PACs jumped nearly fivefold, to
433. The number nearly doubled again in the next two
years, and by 1986 it exceeded 1,700. But even so, things
weren't working the way Vander Jagt had hoped.

Vander Jagt assumed in those days, as did many other
Republicans, that business PACs would become a political
treasury of the GOP. Typically, 95 percent of all labor PAC
money went to Democratic candidates. "It never even occurred to me that if business formed PACs the great bulk of
the money wouldn't go to Republicans," Vander Jagt said.

But Democrats claimed a big share of the new business
money from the start. Business PACs gave heavily to incumbents of both parties. When they gave to non-incumbent Republicans, it most often was in races where the seat
was vacant and there was therefore no worry about offend-
ing an incumbent Democrat. Very little business money
flowed to challengers. That was a shock to Vander Jagt.

After the 1976 campaigns he briefed President Ford on the
disappointing way that business PAC money had been
spent. To be sure, business-related PACs more than doubled
their donations in that election to $10 million. Their com-
bined giving actually exceeded that of labor for the first
time; union PACs gave $8.2 million. But Vander Jagt's fig-
ures showed that only 4 percent of the swelling flow of
business donations had gone to GOP challengers. He had
expected much, much more, and so had President Ford.

"Ford wouldn't believe me; he didn't think it was possible," Vander Jagt recalled. "So I wasn't the only stupid one."

Though Democrats promoted the notion that Republicans had a massive money advantage, it was always the
Democratic candidates who enjoyed the real financial edge;
the fear after 1980 was that Republicans were redressing
the balance. The Democratic *party's* financial weakness
was an old and familiar story. The Democratic National
Committee was still paying off debts from the 1968 presidential campaigns of Hubert Humphrey and Robert Kennedy.
Political reporters were naturally alert to the growing size
of Vander Jagt's war chest at the National Republican Con-

gressional Committee, and to the splashy advertising campaigns of the big, conservative PACs. Headlines played up
the Republican campaign committee's 13-1 advantage over
its Democratic rival.

It was much harder to track what was actually going on
where it mattered, adding up the combined spending of
2,000 House and Senate candidates and breaking that down
by party and by whether the candidates were incumbents
or challengers or were running for open seats. The Federal
Election Commission published official figures, but only
long after the elections were over. By then most reporters
had stopped paying attention. But the truth was that Democrats outspent Republicans. Even in the 1980 elections, in
which Democrats and many political reporters came to believe that Republican money was responsible for several
victories, it was actually Democratic congressional candidates who, overall, spent more money, raised more money,
and received more donations from political action committees. The GOP triumphed, not because its candidates had
more money, but because they had enough and had it when
it mattered, enabling them to catch the wave of popular
discontent and ride it into office.

Democratic candidates, who more often than not were
incumbents running for re-election, not only got 94 percent
of the labor PAC money in 1980; they received 44 percent of
the donations of trade and professional groups and 36 percent of the corporate-sponsored PAC money as well.

For a time it seemed that the Democratic era of dominance might be ending. Business tilted even more toward
the GOP in the 1982 elections in spite of Coelho's efforts.
Many business PAC managers had been captivated by the
idea that Republicans would be able to complete their takeover of Congress. Optimistic reports flowed from the Republican campaign committee on prospects for its candidates.

But that optimism wasn't well founded. The economy
plunged into the worst recession since World War II. Democrats bludgeoned Republicans for supporting the painful

budget cuts instituted by the Reagan administration, including proposals to restrain automatic increases in Social Security and old-age medical benefits. Their message was that the GOP had gone too far, that the "Reagan Revolution" was too radical. Then, in October, the unemployment rate rose into double-digit range.

Ten percent unemployment was a psychological tripwire. Within days after the October jobless figures hit the headlines, Republican poll takers in race after race watched their candidates' support shrivel. The 1982 elections turned into a debacle, with the Republicans losing twenty-six seats in the House. But it was also a wrenching experience for business PACs. Managers who invested too heavily in GOP losers had a lot of explaining to do. Among the Democrats who won, for example, was James Olin of Virginia, the former General Electric executive whom business PACs refused to support.

PAC directors felt betrayed by the Republican congressional committee. "It was just a general sense that we were not being played fairly," recalled Peter Lauer, director of the American Medical Association PAC. "We were not given realistic assessments." Coelho took a page from Jimmy Carter's book, promising the special-interest givers that he would never lie to them about the prospects of his candidates. Lauer said, "Tony worked on that, because he . . . heard from a lot of us of our dissatisfaction."

The 1982 defeat took the heart out of GOP hopes for a business-financed political revolution. Coelho meanwhile became much more brash in his approach to business PACs. He stressed over and over that Democrats retained a commanding majority in the House and that the committees important to business continued to be headed by Democrats. Businessmen would have to deal with Democrats on legislation important to them, whether they liked it or not. "His argument is that we should always go with the winner, that we should never do anything that isn't related to our business interests," said Albert Abrahams, a top Washington hand at the National Association of Realtors.

Abrahams, a Republican, disagreed with that. "We *should* be something of an instrument of change. Just being for the guy who is in is no way to get anything done." But that view was fading even among the Realtors, and among other PAC officials as well.

Funds started to flow back toward Democrats. In the 1984 campaign, even with the economy booming again and Ronald Reagan riding a wave of popular support to a forty-nine-state sweep in the presidential campaign, polling 59 percent of the popular vote, business PACs pulled back from supporting Republicans in House and Senate races.

The Realtors PAC actually reduced the amount of money it gave to Republicans during the 1984 elections by about 3 percent, to $1.6 million. Meanwhile, it increased the amount for Democrats by 73 percent, to $877,349. In 1982 it had given $3.17 to Republican candidates for every $1 for Democrats. In 1984 the ratio dropped to $1.77 to $1.

Coelho's marketing tactics sometimes resembled a legal version of the old protection racket, as when he used a heavy-handed tactic against the National Association of Home Builders. During 1984 the fast-growing Home Builders PAC was bucking the trend, leaning even more heavily toward Republicans. Fully 56 percent of its money went to GOP candidates in that campaign, up from 52 percent in 1982 and 42 percent in 1980. House Democrats were especially upset that the Home Builders refused to support a Democratic incumbent with twenty-two years' seniority, Joseph Minish of New Jersey, a party stalwart who was a personal favorite of Speaker O'Neill. Minish was struggling in a district that had suddenly become hostile territory after being redrawn under a court order to include a suburban, Republican majority. Many of his new constituents didn't know him.

Coelho engineered an attempt to extract $5,000 from the Home Builders for Minish. A letter sent to the Home Builders' chief lobbyist, Robert Bannister, noted that Minish was the third-ranking Democrat on the Banking Committee, which handles subsidy programs worth billions of dollars to builders. It carried the signatures not only of Coelho but of Speaker O'Neill, Majority Leader Wright, Banking Committee chairman Fernand St Germain of Rhode Island, and Ways and Means chairman Rostenkowski, who dealt with tax breaks worth billions more.

The signers said re-election of "our dear friend" Minish is "a number one priority" and deserves "the maximum financial contribution" of $5,000.

The extraordinary letter contained a clear threat: "The NAHB has a good relationship with Democrats in the House and we would like to see that relationship continue and grow. Your action in this race causes us to be concerned that the relationship will be damaged."

The Home Builders opposed Minish in that race primarily because the Republican, Dean Gallo, was a prominent builder and real-estate developer himself and a long-standing member of the NAHB. They were quite naturally supporting one of their own. Nevertheless, Coelho, O'Neill, Wright, St Germain, and Rostenkowski insisted the Home Builders had a duty to donate to Minish, too.

Actually, although the liberal Minish did vote consistently in favor of federal subsidies for building low-income apartments, programs that had provided a bonanza for developers, his overall voting record was rated a poor 41 percent by the NAHB.

The Home Builders resisted the pressure to give, but the letter caused great concern and prompted a pained and defensive reply from Bannister. "Dear Tony," he said. "In the past two elections, we have contributed over $1,180,000 to Democratic candidates for Congress. In the last election, we contributed to 214 Democratic candidates and to 234 so far this year." He diplomatically omitted mention of the increasingly Republican tilt of the PAC, but added pointedly, "It should be remembered that we are a business organization, not organized labor." In the end, Minish lost overwhelmingly, polling only 44 percent of the vote. His disclosure reports showed he finished with $269,000 in unspent campaign funds, money he was legally entitled to keep.

A few days after the 1984 elections, Coelho showed his pleasure at blunting Republican business PAC donations. "At the same time they [business PACs] were killing us they were coming to us for legislative solutions," he said. He said he had gone to more than a hundred business groups with a single message: Democrats "are going to retain control of the House for the remainder of this century. . . . We have the advantage. We're the incumbents. They have to beat us."

Now the Republicans felt betrayed. Richard Cheney of Wyoming, chairman of the House Republican Policy Committee, wrote a memo to his fellow GOP House members in June 1985 that reflected the frustration that many of them were feeling. "I have been, and continue to be, a strong believer in the PAC system," he wrote. "But I do think we Republicans need to remind our friends in the PAC community that we are determined to become the majority party in the House of Representatives, and that we do not look kindly on organizations that help the Democrats perpetuate their majority."

The memo included a study by his staff purporting to show that in "the 25 closest House races" of 1984, Democrats not only got most of the union PAC money but also received 9 percent more of the corporate-sponsored PAC donations as well. That turned out to be wrong: the study actually included only twenty-five races in which Democratic incumbents were being threatened, ignoring close contests for vacant seats and races in which corporate PACs had rallied to defend sitting Republicans. It also failed to count receipts that came in late in the campaign, when business PACs tend to give heavily. But even though it stretched the facts, the Cheney study showed how bitter Republicans were becoming over the performance of their offspring, the business PACs.

"It is clearly mistaken to regard corporate PACs as the baileywick [sic] of Republicans," the Cheney study said. "It is vitally important that we reconsider the current relationship between PACs and the House wing of the Republican party. . . . We should make it abundantly clear to our allies in the PAC community that we expect them not only to support deserving incumbents but also to provide needed financial resources for promising Republican challengers."

Cheney might as well have been old King Lear making empty threats. Republicans weren't in any position to put the squeeze on business PACs. They were in the minority. They controlled no committee chairmanships. What could they do for the business PACs, or to them, for that matter?

Actually, Cheney was showing himself to be something of a slow learner when it came to PACs, as were most of his Republican colleagues. He had been present in the White House, as Gerald Ford's chief of staff, when Vander Jagt gave his briefing on the dismal support that corporate PACs gave to Republican challengers in the 1974 elections. Now, ten years later, those PACs were merely reverting to type. As a group, they remained far more interested in currying favor with the ruling faction than in promoting the free-market ideology the Republicans championed.

Coelho got hold of a copy of the Cheney memo and took it as high praise of his own performance. He circulated copies to PAC managers himself, with a cover letter that played heavily on his I'll-never-lie-to-you theme.

"Obviously frustrated by our strong showing last year, House Republicans are still looking for alibis and resorting to thinly-veiled threats and false accusations," Coelho said. The GOP projection of a gain of thirty to forty House seats hadn't come true, he noted. He accused Vander Jagt's committee of bamboozling PAC managers with "blue smoke and mirrors."

Coelho and Vander Jagt would continue their tug-of-war through the 1986 elections. But for the GOP the zest had gone out of the game.

5

"The PACs
Are Whores!"

*How, then, can you expect what they call "busi-
ness men" to turn into politics all at once and
make a success of it? It is just as if I went up to
Columbia University and started to teach
Greek.*
—GEORGE WASHINGTON PLUNKITT

Along the 1986 campaign trail, Guy Vander Jagt felt frustrated and betrayed. "The PACs are *whores!*" he exclaimed.
    In the struggle for business money, Coelho had won.
    The idea that Republicans might take over the House had
long since faded. Vander Jagt would be pleased simply to
hold on to the House seats Republicans already possessed.
Coelho was predicting he'd score a net gain of perhaps ten
to fifteen seats. The PACs were convinced that Vander
Jagt's cause was hopeless, and their money flowed accordingly.
    Some business groups were now so eager to please the
Democratic leadership that they were giving to Democratic
candidates who weren't incumbents. In Louisiana they
were siding overwhelmingly with a Democratic candidate,
Tommy Hudson, whose list of business donors ran al-
phabetically from Abbott Laboratories to the Yellow
Freight System. He was collecting what would amount to

$185,000 from PACs, mostly business groups. That was a large sum for any non-incumbent House candidate, but particularly for a Democrat. His business donors included the American Bankers Association, the National Automobile Dealers Association, Shell Oil, Tenneco, and Drexel Burnham Lambert. Judging Hudson by his list of donors alone, one would swear he was a Republican.

Vander Jagt complained that business PACs feared to appear partisan. "They're always looking for conservative Democrats," he said. "And they do not understand the importance of control." If Republicans could gain a majority, he argued, they would oversee committee chairmanships and the Speaker's chair and with them the flow of legislation.

Labor understood that principle. For example, union PACs were giving very little to Hudson's Republican opponent, Richard Baker. Baker was an ex-Democrat from a blue-collar district who ran up a pro-labor record as a state representative. But labor PACs deserted their old friend when he became a Republican. The Republican Baker would eventually win his election, even without much PAC support. But elsewhere business PAC money was helping non-incumbent Democrats to victory.

In Salt Lake City, liberal Democrat Wayne Owens, a former member of the House, was running to regain his old seat. He was having trouble collecting some PAC donations, and Coelho came to his aid.

A number of PACs had promised money to Owens but hadn't come through. Coelho was particularly interested in the Realtors, whose Utah local had endorsed Owens and committed $5,000. He heard that the national directors of the PAC were delaying the check and talking about reducing it to $2,500.

Owens had courted one Utah Realtors official after another, lobbying for money. He had been a House member before but lost a bid for the Senate in 1974. While in office he compiled a liberal voting record, but he told PAC executives he had changed. One Realtor said, "He now indicated

that he had learned his lesson, that he was far more conservative and he knew what he had to do to win." PAC
officers in Utah urged a $5,000 donation on April 18, but now
in June the national board of the PAC was still deferring a
decision.

Some national PAC leaders wanted to keep the door open
for the Republicans. If the Realtors, the largest of all business PACs, gave a $5,000 donation to the Democrat so early,
it would be taken as an emphatic vote of confidence in
Owens, and lesser business PACs would get the message
that he was acceptable to business and probably would win.
They would classify Owens as a safe investment, and more
money would flow from those wishing to please Coelho and
the Democratic leadership.

Coelho met with Realtors PAC officials in Washington, and he wasn't subtle. "He berated them rather lust-
ily for failing to support some of his guys," recalled one
participant, a seasoned operative. "Even I, with all
my years in politics, was surprised by the ferocity of the
attack."

PAC leaders, perhaps anticipating Coelho's arrival, had
approved the full $5,000 for Owens the day before the meet-
ing, although the check wasn't received until some time
afterward. Coelho angrily demanded support for other
Democrats as well. He criticized the Realtors particularly
for withholding funds from Richard Stallings, a freshman
Democrat from Idaho who had compiled a flawless voting
record on the measures that the PAC chose for keeping
score. In Stallings's case Idaho Realtors were hoping to
recapture the overwhelmingly Republican district for the
GOP, which had lost it only because the previous incumbent, George Hansen, had been convicted on four felony
counts of falsifying his personal financial disclosure forms
and was later imprisoned.

Coelho went to the Realtors meeting vowing to hammer
away. "I really want to hit them over the head," Coelho told
his staff beforehand. "The locals are asking that he [Stall-

ings] be given $5,000, and Washington is delay, delay, delay. We really need to go after these people."

The meeting grew heated. "I don't know why I've even been wasting my time here," Coelho said. But he had achieved the desired effect; within weeks the Realtors remitted $5,000 to Stallings, too.

The money the Realtors sent to Owens helped his PAC total grow to $385,000, the highest ever received by a non-incumbent House candidate, Democrat or Republican. While most of Owens's PAC funds were coming from labor unions, environmental and peace groups, pro-Israel PACs, and other generally liberal groups, he also received funds from more than sixty business groups, including life-insurance salesmen, trial lawyers, auto dealers, out-of-state banks and utility companies, and corporate giants including Chrysler, General Electric, Standard Oil (Ohio), U.S. Steel, and Warner Communications.

Owens's Republican opponent, Tom Shimizu, didn't do nearly so well, despite vigorous promotion among PAC officials by Vander Jagt's committee. Shimizu managed only $108,000 in PAC funds all told.

Driven by expediency, the Realtors eventually supported both candidates in the Utah contest. The initial $5,000 to Owens, which went to reduce his debt from a primary campaign, was followed by a $1,000 donation to his general-election effort in September. The PAC gave $5,000 to Shimizu in October, too late to help him with other business PACs. Owens, aided by his superior finances, won with 55 percent of the vote. Afterward, in December, the Realtors sent him an additional $4,000 to retire general-election debts, raising the total for the year to the legal maximum of $10,000.

In Idaho, the early money from the Realtors helped Stallings amass nearly $300,000 from PACs, including many business groups. Stallings spent $470,000 to win with 54 percent of the vote.

Business PACs were still growing and still giving mostly

to Republicans, but they were more docile now, almost apologetic. Even Dow Chemical, one of the leaders in the formation of Republican-leaning business PACs, felt compelled to consult Coelho's committee when making donations through its PACs, which had grown in number to nine.

"I gave a presentation to the 9 directors of the Dow Chemical PACs," the DCCC's field director, Marcia Hale, wrote in a July memo. "They told me they were interested in losing their reputation as being Republican PACs and would like a list from us of Northeastern Democrats [incumbents] that they could give to this year."

In the end Dow's PACs remained staunchly partisan, giving 93 percent of their money to Republicans during the entire 1986 election cycle. Dow PACs gave only $20,600 to a total of 34 Democratic congressional candidates, while providing $273,975 to 148 Republicans.

Other business and trade groups were falling into line, however. A July memo from committee staff employee Murray Rapp said that the Republican-leaning American Medical Association PAC, known as AMPAC, was sending $5,000 to Democratic candidate David Skaggs, who was running for an open House seat in Boulder, Colorado.

The AMA's PAC usually supported Republicans, but in this case Skaggs, as a member of the Colorado House, had sided with doctors and insurance companies in their fight to restrict the awards that patients can win when they sue physicians for malpractice. The effort, being pushed at both the state and the federal level, was known as "tort reform"—"tort" being the legal term for the cause of a lawsuit.

Skaggs had introduced tort-reform legislation in Colorado, earning the admiration of AMPAC. And his likely GOP foe, Mike Norton, had been a lobbyist on the other side.

Skaggs, interestingly, also received $8,000 from the Association of Trial Lawyers, who oppose the sort of limitations on legal judgments sought by the doctors. The Trial Lawyers were giving defensively, a common phenomenon. Just as some business PACs give to both sides in a political race, candidates gladly take from both sides in a lobbying fight. In fact, one of the reasons PAC money was mushrooming was that business lobbies hated to be outdone by their rivals. For House candidates this special-interest bidding produced a happy result: lots of funds and a built-in defense against criticism. They could say, "I wasn't influenced; I got money from both." Helped along by his business PAC money, Skaggs defeated Norton with 51 percent of the vote.

The reason that Democrats like Skaggs, Stallings, and Owens received significant support from business and professional PACs was that the donors cared more about particular bills than about any broad philosophy of free-market economics. Vander Jagt thought businessmen had a moral commitment to fostering free enterprise and minimal government. Coelho figured that corporate managers were interested in preserving their companies' short-term, after-tax profits. When Republicans talked about being pro-business, they were speaking of freedom from government regulation. When Democrats said they were pro-business, they more often were touting federal subsidies or tax loopholes. Coelho appreciated, as Vander Jagt at first did not, that business PACs gave mostly to open the doors of the lawmakers who controlled the good things the federal government had going.

One such PAC manager was Robert Bannister, who came to the National Association of Home Builders as its chief lobbyist in 1978. Its PAC made only $52,635 in campaign contributions that year. Bannister didn't feel like a "player" in the Washington money game. He made speeches at meetings of the association, saying that having only the 156th-rated PAC "just didn't make any sense."

He told his members he suffered humiliation one day when he had been on the job only a few months. He paid a call on an unimportant member of the House, one so junior that his office was in one of the uncoveted warrens on the uppermost floor of the Cannon office building. Yet even this lowly backbencher kept Bannister cooling his heels for long past the appointed hour. From the reception area Bannister could see through the door, which was slightly ajar, that the congressman was doing nothing more important than reading a newspaper.

"That told me the guy didn't see housing as important enough to put down the funnies," Bannister said. His point was that the Home Builders weren't being accorded proper respect on Capitol Hill. Something should be done, and what needed doing was to amass a giant PAC. The Home Builders did just that, pouring out just over $1 million in donations in the 1982 elections, $1.6 million in 1984, and nearly as much in 1986.

Bannister said the Home Builders then received respect. At the association's conventions, a dozen or more House and Senate members were seen at hospitality suites where drinks were poured for members of the PAC's "Capitol Club," an elite group whose members contributed the legal maximum of $5,000 a year to the PAC.

Bannister wasn't the only lobbyist who felt compelled to give. After the 1986 election the Center for Responsive Politics interviewed fifty PAC directors and lobbyists, promising them anonymity to encourage candor. It reported that the PACs privately felt victimized by the campaign finance system, "yet, the fear of losing access compels them to continue. . . . Among the problems PACs say exist are the detrimental effects of large sums of money on campaigns, the pressures of and time wasted in fundraising, the problems challengers face in raising money, and increasing public cynicism about the electoral system."

One lobbyist was quoted as saying: "I discovered, after my best efforts of two or three years to visit with members of Congress, that those who made regular contributions had much easier access, and consequently I persuaded our organization to authorize a small PAC." Another said, "Well, frankly, I had a hard time maintaining a great deal of respect for a member of Congress—when I was trying to talk to him about an issue, he would change the issue to whether my PAC would contribute to him."

Some of those quoted expected more than mere access.

One said he gave to get "sympathetic access—a guy who basically wants to help you as opposed to a person who is sitting there saying, 'm'hm, 'm'hm." Another admitted seeking a specific quid pro quo: "In one case we gave to a member thinking that we would get something, and it didn't work. We'll never give to that member again." Yet another felt compelled to give as a sign of appreciation for support on legislation: "There is no question that if we went to them time after time and never showed any support for them when they came to us at election time, we'd wear out our welcome pretty fast." Still others feared they would be blacklisted if they turned down requests for money. "If you don't give . . . the physical door isn't closed, but there may be a hidden veil up there," explained one. Another said, "I've had them say, 'Well, I like your organization but you haven't given me a contribution.' " Yet another quoted a senator as saying with the deepest of cynicism, "I've had people who contribute to my campaign, and they get access; the others get good government."

As PACs spent more and more to buy access, the lawmakers became more and more dependent on them. House members elected in 1976 got an average of 25.6 percent of their campaign funds from PACs. But those elected in 1986 would rely on PACs for 42 percent of their campaign receipts. Lawmakers of both parties leaned more and more on PACs, and less and less on the voters, to finance their campaigns.

The election laws encouraged PAC dependency. Citizens were allowed to give only $1,000 per election to a House or Senate candidate, and relatively few could afford to donate such a sum. But PACs were allowed to give up to $5,000 per election. For incumbents especially, the law made it much easier to raise money from special-interest groups than from constituents.

The reliance on PAC money was also growing in the Senate. Senators elected in 1976 got less than 15 percent of their election funds from PACs, a figure that rose to 27 percent in the 1986 elections. But the PAC habit was most acute in the

House, where Democratic incumbents commonly received more than half their re-election funds from PACs and much of the rest from lobbyists and business executives. A few House Democrats had entirely given up raising money from their own constituents and simply held a few Washington receptions every two years to extract money from the industries that did business before their committees.

Money had always been important, as Lyndon Johnson had demonstrated during his brief fling at dispensing campaign funds to fellow House members. But this was something new, and it had deep-reaching effects. Before, there had been political profit in working on committees such as Public Works, which dispensed highway projects, dams, and other traditional forms of largesse, and Education and Labor, especially during the Great Society period of expanding social programs. Now the tax-writing Ways and Means panel, always important, became even more so. Not only did it dispense favors through the tax code, trade legislation, Social Security, and federal medical-insurance programs, but it attracted the most money from special-interest groups and businessmen. Energy and Commerce became another hot committee, its members receiving almost as much PAC money as the tax writers. Banking, once desirable only because of the federal housing subsidies and urban-aid programs it dealt with, had become a magnet for money from financial institutions and real-estate developers.

Coelho encouraged and assisted candidates in their quest for PAC dollars. One morning in May 1986 the committee put on another of its "meat markets" for candidates and PAC directors. About 150 people milled about in the conference room of the Democratic headquarters building.

A candidate from Illinois, Shawn Collins, worked the group assiduously. Collins, newly married, freshly graduated from the University of Chicago Law School, and unemployed, was a hopeless underdog when he entered the campaign against a popular Republican incumbent, George O'Brien. But O'Brien unexpectedly revealed that he was fatally ill with prostate cancer and announced his retirement. Now Collins was running for a vacant seat. His prospects of being the next congressman had improved markedly.

"When O'Brien dropped out, my fund-raising consultant said, 'Oh, great!' " Collins said to an official of the cattlemen's association PAC. He said Coelho promised to "turn on the faucet." The candidate boasted that a liquor-industry lobbyist asked for several tickets to one of his fund-raising events. Collins tried to sell the cattlemen's PAC official the idea that he was picking up momentum, that both supporters and money were flowing his way. He was marketing himself.

Collins didn't make the sale; he got nothing from the cattlemen. He may have exaggerated about the liquor lobby too, because he received nothing from them either. But by the end of the campaign Collins would realize $128,000 from PACs, including $5,000 from Coelho's Valley Education Fund. Collins also got help from Ways and Means chairman Rostenkowski of Illinois, in the form of money from two normally Republican industries that were very worried about a massive rewrite of the tax bill currently underway. The PAC of the Chicago Board of Trade, made up of commodity brokers eager to avoid paying income taxes on their trading profits, gave Collins $3,000. And he received $5,000 from a group of prosperous life-insurance salesmen, called ALIGNPAC, which was lobbying hard to prevent federal taxation of the policies they sold. Collins raised slightly more PAC funds than his Republican rival, a state legislator, and fell just short of defeating him, with 48 percent of the vote.

Since the aim of the "meat-market" events was to sell candidates, it paid to put the best merchandise up front. "Only about 10 percent of these guys can win," said the campaign committee's PAC director, Tom Nides. He subtly tried to steer the candidates with the best prospects to donors with money to give. A few weeks earlier, he had attempted a more formal arrangement, but it was a disaster.

He forced candidates to stand behind tables, each with a name card and a place to display his or her literature. It looked like a string of kissing booths. PAC managers huddled around the "hot" candidates and left the others stranded, embarrassed, and angry.

"We got so much heat for it, we had to do it this way," said Nides. "I still wanted to put them at tables. The PAC directors don't have to waste their time with the losers that way." In August the campaign committee tried another approach. This time it brought in its candidates in relays, with an A list of the most promising candidates coming in one day and B and C lists present at other times. Collins was among the forty-five candidates who made the A list.

Coelho pushed candidates hard to raise PAC money if they seemed to be lagging. One such aspirant was Dave Nagle, a former Democratic party chairman in Iowa. He was given a good chance of picking up a House seat being vacated by a veteran Republican. The Republican candidate, John McIntee, had stumbled badly by suggesting that Iowa's economically strapped farmers might get around a shortage of grain-storage facilities by leaving their crops in the fields during the winter. Farm experts later said this would cause most of the corn to rot, and McIntee had been trying to live down his gaffe ever since.

Coelho's staff reported that Nagle was getting favorable news coverage but lacked money. Aides worried that he hadn't paid sufficient attention to getting PAC funds. It was recommended that he begin courting labor unions to raise the needed dollars quickly.

Nagle had collected only about $30,000 from PACs. Within a month he raised $42,000 more. But in mid-September one aide reported that Nagle's biggest problem still was fund-raising, and he urged Coelho to hammer the candidate to solicit more from PACs. Coelho's staff thought Nagle's campaign was well organized, sending the right message to the voters, and even accumulating a respectable amount of money from his own constituents. But still they fretted that too little PAC money might cost him the race; it was considered the one weak element in his campaign.

With Coelho urging him on, Nagle got a total of $172,000 from PACs, mostly from labor unions, peace groups, pro-Israel PACs, and the Valley Education Fund, which gave $5,000. He also received money from foreign-car dealers, Philip Morris, the banking industry, and other business groups. In the end he raised nearly $2 from PACs for every $1 from individual donors. He won with 55 percent of the vote.

In the end, Coelho completely routed the threat of a PAC-financed Republican revolution. But he did so at the cost of making his own party substantially dependent on special-interest money. When the money was counted after the 1986 election, PACs had given $87.4 million to House candidates, and Democrats got 63 percent of that. House Democratic incumbents who ran for re-election in 1986 realized $41 million from PACs; Republican incumbents received $25 million. Democratic incumbents relied on PACs for 49 percent of their re-election funds, compared with 38 percent for Republican incumbents.

Even in contests for open seats, Democrats received $7.1 million in PAC funds and their Republican opponents got $5.2 million. The disparity was wider yet among challengers. PACs gave $6.6 million to support Democratic candidates running against Republican incumbents, compared with $2.4 million for GOP challengers.

Labor and liberal PACs gave heavily to Democrats, as always, but this time business PACs dispensed their funds almost equally to both sides. Of the money that corporate PACs gave to House candidates, Democrats received 48 percent. For trade-association PACs the figure was 52 percent. In financing GOP challengers, business PACs did no better than they had when a shocked Vander Jagt reported his early findings to President Ford a decade earlier. Less than

3 percent of the corporate PAC funds in House races went to GOP challengers.

However the statistics were sliced and juggled, the PAC system was clearly working to keep Democrats in office, and in the majority.

6

"The Process Buys You Out"

*The day may come when we'll reject the money
of the rich as tainted, but it hadn't come when
I left Tammany Hall at 11:25 a.m. today.*

—GEORGE WASHINGTON PLUNKITT

Tony Coelho was spinning out a dream he had, that one day his campaign committee would be weaned of its reliance on special-interest money. He was progressing, he said, toward a time when the party would run mainly on the donations of rank-and-file Democrats. But as he spoke over lunch at the Democratic Club, reality intruded. A lobbyist for a scandal-ridden Wall Street brokerage house, one of Coelho's biggest financial backers, stopped by his table and began complaining about the newest round of criminal charges tarnishing the firm's image.

"We had some more indictments announced yesterday," said the lobbyist, Mary Jo Jacobi, of Drexel Burnham Lambert, Inc.

"Oh, really?" Coelho said. "Is this all part of Dennisgate?"

A spectacle of greed was just starting to unfold on Wall Street. Dennis B. Levine, a thirty-three-year-old managing director of Drexel, had been arrested a few days earlier and

accused of reaping $12.6 million in illegal profits from in-
side information. He eventually would plead guilty to
charges of securities fraud, tax evasion, and perjury, and go
to jail. Drexel officials would cut his photo out of the firm's
annual report and replace it with that of the new head of
its mergers and acquisitions department, Martin Siegel. But
Siegel too would soon plead guilty to felony counts of illegal
trading and tax evasion during his time at another company. Eventually, the trail would lead to the conviction of
one of Drexel's biggest customers, Ivan Boesky. After that,
federal prosecutors would turn their attention to the heart
of Drexel's operation, the California-based junk-bond department that fueled the takeover mania. The investigation
would continue well into 1988, leaving Wall Street wondering which Drexel executive might be indicted next.

The indictments of which Drexel's lobbyist spoke were of
five young Wall Street professionals, who later came to be
called the "Yuppie Five." They included one employed by
Drexel. He would eventually be barred from the securities
industry and sentenced to probation and community service on charges of mail fraud and attempting to obstruct a
Securities and Exchange Commission investigation.

"Our guy was a research analyst, very low-level," the lobbyist said. "And the money that they got, I give Dennis
credit, if you are going to ruin your career you do it for a
very big number. We hate it worse than anybody," she said.
"It makes the firm look bad."

Later, Drexel would look even worse. Its star financier
Michael Milken, who had become one of the wealthiest men
in the United States through dealings with men like Boesky,
would eventually be hauled before a House subcommittee to
explain some of the methods that helped him amass his
wealth. He would invoke his Fifth Amendment right to remain silent. But Coelho would stick by his friends at Drexel
through thick and thin; just weeks before Milken pleaded
the Fifth, Coelho said at a Drexel-sponsored conference
in Los Angeles: "I am here tonight to show my respect

and deep admiration for Michael Milken, my very good friend. . . . He is constantly thinking about what can be done to make this a better world." Coelho accepted a $2,000 speaking fee for the event.

Drexel needed a lobbyist because, even before some of its officials were exposed as criminals, its business methods were so controversial that some members of Congress proposed legislation to force it to change. Drexel was previously a small-time player among securities firms, but it had grown to wealth, power, and notoriety during the wave of corporate mergers, buy-outs, and raids ushered in by the Reagan administration's relaxed policies on enforcement of federal antitrust laws. Drexel pioneered the use of junk bonds—which carried high interest rates and high risks for buyers and large profits for Drexel—to finance such raids and takeovers. Congressional committees debated fitfully whether to crack down on the corporate raiders, Drexel's clients, or at least to restrict purchases of the risky bonds by federally insured savings institutions, including some of Drexel's biggest customers.

While Drexel had been working to head off any such threats to its profitable business, company officials, some of whom measured their yearly income in the millions, had been spreading around hundreds of thousands of dollars in campaign contributions. The firm not only had a fast-growing political action committee that would dispense $253,500 to candidates and party committees in the 1986 elections; its officials organized fund-raising events for key lawmakers that produced substantial additional sums from Drexel executives and customers. Coelho's committee was a principal beneficiary.

Drexel's PAC gave $15,000 to the campaign committee in 1985, and would give another $15,000 soon after Coelho's chat with its lobbyist. Drexel clearly viewed its connection with Coelho as special; his committee was the largest single beneficiary of its PAC during the 1986 campaigns. Furthermore, officials in Drexel's West Coast office were responsible for raising $35,000 to $50,000 each year for an annual series of California fund-raising events that Coelho sponsored.

To attract such backers, Coelho set up the Speaker's Club. Membership was purchased by making large gifts: $5,000 per year for an individual, $15,000 for a PAC. A brochure used to court new members explained what these big donors got for their money: "Members of the Speaker's Club serve as trusted, informal advisors to the Democratic Members of Congress."

Donors bought the right to give advice to the rulers of the House. There was no guarantee that the advice would be followed, of course. That could have been construed as bribery. But the advice was to be "trusted."

The brochure also carried, in oversize type, a quote from Speaker O'Neill: "I have learned to listen. Tell us what you think—at a time and place where we can really hear what you have to say." That should have sounded seductive to lobbyists.

Much of Coelho's sales appeal was just innocent pandering to the egos of wealthy donors; benefits included "a durable set of luggage tags" with insignia "to distinguish you as a club member." The club's two big events were a golf-and-tennis outing and an annual dinner advertised as "one of the Capital's most important social events." But donations also bought access, the Washington equivalent of the inside information Levine misused. Profiting from non-public information on Wall Street could be a prison offense, but not the lawmakers' trade in legislative access. Club members were promised they would "gain valuable information" during "exclusive" briefings on tax, budget, and regulatory matters. "You get the real story," the brochure said.

Club members also could "obtain personal assistance in Washington." Coelho's staff would arrange for anything from a hotel reservation or tickets to a concert to meetings with members of Congress for a businessman who had troubles with federal regulators or a proposed new law. The point was backed up by a quote from a donor whose name wasn't given but who was identified as a member of the club: "Let's face it, Congress is involved in my business. That is why I need to be involved with Congress. The Speaker's Club provides me with the high level contacts I want."

Robert Bannister, the Home Builders' lobbyist, said that paying $15,000 a year to join the club improved his trade group's relations with Speaker O'Neill. "Prior to that, I didn't have a lot of opportunity to meet with the Speaker on a social basis," he said. Bannister added that he especially liked getting his legislative intelligence straight from the highest sources. "They'll have Danny Rostenkowski at the appropriate time on the tax bill, Bill Gray [chairman of the Budget Committee] at the appropriate time in the budget process."

Coelho's access peddling, like much of what he did at the Democratic campaign committee, began as imitation of techniques first invented by Republicans. The GOP had been marketing contacts with its own most powerful policy-makers since capturing the White House and the Senate in 1980. The Republican National Committee's "Eagles" club cost $10,000 a year, and entitled members to meet with Cabinet officers, Senate committee chairmen, and even the President himself. Business lobbyists who gave $5,000 in PAC funds to President Reagan's re-election effort in 1984 became members of a "Presidential Forum" and were promised face-to-face meetings with administration officials on taxes, trade policy, and military spending, among other subjects, plus special privileges at the party's national convention. The limit-skirting "bundling party" staged by the Republican congressional committee, at which PAC managers posed for pictures with the President after donating $20,000 to GOP House candidates, was only a variation of this access-peddling game.

During 1986 the administration was pushing a massive rewrite of the tax code, making its tax experts particularly valuable as fund-raising agents. As the debate on reform heated up, Secretary of the Treasury James Baker traveled around the country giving briefings in return for campaign donations. One such session had to be canceled when a too blatant invitation attracted unwanted publicity; it specifically solicited corporate funds for the Georgia state GOP. Corporate money was legal in Georgia politics but not at the federal level, and this solicitation was too reminiscent of the illegal corporate funds donated to the 1972 Nixon campaign that were uncovered as part of the Watergate scandals. Worse, the Georgia GOP advertised Baker's presentation as a "tax seminar" for businessmen from the Atlanta area, emphasizing the connection between tax legislation and campaign money.

Both parties took such embarrassments in stride. Selling access to the powerful produced too much money for them to fret about appearances. "The Republicans had their Eagles, and they were damned successful," said Michael Fraioli, staff director of the Speaker's Club. "What have the Democrats got? We didn't have the President of the United States, but we had the Speaker of the House."

Coelho said he wanted to move the party away from reliance on big donors and he put great stock in small gifts raised through computer-addressed letters. He said he envisioned a financially secure party organization, more influential with its candidates than any PAC or moneyed interest and itself beholden only to a mass of rank-and-file members who sent in small donations through the mail.

"Direct mail is fabulous right now," Coelho said. "It's going to be over 50 percent of our money, gross." He predicted rapid future growth in these small donations, with no strings attached. "We've got to go to 90 percent, that's where I wish. If I had the stamina I'd stay another two years, because I think in two more years you could move it to 80 percent or more."

But Coelho's dream wasn't coming true. Prospecting for new givers through the mail was expensive and only marginally productive. Coelho tried harder than any other Democrat to raise small donations from rank-and-file citizens, but ultimately he failed to build anything close to the broad base of donors enjoyed by the Republicans.

The reason was simple: the best-educated, highest-income groups of liberal and progressive Americans weren't buying what Coelho and the Democrats were selling. They gave instead to groups like Common Cause and People for the American Way. In 1986 Common Cause claimed 279,000 dues-paying members, while Coelho had 260,000 donors. Common Cause received $10.6 million in 1986, far more than the campaign committee realized from all sources.

Democrats often tried to excuse their failure to attract more financial support from ordinary citizens by saying Democrats were poor, Republicans were rich. But that alibi was inadequate, despite the obvious truth that the richest Americans tended to be Republicans and the poorest were overwhelmingly Democratic. The fact was that millions of well-heeled Democrats and political independents sympathized with the party's noblest themes—compassion, peace, and fairness—but withheld donations.

Extensive polling in 1987 by the Gallup Organization for the Times Mirror Company found two sizable groups of upper-middle-class, politically sophisticated Americans who tended to vote Democratic but who gave little to the party. Among a group it called "60's Democrats"—well-educated people who favored government spending on social programs and strongly identified with peace, civil rights, and environmental movements—51 percent had incomes exceeding $30,000 a year but only 11 percent said they had given money to a political party committee. Another group, called "Seculars"—non-religious people favoring cuts in military spending and opposing both school prayer and legal restrictions on abortions—naturally recoiled from Reagan-style Republicanism and sympathized with Democrats. Of the "Seculars," 49 percent had incomes over $30,000 but only 8 percent gave to a party committee. By contrast, the highest levels of party giving were reported by a Republican group called "Enterprisers." Of that group, 24 percent reported giving to a party committee. And while it was the most affluent segment in the study, with 61 percent reporting incomes exceeding $30,000 annually, it was outnumbered by the other two upper-middle-class groups, which leaned toward the Democrats. "Enterprisers" made up 10 percent of the population, while "60's Democrats" and "Seculars" together constituted 16 percent.

Coelho's direct-mail targets were largely aging pensioners worried about the future. A marketing analysis conducted for his committee in 1985 showed that nearly two-thirds of its donors were over age fifty-five, and 37 percent were retired. To appeal to them Coelho used the names of Speaker O'Neill and Florida Rep. Claude Pepper, who was born in 1900 and was the oldest member of Congress. Like many other direct-mail promoters, Coelho played on his donors' fears; a letter sent in early 1985 said, "A MOVE IN CONGRESS TO SLASH MEDICARE BENEFITS COULD COME QUICKLY," and asked for donations to the campaign committee to "stop Republicans from cutting aid." The committee sent out 1.3 million copies of that letter, carrying O'Neill's signature. It pulled in nearly twice as many new donors as the experts had expected. But O'Neill withdrew the use of his name on the grounds that the letter was causing needless alarm among the elderly. Coelho later sent more copies bearing his own signature instead, but Coelho lacked the Speaker's appeal and the response was unsatisfactory. Committee officials estimated that with O'Neill's name the committee would have gained 6,500 additional new donors and $350,000.

Kathryn Smiley, Coelho's direct-mail expert, said the marketing study showed what she knew instinctively about her donors anyway: "They don't own recreational vehicles. They don't go cross-country skiing." Families with children generally didn't give; "I have nothing to sell to them."

The party got relatively little support from issue-oriented liberals. Once, Coelho insisted on sending a fund-raising letter stressing the issue of military waste, but it cost more to produce and mail than it brought in. He couldn't find any

Democrat to sign the letter who was seen as able to do anything about the problem, so he signed the letter himself. "I felt that defense waste was an excellent issue for us," Coelho said, "but it just bombed."

Tom Matthews, a direct-mail expert whose firm worked both for Coelho and for Common Cause, put the matter bluntly: "The Democratic party doesn't stand for anything. A lot of our people ought to be Democratic donors, but they don't trust the party."

The Democrats' increasingly cozy relationship with lobbyists and big givers was a sensitive matter; the spectacle of Tip O'Neill golfing with Speaker's Club members wasn't one Coelho wanted featured on the evening news. At a campaign committee staff meeting he learned that a Boston television crew planned to film O'Neill teeing off with big donors during a Speaker's Club affair at the Congressional Country Club. What a sight it would be: thirty-six foursomes roaming the greens, three donors and a senior House Democrat in each. Coelho said no.

"The problem is, they asked Tip first," explained executive director Martin Franks. O'Neill had no objection. Franks suggested a diplomatic way to fend off the unwanted film crew anyway. "Doesn't Congressional have a rule that would keep them out? I'm sure Congressional knows we wouldn't be unhappy." So the TV station's cameras were barred, along with other news reporters.

All this looked terrible to outsiders, and even to many of Coelho's own colleagues. "Pete Stark came up to me the other day," Coelho said. "He said the *California Journal* is doing a story on the delegation, and they want to rate everybody on intelligence, ability, integrity, et cetera. One to ten. And he said, 'I want you to know that I gave you ratings of eight and nine on everything, except when they came to integrity, I gave you a six.' . . .

"He says, 'I'm not being critical. . . . It's just that in order to be campaign chair you have to do some things that nobody else in the party would do, and that's the only way we can be successful, is if you deal with the oil and gas people, deal with the business people. And the people like me, that are purists, we could never do that. But somebody has to do it, you do it great, you really have saved the party and so forth.' "

Coelho didn't think of himself as lacking integrity. "I said, 'Pete, the most important thing for me is to go home at night and for me to be comfortable with myself. I don't have any trouble with that.' I said, 'I don't agree with you. . . . You're entitled to your opinion, but you don't know what I do. And you don't know how I do it and you won't take the time to find out, and I don't care.' . . . But I was intrigued that he had to come up and confess."

A curious kind of ambivalence pervaded Washington. Everybody knew that lobbyists gave money to buy access and, whether indirectly or overtly, to gain some influence over legislation. So the more money lawmakers took, the more most of them professed to dislike it.

Coelho's ethical code was common among lawmakers. Doing official favors for donors was permitted. The unforgivable sin was to make the connection explicit. Coelho told a story that illustrated the point.

"I had a guy who paid to join the Speaker's Club, $5,000," Coelho said. "He joined, and then he had a problem with the government. He brought it to my attention. I brought it to Billy Ford's attention." Ford, of Michigan, was chairman of the Post Office and Civil Service Committee. "They went into it, checked it out, and tried to help him and so forth. . . . It was a complaint against the government in regards to harrassment or something. I can't remember all the details. I hope they did a good job. The bottom line was they couldn't do anything for him. So I told him this."

The way Coelho told the story, the donor then overstepped the line. "He said, 'You know, I gave you my $5,000. I expect better treatment than that.'

"I said, 'That's the end of the conversation. . . . You brought up the wrong subject.' "

Undaunted, the donor showed up at a Speaker's Club reception at which O'Neill was present for the unveiling of his portrait. As the donor attempted to speak to O'Neill, Coelho called in several plainclothes Capitol policemen. "Everywhere he went, they were right with him," Coelho said. "So he came up to me and he said, 'Listen, I am insulted that you are doing that.' And I said, 'You are not going to discuss any of these activities. You can go to anybody you want, say what you want to anybody, but you're not going to do it here. We're going to kick you out. You're not invited. You crashed in. I'll let you stay in here; you crashed in. But you say one damn word, you're out.' "

For Coelho, putting the official machinery of the House of Representatives to work on behalf of a $5,000 donor was no more out of line than giving him fancy luggage tags. He said he became offended only when the donor suggested an explicit entitlement to official favors. "There is a fine line," Coelho explained. "I don't mind [donors] bringing up that they have a problem [with the government]. But don't ever try to create the impression with me, or ever say it—if you say it, it's all over—that your money has bought you something. It hasn't. There's a real delicate line there, and it's hard for people to understand how we do it."

The embittered donor told the story a bit differently. Theodore Gianoutsos was by his own description an eccentric gadfly and outspoken Democrat who in 1983 had been fired by the Reagan administration from a job at the Department of the Interior, allegedly for disrespect. His wife, Françoise, had also been laid off from a federal job at the Office of Personnel Management. The two were avid hunters who wanted to will their modest estate to the government to promote the proper use of firearms and to protect endangered birds of prey. They had haunted the Capitol for years, personally lobbying for the establishment of a National Fish and Wildlife Foundation to receive their bequest.

Though hardly wealthy—they lived in a rented, one-story brick house in a working-class Washington suburb with their two hunting dogs—the couple had given thousands of dollars to Democratic candidates and party organizations since 1980, including $4,825 to the Democratic National Committee and $12,755 to Coelho's committee. In early 1984, when their wildlife foundation bill was stalled in the Senate, the Gianoutsoses asked Coelho for help. "I have absolutely no influence over there," Coelho told them. "If you were a member over there, Ted, we could set you up and you could talk to those people."

Theodore Gianoutsos recalled, "It was absolutely clear to me he wanted more money. We were asking for nothing, and he wanted more." The bill passed anyway and became law in March 1984.

The split with Coelho occurred when the Gianoutsoses pressed too ardently for congressional help regarding the loss of their jobs. They once secured an audience with O'Neill by buttonholing him at a Speaker's Club golf outing. "You've been saying your door is always open," Theodore said. "I'll see you in twenty-four hours," O'Neill replied. After hearing them, however, O'Neill declined to do anything officially. "You ought to get a lawyer," he said. The meeting was in June 1984, but the couple persisted for months. In August they sent a handwritten letter saying, "We did expect a lot of you, because we have always believed in you. . . . WHERE THE HELL ARE YOU NOW, MR. SPEAKER?" Coelho finally tossed them out of the Speaker's Club in October, after the incident at the unveiling of O'Neill's portrait. He said in a letter, "Under the circumstances, I think it is best that we return your dues." Enclosed was a check for $3,825, the installments they had paid during 1984.

Coelho didn't see anything wrong with helping Gianoutsos officially, at least up to a point, because congressmen did favors for constituents all the time. Indeed, they saw that as the most rewarding part of their job. Few elections were won by voting for wise national policies; political survival depended much more on constituent service, lobbying for federal grants for the local college, working to salvage the weapons system produced at the local plant, or writing letters to regulatory agencies about a local businessman's complaint.

Increasingly, however, House members were acting as ombudsmen not only for their constituents but also for their donors. Those who gave money came to be a second constituency, one not envisioned by the drafters of the Constitution. Coelho interceded for a donor from another state just as naturally as he would have for a businessman from Modesto, in his own district. One was entitled to help by virtue of residence, the other by virtue of his currency.

The rising tide of special-interest money was changing the balance of power between voters and donors, between lawmakers' constitutional constituents and their cash constituents. Voters retained the ultimate power to defeat a lawmaker at the polls on election day. But reaching those voters required ever-larger sums of money to buy advertising, postage, opinion polling, computers, and other paraphernalia of modern political campaigns. So donors gained importance at the expense of the electorate. This amounted to a de facto amendment to the Constitution. The constitutional change was ratified, in effect, by the forces of economics and technology, without a vote and without much general appreciation of what was at stake.

Voters still prevailed on any issue if enough of them knew about it and cared strongly enough. But they typically made their judgments based on a wide variety of factors, and most didn't pay close attention until the closing weeks of a political campaign. Donors meanwhile exercised their power to give or to withhold money continuously, as lawmakers stepped up fund-raising from an election-year chore to an annual affair. And when the donors were PACs or professional lobbyists, they paid very close attention to how each member voted, even on obscure amendments in otherwise unwatched subcommittees. The power of the voters was supreme, but infrequently exercised and motivated by diffuse factors. The power of cash constituents was crisply focused, vigilantly exercised, and growing.

Coelho admitted that money was affecting legislation, though he insisted that his colleagues weren't corruptly selling themselves. And he allowed that what was going on was wrong, morally if not legally.

"Your staff or the campaign staff or somebody says, look, you've got to go out and raise $50,000 by X date. All of a sudden the fifty thousand dominates you," he said. "You may not sell yourself; you may not sell yourself at all on any piece of legislation. I'm not saying that. It's that all of a sudden the fifty thousand is consuming you. It's all you can do, that you've got to go out and raise it. You go out and start calling everybody. You're calling in your friends, people you may agree with already, that you're not selling out to."

Things were different when Coelho first arrived in Washington in 1965. Lawmakers then used their time to make laws, but now too much time was spent raising money. "The dynamics have changed, and I think that's an absolute waste," he said.

Did it alter legislation? Coelho at first said no, but then confessed the reality. "It *does* affect legislation. You don't have the people feeling that they can be creative . . . because they've got to raise this fifty thousand, and they don't want to turn people off."

People with money?

"People with money."

He denied that votes were sold overtly. "I think that's what the press keeps on trying to say. And I don't buy that; I have a higher regard for my colleagues. I'm sure it happens with a few, and we find out about those."

Rather, he said, lawmakers withheld proposals that would offend donors. "Take housing. Take anything you want. If you are spending all your time calling up different people that you're involved with, that are friends of yours, that you have to raise $50,000, you all of a sudden, in your mind, you're in effect saying, 'I'm not going to go out and develop this new housing bill that may get the Realtors or may get the builders or may get the unions upset. I've got to raise the fifty thousand; I've got to do that.' That isn't a sellout. It's basically that you're not permitted to go out and do your creativity. I think that's bad."

Whatever the Realtors or the Home Builders or the unions disliked, the lawmakers no longer even considered. "But what the press always tries to do is say that you've been bought out. I don't buy that. I just don't think it's true. I think that the process buys you out. But I don't think that you individually have been bought out, or that you sell out. I think there's a big difference there."

Too often, moneyed interests prevail by blocking legislation they don't want. Consider housing, as Coelho suggested. Homeless people and unskilled, jobless youths crowd our cities. Yet the AFL-CIO, financial backbone of the Democratic party, insists on applying Depression-era regulations to federally subsidized housing, pushing up labor costs and reducing the number of apartments that can be built for the poor. Real-estate developers, a rich source of money for both parties, look for subsidies and tax write-offs as the price for building any such housing at all. The obvious becomes unthinkable: Congress dare not consider training jobless ghetto youths in the construction trades and employing them directly at low but decent wages to build no-frills apartments for low-income renters and buyers. Such a direct program would produce more and cheaper housing units than at present and in the bargain create productive citizens from among the tax-eating welfare class. But it would infuriate moneyed interests.

The psychological, even subconscious effect of money is to chill initiatives that donors don't want. As a practical matter, the outcome is the same as if votes had been sold outright. The effect on national policy and well-being are the same. But Coelho says, "One is morally wrong, in effect. The other is legally wrong. There's a big difference." He sees himself as a law-abiding player in an immoral system.

7

"A Big Rip-off"

This civil service law is the biggest fraud of the age. It is the curse of the nation. There can't be no real patriotism while it lasts. How are you goin' to interest our young men in their country if you have no offices to give them when they work for their party?
—GEORGE WASHINGTON PLUNKITT

"We're talking about the very wealthy of this country getting a big rip-off," Coelho declared. "Somebody's got to say it. Where's Kennedy on this? Where are the goddamn liberals?"

Coelho was presiding over another of his marathon management sessions at the campaign committee. He was working over possible lines of attack to use against Republican candidates. He was railing against tax reform.

The Senate Finance Committee had just approved a radical streamlining of the federal income-tax code. The bill would shut down some of the tax-dodging gimmicks used by the well-to-do, raise taxes on corporations, and eliminate federal income taxes altogether for millions of the working poor. Coelho had convinced himself that the bill favored the rich, and he wanted to kill it. His rich donors would be hurt by tax reform, and they wanted to kill it, too.

"Middle America is not going to benefit from this like the

Republicans are going to benefit from it," Coelho insisted.

Actually, Republicans were ambivalent about tax reform because it would raise corporate taxes. House Republicans nearly succeeded in killing a more modest loophole-closing measure the year before, and only all-out lobbying by President Reagan turned up enough GOP votes to revive it. Now the Senate was moving toward passage of radical reform, wiping out tax shelters and dropping the top tax rate on personal income to 27 percent, down from the prevailing 50 percent rate. On the Senate Finance Committee, both Democrats and Republicans voted for it unanimously. House Republicans were saying the Senate bill was more to their liking. The Democratic leadership was strongly committed to passing a tax-reform bill.

Corporate America, meanwhile, was lobbying to head off the Senate tax bill. PACs and business lobbyists were giving millions in campaign donations in hopes of retaining their own threatened loopholes. So were some of Coelho's donors, who had made personal profits from the very loopholes that the bill would close. Coelho was blind to what thousands of wealthy individuals were perpetrating under current law. Millionaires were dodging taxes through loopholes and accounting tricks. For the wealthy and the crafty, paying taxes had become optional.

Two of Coelho's cash constituents had much to do with that. Coelho had developed a close friendship with Wall Street's kings of the tax-shelter business, Selig Zises and Jay Zises, two brothers who packaged tax loopholes and marketed them aggressively. The firm they founded in the late 1960s, Integrated Resources, Inc., had grown so prosperous from the traffic in tax shelters that its stock was traded on the New York Stock Exchange. They were both generous donors and personal friends of Coelho. "We're like brothers," he said.

The Zises family and Integrated were major sources of money for the campaign committee. In 1985 Selig, Jay, and a third brother, Seymour, personally gave $15,000 to the Democratic campaign committee. That was part of a total of $69,500 given on the same day by twenty-seven officials of Integrated Resources. It was one of the largest sums raised by the campaign committee that year from any single source, and it came from the tax-shelter business.

Through their contacts with their wealthy clients and friends in the deal-making business, the Zises brothers allowed Coelho to expand his nationwide network of backers. "They introduced me to people in Los Angeles, they introduced me to people in Chicago," he said. "So it's not just what they raised; it's the people they introduced me to." In 1986 he was counting on them to organize another New York fund-raising event for the campaign committee, tapping donors for yet another round.

Selig Zises was chairman and chief executive officer of Integrated Resources, which he founded in 1969 with $270,000 in family money. He was then a twenty-nine-year-old dropout from New York University's business school. The company paid Selig and brother Jay, who is chairman of Integrated's executive committee, more than $1 million a year each. They got $1.8 million apiece in 1984. In 1985 Selig received $1.6 million and Jay got $1.2 million.

Integrated sold shelters that allowed its clients collectively to avoid hundreds of millions in federal taxes. It pioneered "net-leased" deals, in which tenants bore maintenance costs and Integrated got the tax benefits of ownership without the headaches. Integrated might buy a hotel from its current operators, lease it back to them for enough to cover mortgage expenses, and sell partnership interests in the real estate to wealthy individuals. They in turn were attracted by the prospect of paper "losses" from depreciation and mortgage interest which could reduce or eliminate their federal taxes on other income. Using various gimmicks, the company offered its clients deductions from their taxable income of $2 or more for every $1 they paid to Integrated. Those in the 50 percent tax bracket could lower their federal taxes by $1 or more for every $1 paid to Integrated, and get a partnership interest in a piece of real estate in the bargain. The idea was to cash in the real estate in five or ten years for a big profit which itself would be taxed at a favorable rate as capital gain, or even protected from taxation totally by some fresh tax-shelter deal.

Integrated's clients were, in effect, buying real estate with other taxpayers' money. For ordinary working men and women, the tax system merely subtracted from their paychecks. But Integrated's clients were buying hotels instead of paying taxes. Integrated became the largest single syndicator of tax-shelter deals. It employed a sales force of more than 2,000, helping to make tax avoidance a way of life for a whole class of society. The idea took hold among thousands of wealthy people—and even a few members of Congress—that paying taxes was for suckers. About 200,000 people bought into Integrated's tax shelters before the Senate Finance Committee drafted its bill to shut down the game. Meanwhile Integrated took a cut of each deal, in the form of fees for organizing and managing them. It received about $150 million in such fees in 1985, according to *Fortune* magazine.

Such deals not only helped enlarge the federal budget deficit and skewed an income-tax system that was supposed to put the heaviest tax burden on those most able to pay; they also caused economic waste. They sucked hundreds of millions of dollars into existing real estate, driving up prices while creating only a bigger federal budget deficit and profits for Integrated. As *Forbes* magazine described one such deal, Integrated bought twenty Days Inn hotels for $30,000 a room, a 50 percent markup over the amount the owners paid to buy them a short time earlier. Integrated then sold the hotels to tax-shelter clients for $38,000 per room, or 90 percent over the original price. Since Integrated's customers were shopping with the government's money, there was little incentive for them to be fussy about the price.

Tax reform was a financial catastrophe for the Zises brothers. Earlier and far less drastic bills had buffeted the company's stock and set Integrated searching to diversify into insurance, mutual-fund management, and other lines of business. But Integrated's profits were still heavily dependent on sales of tax shelters when the Senate Finance Committee approved a bill on May 7, 1986, that would shut down tax shelters almost completely. The bill would severely restrict the use of "passive losses" from such deals to offset other, taxable income. The paper "losses" that Integrated's accountants had so creatively put together would suddenly be worthless to most clients. Congressional experts figured the Senate bill would effectively reclaim an estimated $18 billion over five years from tax-sheltered real-estate deals.

The Zises brothers and the real-estate industry complained that reform had gone too far, because it would gradually shut down existing shelters as well as prevent the formation of new ones. They said that it was retroactive and therefore unfair to people who had bought into tax shelters believing the deals would reduce their taxes for years into the future. Wall Street reacted swiftly, sending the stock of Integrated into a tailspin. It plunged 16 percent to $30.75 per share on the day the Finance Committee acted, making it the biggest loser on the New York Stock Exchange that day. The drop continued in the ensuing days and weeks, clobbering the net worth of the Zises brothers, who owned more than 870,000 shares of their company's stock. The value of these shares fell by nearly $8 million by the end of the week, and by $14 million at the end of the year. They lost additional millions from their own stakes in the tax-sheltered partnerships Integrated had sold.

With a big part of their personal fortunes disappearing, it was small wonder the Zises brothers didn't like the bill. They told Coelho that they were being hurt badly. They meanwhile begged off plans to sponsor another New York fund-raiser for the campaign committee.

They weren't the only multimillionaire friends and donors of Coelho affected by the tax bill. The wine-making Gallo family took an intense interest in it. And in their case, Coelho intervened personally, giving some discreet behind-the-scenes advice. As much as he professed to be against tax breaks for the rich, when it came to the Gallo clan, he found himself on the side of a provision that could benefit only the very wealthiest families in America.

Ernest and Julio Gallo, two sons of Italian immigrants, were one of America's great success stories. Starting with only $5,900 between them at the end of Prohibition, they amassed a family fortune estimated at $700 million from a business that made, bottled, and distributed one-fourth of all the wine sold in the United States. Besides the jug wines and varietals whose labels have made the Gallo name a household word, their brands included Boones Farm, Thunderbird, Carlo Rossi, and Bartles & Jaymes. Intensely private, the brothers avoided reporters. Their winery offered no public tours.

Both in their late seventies, the Gallo brothers naturally looked to how they might pass on the family empire to their heirs. The tax bill was a threat to those plans. It would tighten up a largely unenforced provision of the inheritance-tax system that placed a special 33 percent tax on bequests that skip generations. The tax was designed to catch families that tried to avoid a whole generation's worth of inheritance taxes by making bequests directly to grandchildren.

The Gallo brothers hired a Washington lobbyist, John Winburn, to work on the generation-skipping tax. They aimed to get an exemption to allow each couple to pass on $4 million tax-free to each grandchild, or even great-grandchild.

This was no small item for the Gallo clan. The two brothers between them had twenty grandchildren and six great-grandchildren, who thus stood to avoid tax on a total of $104 million in bequests.

The exemption could benefit other families too, but only those with great fortunes and lots of grandchildren. Less than 1 percent of all estates paid any inheritance tax at all under prevailing law, and only a few of those—families with millions to pass on and some grandchildren to give them to—could take advantage of the proposed change. One

Democrat who opposed the measure in committee, Frank Guarini of New Jersey, denounced it as a needless gift to multimillionaires at the expense of "Joe Six-pack."

"It has no purpose in tax reform. It has no social benefits. It argues for giving more benefits to the rich people," Guarini said.

Nevertheless, the Gallo winery was in Modesto, in Coelho's district. Furthermore, the Gallo clan were generous campaign contributors, practically a one-family PAC. The Gallo brothers and their wives and children had given at least $325,000 in campaign donations during the several elections before the tax-reform debate. They were still giving heavily while lobbying for estate-tax relief. They could hardly be called loyal Democrats—they donated to both parties—but Ernest, Julio, and various other members of the Gallo family gave $33,500 to the Democratic Congressional Campaign Committee during the 1986 elections, plus $5,000 to Coelho's Valley Education Fund and $5,220 to his re-election campaign fund.

When the Gallos turned to their congressman for help, Coelho set aside whatever reservations he might have felt about favoring the rich. "They have always been good supporters of mine, and before me of my predecessor," Coelho said at the time. He advised them that relief might be obtained if it applied to an entire class: "I told the Gallos when they talked to me that there was nothing we could do for them [specifically], that if it was done it would have to be done generically." He spoke a number of times to a sympathetic member of the tax-writing committee, Ed Jenkins of Georgia, who disliked the generation-skipping tax anyway, and who pushed the Gallo measure forcefully.

Helped by Coelho's counsel, the Gallo brothers prevailed in the House. The Ways and Means Committee approved their provision by a 24–11 vote, and in December 1985 the House adopted it without debate as part of the larger tax-reform bill. The Gallo clan then spread around more campaign donations to Senate Republicans as they were considering the bill. During a one-week period in late March and

early April of 1986, Ernest, Julio, and their wives gave
$29,000 through a committee set up by Senate Majority
Leader Bob Dole of Kansas, a senior member of the tax-
writing Finance Committee. The total included $20,000 for
Dole's personal PAC, Campaign America, and $5,000 for
Sen. Steven Symms of Idaho, whose family is also in the
wine business and who was also a member of the Finance
Committee. Dole was among the House-Senate conferees
who accepted the House-passed Gallo amendment as part
of the final version of the bill. It was passed and signed, a
small victory for some big donors.

It wasn't hard to see why Coelho was emotionally opposed
to closing tax loopholes; he had fought hard to retain them.
To tell him that the tax system favored the rich and dis-
torted the economy was like arguing the evils of the spoils
system to Boss Plunkitt. Coelho saw the tax code as yet
another opportunity to use the power of government to help
people. He denied that he favored tax loopholes to get campaign contributions from people like the Zises brothers or
the Gallo clan, yet the campaign contributions still flowed.
It was a new form of the old patronage game, part of the
business of politics.

Like his predecessor and mentor, B. F. Sisk, Coelho lob-
bied openly and energetically for the most criticized of all
special-interest tax breaks, those received by independent
oil and gas drillers. In 1982 Coelho collided with Speaker
O'Neill and Ways and Means chairman Rostenkowski over
oilmen's tax breaks. To Democrats from oil-consuming districts, like the Northern cities represented by O'Neill and
Rostenkowski, the tax breaks given to oil and gas drillers
were the worst of all loopholes. Those who benefited came
from the oil-producing states, Texas, Louisiana, Oklahoma.
Some also were from Coelho's district, which contained the
sizable Coalinga oil field, and some of Coelho's constituents
and donors wanted to retain them.

Drillers had been a traditional source of money for Democrats from the days when Robert Kerr of Oklahoma was
head of the Senate Finance Committee, Sam Rayburn of

Texas was Speaker of the House, and Lyndon Johnson was Majority Leader of the Senate. By 1980, however, oil money was flowing to Republicans. The Democratic administration of Jimmy Carter had set price ceilings on domestic oilmen when an Arab embargo sent world prices skyrocketing, and won enactment of a "windfall profits tax" that drained away some of the benefit of the higher world oil prices. Carter also offended the deeply conservative, patriotic sense of these millionaires by giving up U.S. control of the Panama Canal and failing to free American diplomats held hostage by Iranian extremists. In the 1980 elections donations from conservative oilmen helped finance the Republicans who defeated a number of senior House Democrats and seriously threatened Majority Leader Wright.

In 1981 and 1982 Coelho traveled through the Southwest hoping to recapture some of the oil money for Democrats. He had the blessing of O'Neill. "I had told him I was going to go after the oil interests," Coelho said. "And he encouraged me to. He said, 'Look, the oil people, the independents, have always been good friends of the Democratic party in the past. They went away from us, and in 1980 they played a major role against us. If you can neutralize them at least, it would be very helpful to us as a party. If you can't get money from them, from a strategy point of view if you can just slow them down, take some of the heat out of it, it would help us out strategically.' "

But the Speaker changed his mind when a group of conservative Republican oilmen from Texas came gunning for him. They began a very public effort to finance a GOP candidate to run against O'Neill in the 1982 election. The Republican, Frank McNamara, eventually spent $817,000 in an ill-advised and hopeless attempt to oust the solidly popular O'Neill.

The Speaker was enraged when he first heard of the oilmen's plans to stage a coup. He told Coelho he had decided to punish the GOP drillers by stripping all oilmen of their tax breaks.

"He wasn't going to do any intellectualizing with them;

he was going to teach them a lesson," Coelho recalled. "He said, 'I know you've been working with these folks. I just want to tell you I'm going after them; knock everything out.' "

At the time, Congress was considering a bill to raise taxes on business, having given away too much the previous year, when Democrats tried to outdo Republicans in awarding new breaks for business. The bidding war produced a law that almost nullified the income tax for corporations. The giveaways cut federal revenues so deeply, and so enlarged the federal budget deficit, that Congress was looking for new sources of revenue only a year later. As always, there were proposals to end special treatment of the oil industry, but Coelho had been pleading against increasing independent oilmen's taxes.

Privately, Coelho argued that the Democratic party needed their campaign donations. Oil lobbyist Dan Dutko said many Democrats found that argument compelling. "He basically had everybody betting on the come and saying, 'Coelho, if you're telling us this about the independents coming your way and everything, O.K.' "

Dutko was in the Capitol the day that O'Neill summoned Coelho to his office. When Coelho emerged, Dutko recalled, he was "white as a sheet . . . white and almost shaking.

"Tony painted a picture . . . of the wounded lion roaring when he walked in that office. And I can picture the Speaker doing that. Just *roaring.* And he said, 'I *want* those sons of bitches!'

"Tony came out and said, 'I don't know what you guys are going to do. We can't do anything to get those contributions [to O'Neill's opponent] back. But you better start scrambling.' "

"I was upset," Coelho conceded. "Danny [Rostenkowski] was in the room. This [ending breaks for oil drillers] is what was going to happen." Coelho feared that if O'Neill and Rostenkowski succeeded, the wildcatters would conclude that Democrats were hopelessly anti-business, and that he, Coelho, couldn't be believed.

"I was out there saying [to the oilmen], 'Look, there's no reason for you to kill Democrats. I happen to be one who is one of your biggest advocates, because I believe. Not because you've helped me, because you haven't. But I just believe in the industry and I believe in independent oil.'

"And I'd been all over the country preaching that. And all of a sudden now they were saying that Democrats just wanted to kill independent oil. And Tip was now saying, 'You're right. Kill 'em.'

"And so I was concerned that it would destroy my credibility . . . so I organized an effort to beat him back. And we beat Danny and Tip in the Democratic Caucus."

The Senate had passed a $98.5 billion tax increase, undoing many of the breaks that had been handed out the year before. It was being billed as the largest peacetime tax rise the country had ever enacted, but it left the breaks for oilmen intact. O'Neill and Rostenkowski came up with an alternative that would have cut deeply into the oilmen's tax preferences. But Coelho's rebellion, joined by Majority Leader Wright and other oil-state congressmen, succeeded in convincing House Democrats to simply accept the GOP-controlled Senate's bill and to label it as a Republican tax increase. It was an appeal to cowardice; Democrats could vote for a tax rise while denying responsibility for it. And it carried the day.

Word of the bitter fight quickly leaked out from behind the closed doors of the caucus meeting. The Washington *Post,* quoting unnamed sources, said one of O'Neill's Massachusetts colleagues, Rep. James Shannon, complained that the Ways and Means Committee "is a tax-writing committee, not a fund-raising committee." Rostenkowski declared that the oil industry had "blown him out of the water." Coelho didn't try to hide his motives. "I know the business and I represent it," he said.

That 1982 battle helped boost Coelho's reputation among oilmen and among his colleagues from oil-producing states, but it didn't endear him to O'Neill or Rostenkowski. Then, in late 1985, came an episode that heightened their suspicions further. Through a combination of political logic and sheer force of personality, Coelho attempted to unite the strangest of political bedfellows: Jews and oilmen.

Coelho called his odd alliance the Council for a Secure America, and formed it specifically to lobby both for tax breaks for oil drillers and for U.S. aid to Israel. To Coelho, the organization made perfect sense. Jewish friends of Israel feared that U.S. support for the embattled Israeli state might evaporate if the United States became more dependent on imported oil from Arab countries. They worried that anti-Semitism would erupt along with gasoline shortages should Arabs impose another 1970s-style embargo on oil shipments. Encouraging more production of U.S. oil would cut that risk. Oil drillers, of course, argued that they needed tax incentives to continue exploring for additional domestic supplies. Therefore, Jews and drillers could find a common interest supporting government subsidies for oilmen.

Coelho echoed the sentiments of the pro-Israel lobby perfectly, going so far as to say that Arabs once had "control" of American foreign policy: "I predict to you that within five years we're going to be energy-short, and the Arab nations are going to control our foreign policy again as they did in the past. I think it's wrong for us to sit here and let it happen. We're going to become dependent upon those folks, and they don't want us to have a free foreign policy. They want to dictate to us what our foreign policy is."

Coelho had no foreign-policy experience. In the House he sat on the Agriculture Committee and the Committee on House Administration, which oversees election laws and the lawmakers' own internal bureaucracy. What he knew of foreign policy he had learned through the political process, not through academic study. He traveled to Israel, a pilgrimage important for those who wish to advance to high rank in national Democratic politics. His ideas reflected the political reality that Jewish Americans vote overwhelmingly for Democrats and are the largest single source of campaign donations for the Democratic party and

Democratic presidential candidates. Coelho was simply siding with his friends and donors.

To forge the coalition of Jews and oilmen Coelho turned to Dutko, the oil lobbyist, and to Selig Zises, the tax-shelter promoter he first met in Israel. They persuaded one of Dutko's clients, Dallas oilman Frank Pitts, to serve on the board. Coelho threw a kosher dinner at his suburban Virginia home in late 1984 "to get the marriage moving," as he put it. About forty guests attended. They included representatives of the Israeli embassy, the head of the American-Israel Public Affairs Committee (the leading pro-Israel lobbying group in Washington), and Jim Wright. At the dinner, Pitts complained to the pro-Israel donors: "Most of the people you in the Northeast have supported . . . have not voted very much for legislation that would be conducive to a strong oil and gas business."

Politics does indeed make strange bedfellows, but bundling together Jews and oilmen was as curious a political proposition as Washington had seen in a long time. Jews are traditionally liberal on social issues, constituting a major force in the civil-rights and trade-union movements. They tend to live in the oil-consuming Northeast. Their perennial lobbying goal was passage of foreign-aid bills providing money for Israel. Independent oil and gas drillers, on the other hand, tended to be Protestant free-enterprisers from the Southwest, not overly tolerant of unions or civil-rights activists and instinctively opposed to sending U.S. tax money to Israel or any other foreign country.

To the buoyant Coelho, bridging such a cultural chasm was an exercise in person-to-person missionary work. To outsiders, it seemed like a brazen play for campaign funds. One antagonist of the oil industry, Edwin Rothschild of the Citizen-Labor Energy Coalition, said he thought Coelho "sees this as a way to finance the Democratic party."

Appearances weren't helped by Zises's being a tax-shelter promoter. However much it may have been in Israel's interest to encourage U.S. oil production, the tax breaks being sought by the Coelho coalition were also in the personal financial interest of Zises. Integrated Resources, in fact, was losing money on its line of oil-drilling ventures. Cutting tax breaks for drilling would only make matters worse.

Integrated's oil deals lost $11 million in 1983 and were in the red again in 1984. As the coalition was gearing up, Integrated was telling its stockholders that its outlook for earnings was "uncertain due to the proposed tax-law changes." Integrated eventually discontinued its energy tax shelters in mid-1986, booking a loss of $10.4 million. That, along with tax reform and other problems, battered the company's earnings and helped produce a net loss of $1.73 per share of common stock for 1986, a sharp reversal from the $2.04-per-share profit posted the year before. Selig Zises clearly had a personal commitment to aiding Israel. He gave heavily to pro-Israel PACs, and brother Jay later became head of the largest of those pro-Israel political funds, National PAC. But the Council for a Secure America was good for business, too.

When Coelho formed the council, the Treasury Department was proposing cutbacks of tax breaks for oilmen. Most alarming to the drillers was a proposal to end the practice of writing off their intangible costs immediately, rather than following the normal practice of deducting such costs gradually over a number of years. That one proposal could have increased the tax bite on drillers by $5.6 billion a year, the department estimated.

Coelho's group drew up a $300,000 budget for its first year and began doing business out of Dan Dutko's offices. It sponsored what Dutko called an "educational teach-in," flying four New York congressmen to Texas to tour an oil field and, incidentally, meet potential donors. One of the four was Thomas Downey of New York, a member of the Ways and Means Committee, who hadn't been very sympathetic toward the oilmen. After he returned, he said, "What they convinced me of is . . . the potential for serious harm if we don't stand for a strong domestic industry."

The council didn't work very well, however; it was simply viewed with too much suspicion. Rostenkowski criticized it publicly and adverse editorials and articles appeared. "You look at it and it looks so obvious that it's a money-raising thing that I understand what they're saying," Coelho conceded later. He attempted to distance himself and the campaign committee from the project, but without him it floundered. The council had no detectable impact on the tax bill. But it raised questions about Coelho that damaged his credibility when he raised what he said were principled objections to the bill as it took on its final shape in the summer of 1986.

Coelho remained emotionally opposed to tax reform. "I just had real trouble with the bill," he said. Dropping the top rate to 27 percent for individuals was only part of what disturbed him. Coelho wanted to retain some of the very tax breaks the bill would dispatch. "I do believe in shelters, as long as they are for humanitarian needs, as long as they are for helping out the handicapped or the elderly, or things that the government won't spend money on that we need to have, and we get the wealthy to do it for us and we give them a tax credit. I don't have any trouble with that; I think that is good, social, public policy."

Coelho, in short, clung to the very philosophy that had produced such a scandalously inefficient tax system in the first place. He wanted a system with high nominal rates, to which he and his colleagues would grant special waivers for socially desirable investments. That was a fine theory, but in practice it had turned the tax system into a gigantic pork barrel, from which Congress dispensed tax breaks for non-needy groups. Gravel-pit owners got a depletion allowance like oilmen. Some fast-food restaurant owners received low-interest mortgage loans financed with tax-subsidized industrial revenue bonds. The system fostered widespread tax avoidance by the well-to-do, including the clients of the Zises brothers. "There were a lot of abuses," Coelho agreed. "And I resented it, and I thought the Ways and Means Committee should spend more time going after the abuses." He said the reformers should have "used a carving knife instead of knocking the whole thing out."

But because he had built his reputation in Congress as a money-raiser, his colleagues were skeptical. "People suspected that I was trying to kill the bill for these other folks," he says. "Some folks were very critical of me because I wasn't playing a very positive, public role in trying to get the bill passed. Well, there was no way I could play a positive role to get the bill passed because I didn't *believe* in it."

8

"It's Not My Personality"

I mourn with the poor liquor dealers of New York City, who are taxed and oppressed for the benefit of the farmers up the state.
—GEORGE WASHINGTON PLUNKITT

As the debate on tax reform unfolded, it became a bonanza for members of the tax-writing committees, displaying the sickness of the PAC system as never before.

The tax bill exposed an election system out of control. Powerful incumbents could raise so much special-interest money they could bury their opponents, and in some cases avoid the annoyance of an election entirely. Selecting congressmen had become a two-step process. Elections were held first in Washington, by PACs and lobbyists who voted with dollars, and only later in the home districts, where voters cast real ballots. Incumbents could win PAC elections so decisively as to remove voters from the process entirely.

One of the top money-raisers among the tax writers was Rep. Sam Gibbons of Florida, the second-ranking Democrat on the committee. At sixty-six he had been in the House for nearly twenty-four years, and Coelho feared he might have lost a step or two politically. The Tampa congressman's district leans heavily to Republicans in most national elections. It gave Ronald Reagan 63 percent of its vote in 1984. Gibbons hadn't faced serious opposition in many years, but in the 1984 election a conservative Republican candidate took 41 percent of the vote, sending off alarms at the campaign committee. Coelho feared his Tampa colleague was at the top of the Republicans' hit list. He arranged for outside political consultants to make over Gibbons's House office to maximize the vote-getting appeal of his official mail, travel, and staff. And he pressed Gibbons to capitalize on his position on the tax-writing committee to raise sizable funds.

Gibbons had spent $93,000 getting re-elected against token opposition in 1982 and laid out nearly $300,000 against the more serious threat in 1984. But those sums were nothing compared to what he raised, urged on by Coelho, for the next election. By the end of 1985 Gibbons had deposited $421,000 in his re-election committee's bank account, the bulk of it raised from PACs, Washington lobbyists, and non-Florida business interests. Gibbons's cash constituents included tobacco companies fighting to roll back the federal excise tax on cigarettes, drug companies that wanted to keep a tax haven in Puerto Rico, and equipment-leasing firms that profited from special tax credits given for purchases of capital goods.

Gibbons was an opponent of tax reform, and while he was fighting against it in the Ways and Means Committee, money was flowing in from all around the nation, especially from corporations that liked the tax system the way it was. Boeing of Seattle gave him $1,500 in 1985 and another $1,500 the following April. In the years 1982 through 1985 Boeing made $2.3 billion in profits but paid a net total of nothing in federal income taxes. American Telephone & Telegraph gave $10,000 during the campaign: $5,000 for the primary election and $5,000 for the general. AT&T paid net federal income taxes of zero on corporate profits of $25 billion during 1982–1985, placing it at the top of a list of "corporate freeloaders" issued by Citizens for Tax Justice. Ashland Oil donated $4,000. Ashland's four-year profits exceeded $500 million, but its net federal income taxes were zero. Grace & Co. gave $2,000; it paid no tax on four-year profits of $483 million.

Gibbons got $1,000 from the American Horse Council, representing thoroughbred breeders who wanted to keep the right to claim rapid depreciation for their animals. Congress in 1981 had shortened the tax depreciation period for horses to three years from five. It was part of a tax reduction for business that Congress passed that year with the professed aim of encouraging investment to "reindustrialize" the nation.

By the end of the two-year election cycle, Gibbons had raised just over $900,000, including $572,210 from PACs. The only other House candidate to receive more from PACs was Jim Wright.

Gibbons's fund worked better than Coelho had hoped. Despite his somewhat weak performance in the 1984 campaign and the increasingly Republican bent of his district, the GOP couldn't recruit a candidate willing to run against an incumbent already sitting on such a re-election fund. His cash constituents decided the election, relieving his voting constituents of the chore of making a choice on election day.

Apologists for the PACs say they have a positive effect, getting people involved in the political process through writing checks. But in this case, the checks suppressed the involvement of voters. Defenders also insist, publicly at least, that campaign money doesn't affect lawmakers' votes. And to be sure, academic researchers who have attempted to apply their statistical calipers to the effect of money on votes have generally concluded that lawmakers still seem to be swayed more by party, region, or personal philosophy than by money. But the tax-reform fight showed that PACs are growing and lobbyists are giving precisely because they believe that one way or another, votes are affected. And their belief is based on hard personal experience.

PAC managers don't mince words when communicating privately to their own donors. Early in the tax debate John J. Koelemij, president of the Home Builders, appealed to the association's members to give money to defeat tax reform, then being advanced as a tax "simplification."

"I need you to join me in supporting BUILD-PAC, our political action committee, with a financial contribution," he said. "I need you to join me in lobbying Congress against some of the devastating tax proposals contained in these 'tax simplification' bills."

Builders were fighting to preserve, among other things, deductibility of mortgage interest on vacation homes, tax-exempt treatment of bonds to finance low-rate mortgages that state and local governments like to disburse to favored groups, and fast write-offs of apartment buildings. To protect this tax-based patronage, the builders had to deliver dollars, just as Tammany's workers once had to deliver votes to keep their municipal jobs.

"A strong political action committee will make the difference between victory and defeat when we take our case to Congress," Koelemij said. "If there's one thing they understand in Washington, it's the kind of political clout BUILD-PAC, our political action committee, has earned."

The money worked, according to Koelemij's successor, David C. Smith. "I've seen for myself how BUILD-PAC opens doors for our industry on Capitol Hill," he said in a 1986 brochure for members.

The tax bill, of course, was only the most dramatic example of lobbyists giving money to influence legislation. With Washington proposing to regulate or subsidize practically every kind of business activity, money was spread around accordingly.

Auto importers wanted to defeat proposals to curb sales of Toyotas. Beer wholesalers—they have named their political fund SixPAC, of course—sought changes in antitrust laws to allow them to impose regional monopolies. Dairy farmers hoped to continue federal price supports for milk, cheese, and butter that cost taxpayers billions of dollars and raised food prices for consumers by billions more. Commercial bankers aimed to get into investment banking, and investment bankers wanted to keep them out. Television station owners desired easier license-renewal procedures. Insurance companies and personal-injury lawyers feuded over proposals to limit damage awards. Physicians opposed attempts to hold down the fees that Medicaid reimbursed. Truck operators, still smarting over an increase in diesel-fuel taxes and the loss of protective economic regulation, wanted a uniform national driver's license for truck drivers, an end to the 55-mile-per-hour national speed limit, and increased federal spending to repair the interstate highway system. All of these groups gave money to protect their patronage.

Even obscure industries felt they needed PACs. During the 1986 campaigns the private ambulance industry, represented by the American Ambulance Association, believed that it was threatened by a Reagan administration proposal to cut Medicaid payments for ambulance services by as much as two-thirds. The association's lobbying firm, A-K Associates, later boasted that when the cuts were proposed "the association's officers and government relations consultants swung into action—on both the lobbying and the PAC fundraising fronts." The political fund, AMBUPAC, hadn't raised more than $15,000 previously. But with a cut in government insurance payments threatened, sixty-nine donors were persuaded to give $1,000 each, and the PAC's total receipts rose to $82,000. Meanwhile, the industry's lobbyists complained to members of Congress. The administration withdrew its proposal. And far from denying that money influences legislation, A-K Associates issued a press release to boast of its success.

The chief beneficiaries of this PAC fever, of course, were the incumbent members of the tax-writing committees. Gibbons wasn't the only one raising funds to keep himself in office. Republican Robert Packwood of Oregon, chairman of the Senate Finance Committee, realized more than

$1 million from PACs, nearly all of it during 1985, when the tax bill was being worked over in the House and, earlier, by administration officials who consulted closely with Packwood in the process. Many of his donations from individuals came from outside Oregon, given by business executives and lobbyists seeking Packwood's aid in keeping their loopholes.

Members of the lobbying group ALIGNPAC gave Packwood more than a quarter of a million dollars. The donors were life-insurance salesmen whose products sold well because the interest on the cash value of life insurance isn't taxed in the same way as interest on other forms of savings. Packwood fought to preserve that loophole, which was one of the biggest tax breaks to survive in the bill that eventually became law.

Like Gibbons, Packwood was no friend of tax reform, at least in 1985. When the Reagan administration proposed wholesale elimination of loopholes, he said he rather liked the tax code the way it was. And like Gibbons, Packwood raised such enormous sums that he scared away the opponents who would have had the best chance to defeat him. By the start of 1986 two Democratic congressmen—Ron Wyden and Les AuCoin—had concluded that Packwood's financial advantage was too great to overcome.

Packwood's eventual Democratic opponent, Rep. James Weaver, was an eccentric liberal who was so wounded by his own misuse of campaign funds that he had no chance to win. Weaver had dipped into his House re-election funds for $82,000, which he lost in ill-advised speculations in the highly volatile bond market. The House ethics committee later determined this to be in violation of House rules against personal use of political funds. By that time Weaver, unable to raise a serious campaign fund and under pressure from the ethics investigation, had withdrawn from the race. Oregon Democrats had to scramble to come up with a last-minute substitute, or Packwood would have won without an opponent. For all practical purposes, he had won a year before voters went to the polls, by collecting special-interest donations given in the hope of influencing the shape of the tax bill.

The general outpouring of special-interest money sometimes brought the progress of tax reform to a halt. On the evening of November 19, 1985, the drafting of the tax bill had to be interrupted because Rep. James Jones of Oklahoma was holding a $500-per-person fund-raising reception at a Washington hotel. Rostenkowski left the hearing room briefly to attend the event. Campaign-finance reports later showed that Jones, who was running for the Senate, raised $67,000 from PACs during June. Jones at the time was a champion of the insurance industry. The PAC of the Guardian Life Insurance Co. gave $1,000, Massachusetts Mutual Life $1,000, New England Mutual Life $500, Northwestern Mutual Life $500, Prudential $2,000, Security Life of Denver $2,000, and three other insurance-industry groups $1,000 more, for a total of $8,000.

Republicans on the tax-writing panel were also squeezing PACs. GOP Rep. Henson Moore of Louisiana raised $1.4 million during 1985, 23 percent of it from PACs. Moore tried hard to kill the bill. He was also a key figure on a panel that drafted proposals to change taxation of both insurance companies and the products they sell. On October 28, 1985, just two weeks before the panel was set to issue its recommendations, Moore flew to New York City to dine with executives of insurance companies whose PACs had given, or promised to give, at least $2,500 each to his campaign. Moore insisted afterward that all the insurance men got for their money was an opportunity to hear bad news firsthand. "I explained to them that it wasn't going to fly—what they wanted wasn't going to happen," he said. "I'm not there to do what they like, but to do what's right."

Moore's insurance money illustrated vividly the contrast between the voting constituency in Louisiana and his donor constituency in the insurance industry. Even after giving insurance men unwelcome news, he received on a single day, December 29, 1985, a total of $27,550 from insurance agents, executives, and lobbyists from all over the country. The money flowed in from places such as Elkhart, Indiana; Portland, Oregon; Englewood, Colorado; Philadelphia, Los Angeles, Minneapolis, Milwaukee, Fort Worth, Houston, Austin, Atlanta, and Washington, D.C. But his disclosure report shows not a penny that day from anywhere in Louisiana, whose voters he was courting in a bid for the Senate in 1986.

Another example of the power of campaign money was provided by Democratic Rep. Wyche Fowler of Georgia, also a Ways and Means member, who worked on businessmen all over the country for donations to finance his Senate campaign. Then, during a crucial moment on the House floor, Fowler voted to kill tax reform, joining House Republicans in support of a procedural measure to block action on the bill. He sided with his nationwide constituency and against the economic interest of Georgia voters. He then represented a poor district; 65 percent of his constituents were black, and 24 percent had so little income they met the government's official definition of poverty. Thousands of those low-income people, black and white, would have been relieved of federal income taxes entirely under the tax bill that Fowler voted—without any public explanation—against. The bill was saved only by a lobbying blitz by President Reagan, who persuaded enough House Republicans to change their votes. After passage was assured, Fowler also switched and supported the bill.

Fowler was running for election in Georgia, but he was raising money in places like Houston, Dallas, and New York City. His cash constituents included, among many others in the real-estate industry, Coelho's good friends the Zises brothers. In October 1985 Fowler raised $10,500 from the Zises clan and other executives of Integrated Resources.

The Zises brothers help mostly Democrats, but Fowler also got money from Republicans even though his voting record had been in some ways as liberal as Edward Kennedy's. He reaped a total of $6,500 from Dallas real-estate developer Trammell Crow, executives of Crow's com-

pany, and its political action committee. Crow also was
against the bill. He and Selig Zises served together on the
board of the National Realty Committee, a group of the
nation's wealthiest developers and real-estate financiers,
which was lobbying hard to salvage tax breaks for the industry. Crow is such a strong Republican that during the
1984 GOP convention he had sponsored a major fund-raising event for President Reagan. But the quest for tax breaks
can transcend both party and regional ties, moving conservative Texas Republicans to give to a liberal Georgia Democrat.

In all, Fowler received $75,800 from wealthy Texans in
the last six months of 1985, the period during which the tax
bill was before his committee. The Texas money accounted
for 23 percent of his donations from individuals during that
period. Most of it came in on September 30, at an event
organized for Fowler by oil-industry lobbyist Carl F. Arnold. Arnold was also seeking Fowler's vote for continued
tax breaks for oil and gas drillers. He was retained by Quintana Petroleum of Houston. Fowler's disclosure reports mis-
leadingly listed Arnold's occupation as "consultant," and
described two other donors, Corbin Robertson, Sr., and Corbin Robertson, Jr., the top executives of Quintana, only as
self-employed investors.

The special-interest giving disturbed even some who
benefited from it, including Dan Rostenkowski, a veteran of
old-fashioned Chicago machine politics and a protégé of
the late Mayor Richard J. Daley. The Chicago machine, in
its day, was a place where Boss Plunkitt himself would have
felt at home. But that machine disintegrated after Daley's
death, and Rostenkowski converted from the old patronage
system to the new by raising one of the biggest political
funds in the House. That left him with mixed feelings.

One day in mid-1986, not long after he had returned to
Washington from a series of fund-raising trips that produced nearly $300,000 for his personal PAC, Rostenkowski
expressed his ambivalence. The money came from real-
estate developers, stockbrokers, insurance salesmen, and

corporate executives, including the board chairmen of IBM, Paramount Pictures, First Boston, and several other major corporations, all interested in the final shape of the tax bill. Twenty-three executives of Drexel Burnham's Los Angeles office contributed $10,100. Rostenkowski knew why they gave. "It's not my personality," he said. "I'm sure it's my position." He was then picking the Ways and Means members who would be part of a Senate-House conference to draft the final shape of the tax bill.

Rostenkowski, to the astonishment of lobbyists and reporters, had become a champion of tax reform. While drawing up the House version of the bill, he said his stomach turned at the influence that money had on some of his colleagues. "There was on the part of three to five members, on both sides of the aisle, a definite string attached to some corporate lobbyist outside in the hall," he said. "In one instance, a direct link with respect to how much money he could raise in a campaign. That got me nauseated." He said two members "flagrantly violated ethical codes," but wouldn't reveal who they were.

Rostenkowski wasn't so nauseated that he returned any of his own special-interest money, however. He was also more than a little resentful of Coelho, whom he considered a young upstart rising on the strength of his ability to secure campaign funds. Rostenkowski wanted to move up to be Speaker of the House, but his way was blocked by Coelho's ally, Jim Wright. Rostenkowski, in fact, ceased raising money for the Democratic campaign committee so that Coelho couldn't claim credit for it. "I was the biggest fundraiser that he had, until I started to see Tony's moving in for leadership," he said. "If he wants to do that, that's fine with me. But I don't want him to think he's fooling me." Rostenkowski had begun raising funds for a personal PAC, which he first called the Chicago Campaign Committee, a name he later changed to the higher-sounding America's Leaders Fund. He said he quit working for Coelho's committee because "I want to go out and say to people, 'Look, you're giving it to *me* to distribute.' "

Rostenkowski was determined to put the Democratic party's stamp on the tax-reform bill and wanted Coelho to support it. But Coelho went to Speaker O'Neill and complained that the bill dropped the top rate too low, letting wealthy taxpayers off the hook. The Speaker sided with Rostenkowski. Tax reform had always been a Democratic issue before Ronald Reagan began pushing it, first to keep Walter Mondale from using it in the 1984 campaign, later to cut the top rate. Rostenkowski and O'Neill weren't going to let Reagan get to their left. Besides, organized labor was pushing strongly for closing the loopholes that allowed many profitable corporations to pay little or no tax.

Coelho found himself fettered by his open ties to wealthy tax-reform foes. Public attention was being focused on the bill; news stories about its progress appeared almost daily. And however much Coelho opposed it privately, the Senate bill was in fact modeled on a proposal first advanced by two liberal Democrats, Sen. Bill Bradley of New Jersey and Rep. Richard Gephardt of Missouri, a close political ally of Coelho. Coelho found it politically impossible to lobby against such a measure. His public reputation was built almost entirely on his success at raising money from special-interest donors. He would be accused of doing the bidding of the campaign committee's contributors. One of its major supporters was Rep. Charles Rangel of New York, a black congressman representing a district with poor blacks and Hispanics. Rangel, a Rostenkowski ally on the Ways and Means Committee, was Coelho's principal opponent in the race for Majority Whip. If a black congressman from a ghetto district drafted and supported the bill, how could it favor the rich? Coelho was in an impossible bind.

Word spread that Rangel's supporters were preparing to attack Coelho unless he made a public show of support for the bill. That could cost Coelho votes, and possibly the Whip race. He decided he had no choice but to vote for the bill.

"I went to Danny one day, privately," Coelho said. "I said, 'Look, I don't want you to ever say this publicly. I'm taking a lot of heat and I don't give a goddamn. I'm going to vote for the bill. I just want you to know that's where I am. I'm not going to lobby against the bill.' "

Going against the Zises brothers was hard for Coelho. "They helped me raise a lot of money, they could have jerked my chain anytime they wanted," he said. "I expected that this bill would divide our friendship, that we would lose our friendship."

But the Zises brothers accepted the necessity of Coelho's decision. Selig and Jay called Coelho from New York after hearing from others that Rostenkowski was threatening him. "They said, 'Look, we're hearing from some of our friends [on the Ways and Means Committee] that you're in trouble on the Whip's race because you're not doing this thing. This bill devastates us. . . . But you're like a brother to us. And we think its important that you become Whip. We want you to vote for it.' " By that time, passage of the bill was all but assured anyway.

Coelho got a similar call from Grover Connell, a multimillionaire rice broker from New Jersey who had supplied the campaign committee with $50,000 a year and who also was lobbying strongly to defeat the bill. Connell's rice and sugar empire had expanded into the lucrative equipment-leasing business. His personal companies owned about $2.5 billion worth of railroad locomotives, coal cars, airplanes, and other heavy equipment, which were leased and operated by others. His leasing business realized the tax advantages of rapid depreciation, investment tax credits, and deductions on the interest paid on the money borrowed to buy the equipment. His companies don't file public reports of their earnings and taxes, but a typical leasing operation can run up enough paper losses and tax credits to reduce or eliminate taxes on income from other sources. The bill threatened to eliminate much of the tax advantage enjoyed by leasing companies, repealing the investment tax credit and allowing smaller write-downs each year for depreciation. The bill, in short, was going to cost Grover Connell a lot of money.

But he, too, saw the futility of Coelho attacking the bill and called to say so.

"He said, 'I understand you're getting a lot of crap. . . . This bill really hurts me, but I want you to vote for it.'

"I said, 'Vote *for* it?'

"He said, 'Yes, I want you to vote for it. The reason I want you to vote for it is because I think it is more important to the country that you be Whip or Leader or whatever you want to be than that the bill gets defeated.' . . . Interesting phone call."

The Zises and Connell conversations weren't what Coelho had expected. "I was shocked that I was getting these calls," he said. "I couldn't believe that these people would do that." Perhaps he shouldn't have been so surprised, however. Elevating an unabashed friend of tax breaks to the top ranks of the House leadership could be far more valuable to Zises and Connell than persuading Coelho to vote against a bill he was powerless to stop anyway.

The tax-reform bill didn't really favor the wealthy as Coelho claimed. To be sure, the final version dropped the top rate to 28 percent, just one point higher than the Senate version. That seemed superficially to favor the rich. But in fact, the bill shifted a huge portion of the overall federal tax burden away from individuals and onto business, the very corporate America that Coelho thought would benefit. After factoring in the elimination of tax shelters and the closing of a number of other loopholes enjoyed by upper-income families, wealthy individuals got less of a break than the poor. Experts at the bipartisan Joint Committee on Taxation figured that the bill gave most dramatic tax relief to the poorest workers. Initially, in its first year, the bill actually increased the tax burden on the wealthy, quite contrary to Coelho's thinking.

The Joint Committee's figures show how badly Coelho was misled. Tax reform cut the average taxes of families making less than $10,000 a year by 57 percent in the first year, and 65 percent in the second, compared to what they would have paid under prevailing law. The next-poorest class got the next-biggest cut; families making between $10,000 and $20,000 received tax cuts of 17 percent in the first year and 22 percent in the second.

On the other hand, the taxes of the wealthiest taxpayers, those making $200,000 and above, would go up an average of nearly 10 percent in the first year. Their taxes did go down in the second year, but by only 2.4 percent. Less affluent taxpayers received bigger cuts, an average of 6.1 percent for all individuals. Nearly 80 percent of all individuals got a reduction under the tax-reform bill. But that included 88 percent of the poorest and only 56 percent of the wealthiest.

Interestingly, tax reform couldn't have passed without a conversion by Robert Packwood, who switched from a defender of loopholes to a proponent of trading loopholes for low rates. It was his very dependence on special-interest money that led, at least in part, to his rebirth as a champion of reform.

Packwood was politically vulnerable. He was a leading defender of population control and women's right to abortions, but faced a Republican primary opponent who ran mainly on the right-to-life issue and later managed to score 40 percent of the vote, too close for comfort where a splinter candidate was concerned. James Weaver, the Democratic nominee, was attacking Packwood as a tool of the moneyed interests even though his own misuse of campaign funds diminished his credibility. Local news media were criticizing Packwood as well. Furthermore, he seemed to be losing control of the Finance Committee as it began working up its version of a tax bill. He refused to entertain elimination of loopholes for oil, gas, timber (a big industry in Oregon), mining, and agriculture. The committee strayed so far from the goal of tax reform that it began approving new loopholes, including an increase in the amount of income that high-salaried executives could shelter from taxes using 401(k) pension plans. The spectacle was such that the independent *New Republic* dubbed the chairman "Senator Hackwood." Tax reform was perishing on Packwood's watch, and he would enter a re-election fight looking like a hit man for PACs and lobbyists. With a campaign issue like that even his wounded adversary, James Weaver, could conceivably score an upset.

His own political survival at stake, Packwood turned on his donors. He and his chief aide came up with a modified version of the Bradley-Gephardt plan, proposing a drop in the top individual tax rate, largely at the expense of real-estate developers and tax-shelter syndicators. The National Association of Realtors, its leadership dominated by wealthy developers, doubled its $1 million budget for "independent" political spending, through which it could pour unlimited amounts of money into defeating House or Senate members it didn't like. The Realtors considered an all-out campaign to punish Packwood and his party by financing political attacks on enough politically shaky Republican senators to swing the Senate back to Democratic control. The rumor was that the president of the Realtors PAC at one meeting had hung out a sign saying "Lloyd Bentsen for Finance Committee Chairman"—Bentsen was the second-ranking Democrat on the committee, behind Louisiana's Russell Long, who was retiring. Eventually the Realtors cooled off, though they did weigh in with a sizable campaign in support of James Jones, who had backed real-estate interests in the House Ways and Means Committee and who was trying to unseat GOP Sen. Don Nickles, a member of the Finance Committee.

Big donors weren't accustomed to such treatment, but they couldn't publicly accuse lawmakers of going back on a bargain. A few days after Coelho voted for final passage of the tax bill, and as it waited on the President's desk for signing, a disappointed Selig Zises complained to a television interviewer that Congress had unfairly singled out the real-estate industry. Zises chose his words carefully.

"Do you feel betrayed?" an interviewer inquired.

"I don't think any of the people who were involved in the political process wanted any special favors," Zises responded. "What you hope when you support somebody is that they have an ideology that's consistent with yours. I've been around long enough to know that you can't and you really don't ever hope to really influence anybody against their own principles and convictions."

"Will this change your approach to political contributions in the future?"

"We will still be very active in the political process," Zises said. "But I think that in terms of who we support, our dialogue will be much more penetrating."

9

"Good Democrats and Bad Democrats"

Every good man looks after his friends, and any man who doesn't isn't likely to be popular. If I have a good thing to hand out in private life, I give it to a friend. Why shouldn't I do the same thing in public life?
                    —GEORGE WASHINGTON PLUNKITT

Martin Franks, Coelho's top staff man, delivered a glowing report on the Democratic Congressional Campaign Committee's 1986 soft money:

"The $25,000 from the Steelworkers came in this week, and with a letter promising payment of the other 3 installments on the first of July, the first of August, the first of September.

"The IBEW [International Brotherhood of Electrical Workers] is just awaiting an opinion from their lawyer. . . . I will be surprised if we do not have the full $100,000 by the end of the month."

Coelho's campaign committee was consuming substantial sums of soft money, political income used in ways that got around donations limits. Hard money was hard to come by; it had to be raised, spent, and disclosed under the strictures of the election law. But soft money had a special allure. Because of permissive regulators and legal ingenuity, Coelho could find a political use for anyone's check. He didn't have to pass up money from lobbyists who wanted to pay Speaker's Club dues with corporate funds, which would otherwise be illegal. He could legally accept donations from PACs willing to give more than $15,000 a year, which would otherwise be the maximum under the federal limits. He could accept checks from developers, oilmen, or anyone, in any amount, whether or not they had already "maxed out" by giving the annual maximum of $25,000 in federal campaign gifts.

Before Coelho took over the Democratic Congressional Campaign Committee it didn't deal in soft money; every penny was raised under federal limits and disclosed. But in his scramble to catch up with Republicans he was drawn to the stuff, which his lawyers also called "non-federal money" on the theory that it wasn't covered by federal law. He described the situation in early 1985 in a confidential report on the operations of the campaign committee, under the heading "Putting Non-Federal (Soft) Money to Work":

"The DCCC has pushed hard on soft money because the DCCC believes that it is one of the principal ways in which the DCCC can accelerate its catch-up process with the Republicans. . . . There simply is not enough hard money to do everything that the DCCC would like to do. Moreover, it would be foolish to spend hard money that could be used in support of candidates on projects that can be legitimately paid for with soft money."

Coelho built his television studio largely with soft money, starting with an interest-free loan of $400,000 from Pamela Harriman, the British-born wife of former New York Governor Averell Harriman. The Harriman salon in Georgetown was a regular oasis for Democrats seeking financing for their campaigns from wealthy liberals. Pamela Harriman ran her own PAC, Democrats for the '80's.

The Democratic party's new headquarters building, which was being readied for occupancy at the time Coelho wrote his report, was financed completely with soft money, chiefly from labor unions and rich individuals. The party refused to release a complete accounting of those who paid for the building. The three-story structure itself, made of tan-colored brick and darkly tinted window glass, was hardly a grand edifice. From outward appearances it could as easily have housed orthodontists' offices or an Elks lodge. But its completion was cause for rejoicing among party officials. It allowed the three national Democratic organizations—the Democratic National Committee, the Democratic Senatorial Campaign Committee, and Coelho's DCCC—to move into permanent quarters.

The party committees had spent years camping like nomads in various rented offices. The DNC operated for a while in the now-famous Watergate complex, where its rented offices were invaded in 1972 by incompetent burglars. With the opening of the new building the Democratic party had a real home at last.

The Democrats also used soft money to attack President Reagan. Because it could command so little financial support from ordinary donors, the party was forced to fall back on soft money to put on several nationally televised appearances for spokesmen who rebutted Reagan's annual State of the Union addresses to Congress. Networks provided the time free, but the party had to bear the production costs for studio use, cameras, and crews. Party lawyers believed these TV appearances didn't amount to electioneering if Democrats only criticized the President's policies without overtly appealing for votes. "Since the State of the Union is issue-rather than election-related, soft money can be used to pay the costs of production for the State of the Union responses," Coelho said in his report. "Without the help of soft money, it is doubtful whether the DCCC would have been able to afford the four State of the Union programs that it has participated in with the DNC and the Senate Committee."

Democrats paid in soft money for their legal battles over the drawing of new congressional district lines following the decennial census. A good lawyer could win a congressional seat for a client as readily as a good political consultant; the lawyer worked with artfully drawn district lines while the consultant's tools were skillful polling and clever television commercials. But Congress hadn't applied campaign limits and disclosure requirements to money spent for legal fees. "The DCCC has used soft money to support lawsuits and other studies related to the 1980 reapportionment," Coelho wrote, "and is making plans to become heavily involved in the 1990 reapportionment fights." He later launched what he called Project 500, an expensive effort to train hundreds of political workers to assist in the campaigns of candidates for state legislatures. By keeping control of as many statehouses as possible, Democrats could dominate the drawing of district lines in 1991. Soft money was paying for the effort.

Most importantly, Coelho had found uses for soft money that in practice subsidized the campaigns of his House candidates. He said in his report: "In 1984 the DCCC supported a number of state party organizations with soft money. The state party organizations were particularly helpful in registering voters and in getting-out-the-vote drives in critical states. . . . And while the DCCC may not get a direct and tangible benefit for every dollar expended, all candidates will receive considerable spillover benefits from the running of good get-out-the-vote efforts by state parties."

The same thing was continuing in 1986. Coelho gave a large donation of soft money to the Mississippi state party to aid the campaign of Mike Espy, a promising black candidate.

Coelho liked Espy and was emotionally committed to seeing him elected. Espy would be the first black congressman from a rural district in old Dixie since Reconstruction, and would help fill Coelho's prediction of a fifteen-seat gain for Democrats on election day. Another black Democrat had come agonizingly close to winning the seat in each of the previous two elections.

"The issue here is simple: it's a 58 percent black district; a black should represent that district," Coelho said. "There are some people who started off, including some blacks, saying the best way to win that seat is by getting a white that blacks can support. I said, 'No, that's wrong. We need a black that blacks can support. And if whites won't support him, that's the way it has to be.' "

Coelho urged Espy to run, promising him the maximum aid the campaign committee could furnish and vowing to raise as much as $100,000 in additional funds. He worked behind the scenes to help Espy defeat two white Democrats in a primary, narrowly avoiding an expensive runoff election that could have sapped his political strength for the main contest in November. The campaign committee eventually spent $52,742 to aid Espy, within a few dollars of the legal maximum, and touted his race energetically among liberal and union PACs. But Coelho was determined to do even more.

The Espy campaign depended on organizational grunt work, registering black voters and getting them to the polls on election day. The Mississippi state party requested funds from Coelho to help Espy, and Coelho's lawyer, Robert Bauer, repeatedly called the Mississippi state party chairman, Fred Slabach, to work out details.

The legal fiction that made such a gift possible depended on the presence of state supreme court candidates and some aspirants for local office on the ballot in Espy's district. The Federal Election Commission allowed state parties to mix hard dollars and soft dollars in voter drives that benefit both federal and state candidates. The art of using soft money to aid House or Senate campaigns lay in the cleverness with which lawyers allocated the federal and non-federal share of the cost. If there were enough non-federal candidates running, a voter drive could be paid for almost entirely in soft money, even if the primary purpose was to help the congressional nominee. That was the case with Espy.

In late October Coelho forwarded to Slabach a $12,000 check from one of his several soft-money accounts. A cover letter said Slabach was responsible for seeing that it was used legally. "I am depending on your representations," Coelho wrote. Slabach said he passed on $7,000 to a civil-rights group, the A. Philip Randolph Institute, to buy gasoline and hire drivers to fetch black voters to the polls. He put the remaining $5,000 into a general overhead fund, where the party could legally accept soft money, thus freeing other funds to pay for a sample ballot that was mailed to registered voters in Espy's district just before election day. The postcard listed Espy at the head of a slate of local candidates. "Tony Coelho's check was a real big boost to our ability to do that," Slabach said. The state party's entire budget for that year was only about $75,000, including Coelho's soft money.

Neither federal nor state disclosure reports showed a trace of Coelho's soft money. "There aren't a whole lot of regulations on campaign finance in Mississippi," Slabach said. Espy won by a margin of 4,827 votes out of 141,411 cast.

Democrats were quick to denounce similar activities by Republicans. The DNC had threatened to file a legal complaint against the National Republican Senatorial Committee in 1984 for, among other things, making hard-money grants to state party organizations in states where Senate campaigns were taking place. Although the Republicans' grants came from funds that were fully disclosed and raised according to the donation ceilings, Democrats complained that the GOP was using the transfers to get around limits on party financing of Senate candidates. Democratic chairman Charles Manatt said then that the GOP committee was like a "rogue elephant, hemorrhaging money out in all directions." He cited $924,560 in grants the NRSC made to GOP organizations in Senate races. But Manatt was content to grab a few headlines, and failed to carry through with his threat of a legal complaint.

Coelho even used soft money to pay a part of the DCCC's general operating expenses. The committee met 6 percent of its operating costs with soft money in 1982 and 1983, but by 1985 it had more than doubled that. About $1 of every $8 in overhead was being paid in soft money. A committee whose purpose was to elect House candidates was being funded partly by supposedly non-federal money.

Despite all the finely drawn legal distinctions between hard and soft money, the differences in practical political terms were largely academic. Coelho's 1985 report frankly admitted that it hardly mattered whether a donor was paying in hard or soft dollars. A dollar of soft money could be spent for things that a hard dollar would otherwise have to pay for. "Being able to use non-federal dollars to pay for operating expenses has allowed the DCCC to use other precious federal dollars for strictly federal activities," Coelho wrote.

Though both parties were rapidly sliding back to their old practices, taking big donations in secret, the enforcement agency spawned by the Watergate scandals was doing nothing to correct matters. In fact, the Federal Election Commission in 1986 rejected a request by Common Cause to investigate the widespread abuse of soft money. Actually, the FEC was doing less than nothing. Its own regulations were making a bad situation worse: the more soft money Coelho expended for elections via grants to state parties, the more soft money the FEC's rules entitled him to use to pay overhead costs. "The FEC allows the DCCC to offset its operating costs based on a formula involving contributions made to state and local party committees and candidates," Coelho wrote. "Because of the DCCC's recent increased contribution activity to state parties, the DCCC is presently able to increase its offsetting percentage [of overhead expenses] to 12.5 percent." Using one loophole widened another.

Soft-money abuses proliferated out of control. The Republican National Committee had no fewer than seven soft-money accounts, each designed to exploit particular types of state laws. Through these it took in and dispensed $3.7 million in 1984 alone, mostly in corporate funds and subject to no effective disclosure requirement. The Democratic National Committee defrayed much of its general operating expenses from soft-money accounts. While Coelho was paying 12.5 percent of his overhead with soft money, the DNC figured it could legally take care of as much as 40 percent of its own general operating expenses with it. For a time DNC staff employees were receiving two paychecks, one paid in hard dollars and another in soft, on the theory that their time could be allocated partly to federal elections and partly to state and local contests where such funds were legal. In 1987 the DNC accepted the largest single campaign donation to surface since the Watergate scandals, a check for $1 million from Joan Kroc, widow of the founder of the McDonald's fast-food empire. Her check was, of course, entirely soft money. Donation limits were becoming a dead letter.

With the demise of these limits came decay of the only reform that had proven itself to be a real antidote to money's undue influence: disclosure. Each new loophole in the donation restrictions created another hiding place where contributors with suspect motives could secrete their gifts. The effect was unfortunate—the biggest gifts, with the greatest potential for undue influence, were the very ones that were being hidden.

Joan Kroc's $1 million check became known only because the DNC, proud of its good fortune, issued a press release to boast about it. But at the same time, the committee refused once again to open its books fully. A spokesman said that during the first months of 1987 it received $900,000 from business corporations. But which corporations and how much from each, the party declined to say.

The full extent of Coelho's soft-money dependence remained secret as well. He disclosed much of his soft-money income during 1986. But much remained hidden, and he refused a request to make a full public accounting. Nevertheless, a series of memoranda from Martin Franks gave some revealing views of what was going on during the 1986 campaigns.

Franks described soft-money collections for the Capital Trust, a project begun in February 1986. Coelho went to the annual winter meeting of the AFL-CIO in Bal Harbor,

Florida. He met with the presidents of one union after another, over breakfasts, lunches, and dinners. He asked each one to pledge $100,000 to his committee during the year. He called it the Florida Project at first.

The Capital Trust project represented only part of the soft money that fueled Coelho's campaign committee, but it was especially important. Indirectly, the funds subsidized the campaigns of Democratic candidates who used the party's television studio.

Coelho wanted a studio because the Republicans had one. But he couldn't pay for it the way the National Republican Congressional Committee financed its own much smaller facility years earlier. The NRCC spent only hard money to buy its electronic equipment. At the time it didn't need soft money. Besides, GOP attorneys said it would be hard to defend using "non-federal" money to finance a studio employed solely to make television and radio commercials for use in House campaigns.

Republican lawyers weren't nearly so venturesome as Coelho. He paid for studio equipment with soft-money donations, in this case using a loophole for "building funds." Republicans had argued successfully to the FEC that money spent to renovate new office quarters for the party had no connection with any specific federal election and so didn't qualify as a campaign expenditure subject to federal limits. The GOP raised $7 million for a new headquarters building in 1977, all fully disclosed, with no donation larger than $10,000.

Carving out the building-fund exemption theoretically enabled the GOP to accept gifts of any size, from any source. Even so, it financed the structure largely with small donations from its successful direct-mail operation. Guy Vander Jagt's committee disbursed $983,502 in small-donor money into the project in 1978, and the Republican National Committee supplied $583,754 from similar sources. The GOP's building fund eventually did receive corporate donations as large as $25,000 from Atlantic Richfield and $12,000 from

Houston Natural Gas. Republicans had created a loophole that Coelho would exploit.

The GOP ceased disclosing receipts of its building fund in 1980, creating a legal "black hole" where it could hide corporate funds or other gifts. Coelho revealed his own building-fund receipts regularly until the end of 1986, but kept secret the sums of soft money he raised to subsidize recounts, get-out-the-vote drives, or overhead expenses. Building funds and other soft-money accounts had become funds through which both Democratic and Republican party committees were raising and spending millions, without scrutiny from voters.

"We disclosed what the law required us to disclose," Franks said later. "Do you pay more taxes than the IRS requires?"

Coelho stretched the building-fund loophole even wider than Republicans had dared. Soft money was flowing through the TV studio, indirectly subsidizing dozens of House campaigns.

Coelho's venture into the video-production business began in 1983, when he used the Pamela Harriman loan to buy a Capitol Hill town house and some electronic equipment. He wanted to subsidize the production costs of the commercials for Democratic candidates. Officially, according to the committee's press releases, the town-house studio saved Democratic candidates more than $800,000 and was used by more than 250 campaigns to produce more than 600 radio and television commercials, mostly for the 1984 elections.

Coelho wanted to outpace the GOP with a bigger, more expensive production facility. So with borrowed money he installed a studio in the basement of the party's new building. He named it the Harriman Communications Center, after his major benefactor. It was crammed with $2.5 million worth of state-of-the-art video-editing equipment and billed itself as "the newest and most technologically advanced audio and video production house in the Washington, D.C., area." There were two camera crews, a sound-recording studio, and two editing suites staffed by four technicians. A two-channel Ampex ADO manipulated images to look like posters, freeze them, or make them spin or streak across the screen with video swirls and sparkles. A Quanta Q-8 character generator superimposed headlines in a choice of size, font, and color. Practically any video effect that network television audiences are accustomed to seeing could be duplicated.

Coelho financed much of this with soft money. Portable mini-cameras, for example, were purchased with hard dollars. But attorney Robert Bauer concluded that much of the wiring and permanently installed equipment qualified as fixtures of the building and could be financed out of the building fund.

The Harriman Center opened officially in April 1986. It was double the size of the earlier studio, with carpeted halls and walls painted in pastel colors. It put to shame the GOP's facility, which had a single editing room, cluttered with racks of old videotapes and audiotapes, doing double duty as a recording booth.

For a time, the new Harriman Center was also a financial calamity. Six days after the official opening, Coelho was fretting about how to make ends meet.

Producing commercials for congressional elections was highly seasonal work, concentrated in September and October of even-numbered years. Coelho's plan was for the studio to keep fairly busy with non-political work from business clients and with quasi-political work from labor unions and liberal organizations. But as studio director Jim Eury's weekly reports showed all too clearly, the expensive editing suites were standing empty much of the time.

That changed as the campaign season heated up. During October the studio was operating night and day. Candidates were required to use the new studio as a condition of getting financial aid from the campaign committee. The committee would supply a "letter of credit" to entitle candidates to free studio time. Part of the party's donation to the candidates would thus come in the form of free radio and television production services subsidized in part by soft-money donations.

Committee officials insisted they were meticulous about prorating the variable costs of the studio, including supplies and the salaries of its employees. Hard money was used to pay for campaign work, and only non-campaign jobs were reimbursed out of soft money, according to attorney Bauer. But the capital costs of the studio were still being underwritten with $100,000 gifts from union treasuries and other soft grants, and the benefits of those subsidies were being passed along to candidates.

By the time the campaign was over, the committee supplied candidates with just over $500,000 of free radio and television production services. Additionally, the committee gave away ready-made, "generic" television commercials—to which a candidate generally only had to add his or her name, picture, and perhaps a word or two of narration—valued at more than $266,000. Altogether, the free services of Coelho's television studio accounted for more than 37 percent of the financial aid he reported giving to House candidates in the 1986 elections.

Coelho justified his expansive use of soft money by saying he had to catch up to his GOP rivals, but in fact he was caught in a cycle of escalation that was vitiating the basic intent of federal laws prohibiting corporate or union funds in federal elections and calling for full disclosure.

Republicans were happy to see Coelho enlarging the possible uses of corporate funds, which they could tap more easily. Following his precedent, the National Republican Congressional Committee in 1987 began using building-fund money in a three-year program to refurbish its own aging studio, spending $570,000 during the first year for remodeling and for new equipment, including video recorders and an $85,000 Grasslands editing console. By this time the NRCC's gusher of small donations was drying up as the Reagan era faded, and it was being forced to cut staff because of the relative shortage of hard dollars. But old equipment financed with fully disclosed hard dollars could now be replaced using building funds from corporations and wealthy donors. Their identities, just as in pre-Watergate times, were kept secret. The NRCC's executive director, Joseph Gaylord, said the fund received gifts as large as $20,000.

The NRCC dilated the loophole yet another degree, using building funds to purchase three new disc drives for its Wang mainframe computer at a cost of $36,000. This was to expand the capacity of an office-automation and data processing system it had installed in 1981 with $2.5 million in fully disclosed hard money. Now, practically anything bolted to the floor was being classified as a building fixture. Coelho had used building funds to pay for cables linking his own network of microcomputers, but the desktop machines themselves he leased from a labor union.

The expansion of the building-fund provision continued after Coelho left the DCCC. In 1988 the party spent $125,000 through the building fund to install a microwave link between its TV studio and a satellite ground station. This enabled incumbent House and Senate Democrats to beam political broadcasts back to their home states and districts on an instant's notice, enhancing their ability to dominate local news coverage.

The maneuvering was reminiscent of the technological competition between armor and artillery; an advance on one side inevitably led to a compensating innovation on the other. The Federal Election Commission protested none of this, and neither party filed any complaint. To do so would have been, as Martin Franks had said, "the pot calling the kettle."

Coelho borrowed heavily. "Our debt was not onerous, but instead was just like the mortgage on your house," Martin Franks insisted after the campaign. Coelho's committee required something like $500,000 a year in soft money. There simply weren't enough hard dollars to finance such a grand project as the television studio.

Coelho's initial goal for the Capital Trust was to raise an

extra $500,000 in soft money to reduce the debt he would leave for his successor, but soon he was shooting for much more. Franks reported that wealthy donors attending the party's annual Washington fund-raising dinner were turning out to be more generous than expected. "I think we will get double what we are expecting from the Dinner in soft," Franks wrote. "I continue to think that we are in good shape for at least a million, and the question is how far over that we can get."

Coelho was pleased, but kept pushing. He insisted that the staff track the promised donations with a chart that was updated each week. He wanted to know who was giving and who was not. Once, in a memo at the end of June, Franks confessed that he hadn't done anything about collecting for a while. "I will try and do some more calls tomorrow," he wrote.

In a memo the following week Franks reported progress: "Another $25,000 should be in from the Steelworkers next week. . . . I think that $100,000 from the IBEW will be in as soon as they get their sign-off up from their lawyers." He recounted efforts to collect pledges from the marine engineers' union, the seafarers' union, and the carpenters' union and said he was "trying to work out a deal" to get a contribution from the American Federation of State, County, and Municipal Employees. He was pursuing installment payments from the garment workers', painters', and sheet-metal workers' unions.

The seafarers' project was perhaps the most imaginative, requiring days of negotiation among lawyers for both sides. The union purchased $150,000 worth of microcomputer equipment, which it leased to Coelho's committee on unusual terms. Part of Coelho's payment wasn't in cash; instead, Coelho's staff of programmers gave the union help in setting up its own microcomputer network. Coelho was infatuated with computers. The seafarers' soft-money support enabled Coelho to take the campaign committee from working on typewriters to a computer network.

Payments made to the seafarers for this lease were disclosed on Coelho's FEC reports. "Fair market value was paid," Coelho said.

Some of Coelho's donors made quite specific demands. The carpenters' union promised $100,000, then balked at paying the full amount because not all Democrats supported its legislation.

"I made another round of calls this week and the only one that I am a little bit nervous about is the Carpenters," Franks wrote in mid-July. He said union president Patrick Campbell "was still upset about the Southerners." Campbell and other union leaders were still angry over a humiliating defeat administered to labor forces the previous year, 1985. The House fell five votes short of passing a watered-down version of a bill the AFL-CIO had been fighting to get for more than a decade. It would have required employers to notify their workers far in advance of closing a factory or laying off large numbers of workers. In that vote, fifty-four Democrats, including forty-nine from Southern states, voted against the unions. Labor leaders lost face in the eyes of their own members. They blamed the House leadership for failing to whip Democrats into line on the issue. As an AFL-CIO official, Jay Power, said at the time: "We knew who was wrong, who should have been right, and we're going to have a long memory. We are extremely upset and disappointed that so many voted against us."

Coelho personally adopted the next labor-backed bill to come up. This was a measure to protect construction unions by restraining employers from setting up both union and non-union business units, a ploy known as "double-breasting." Coelho energetically rounded up votes for the bill, and the House passed it handily April 17, 1986, by a vote of 229–173.

That wasn't enough for the carpenters, who were telling Franks they still might not give their full $100,000 because too many Democrats deserted them on the plant-closing bill. "I countered with double-breasting," Franks reported in his memo, "but I am not sure that it scored." He was optimistic, though: "I am convinced that . . . we can resurrect this one." And he soon reported, in another memo, "I picked up $25,000 from the Carpenters this afternoon. They promise another $25,000 in the fall and 'will have to see' about the rest."

But the plant-closing vote still rankled. "Again I was told that Pat is worried about good Democrats and bad Democrats," Franks said. Good Democrats voted right; bad Democrats didn't. Franks suggested bringing in the Majority Leader, Jim Wright, to help close the sale. "I suggested that in September we get them together with you and Wright and I think that is what will get them up to the full $100,000," Franks wrote. But the carpenters remained steadfast and refused to give more than $25,000.

Coelho mused about the incident after the election. "The carpenters to this day are still taking it out on the party because they didn't get what they wanted on that. And my point is, 'Look, I don't sell legislation. All I do is try to help you if I think you are right.' "

Coelho argued that the carpenters would be more likely to get their way if they gave more money to the party. "My position on that is that the way you make bad Democrats into good Democrats is by making the party stronger," he said. Coelho was right about one thing: with more money to give, the party organization could exert greater discipline over its members and line up more "good Democrats" to vote the party line. But the party line and the union line tended to merge.

The carpenters weren't the only Capital Trust donors to cause Coelho headaches. The International Ladies' Garment Workers' Union had promised $100,000 and had delivered half of it on May 30. However, the leadership became unhappy with Democratic efforts to secure protectionist trade legislation.

Half the clothes bought by Americans were being made overseas. Low-cost foreign goods were a blessing for American families, but a disaster for the union, which had watched its membership dwindle by half. In concert with textile manufacturers and other affected interests, the ILGWU had pushed through Congress a bill calling for a 30 percent cut in clothing imports from Hong Kong, Taiwan, and South Korea and decreasing shoe imports to 60 percent of the U.S. market, from the prevailing 80 percent level. But President Reagan had vetoed the measure, calling it anti-consumer and likely to provoke a trade war that could hurt farm exports and cost American jobs in other industries. In late July the House prepared to attempt an override of the veto.

Large numbers of textile-state Republicans were sup-porting the bill in defiance of the President, but to put the measure into law over a veto required a two-thirds majority of those voting in each House. The garment workers needed every Democratic legislator they could get. Union president Sol Chaikin made it clear that Democrats should consider the sources of their campaign money when they voted. "He would take every opportunity to say, 'You can't expect help from our union if our workers don't have jobs," said Evelyn Dubrow, the union's vice president in Washington.

The garment workers' union had given $575,688 to con-gressional candidates in 1984, of which 99 percent went to Democrats. The PAC was shrinking along with the number of union members, one reason the union's leaders were willing to use general treasury funds to make soft-money donations. But the PAC would still give $362,292 to congres-sional candidates during the 1986 elections, and 96.5 percent would go to Democrats. Even more than other labor unions, the garment workers functioned as a unit of the Democratic party, and Coelho could ill afford to ignore that reality.

Chaikin wanted Democratic solidarity on the veto over-ride. "He felt very strongly that the Democratic party ought to be on our side," said Dubrow. Matters heated up just before the vote. Chaikin told one of Coelho's fund-raisers that he wanted stronger action by the House leadership. Franks sought assurances that the union wouldn't renege on the second half of the promised $100,000 in soft money.

He reported to Coelho that after hearing about Chaikin's unhappiness with the trade meeting, "I went and personally saw Evy [Dubrow] to see if there was a problem. She assured me there was not and that she was working on getting . . . the second $50,000."

There was hardly a stronger champion of union-backed protectionist legislation than Coelho. He was trying to make the textile vote into a major campaign issue, one reason so many Republicans voted in favor. For months Coelho had been coaching candidates, urging them to support a protectionist line, accusing the Republican administration and its supporters of exporting American jobs. The research staff at the campaign committee devoted much of its time to purveying figures on the worsening U.S. trade balance to candidates in the field. One of Coelho's generic TV ads showed workers vanishing from farms, factories, and offices and blamed Republican trade policies. Coelho encouraged candidates to hold press conferences in front of padlocked plant gates.

The campaigning had its effect: when the vote came to override Reagan's veto of the textile import bill, seventy-one Republicans voted against their own administration's position. But forty-three Democrats voted for Reagan, and against the bill. The garment workers and Coelho fell eight votes short of the total required to override. Still, Coelho got the last installment of the union's $100,000 as scheduled.

Coelho even courted the Teamsters' union, and found that they too mixed legislation and money together. Franks and the campaign committee's PAC director Tom Nides had lunch with Dave Sweeney of the Teamsters to discuss a $100,000 gift. "We heard a lot about some drunk driving issues and some other things that are bottled up in [the House] Public Works [Committee]," Franks reported to Coelho.

The Teamsters were fighting a proposal to banish from the highways any drivers of big, over-the-road trucks who were twice found guilty of driving with traces of alcohol in their blood. Truck owners were pushing for a bill to set national licensing standards for drivers of the big rigs, and it looked as though it was going through. The Teamsters were upset that in one version, which was being pushed by Republican Sen. John Danforth of Missouri, drivers would be subjected to the same blood-alcohol standard that applies to airline and railroad workers, a standard two and a half times stricter than the rule that most states apply to ordinary motorists. Under Danforth's plan, a trucker's license would be suspended if he was found guilty of driving with a blood-alcohol level of 0.04 percent (0.10 percent is the standard for other drivers). A second conviction would cause a trucker's license to be revoked for life. Truckers often were hauling chemicals or other hazardous cargo, so a drunk truck driver posed a much greater danger to innocent bystanders than did ordinary drunk drivers. Franks, however, denied any connection between the $100,000 and the drunk-driving legislation. "In the course of a long lunch with an old friend, Dave Sweeney, we talked about a lot of things as friends do," he said when questioned about his memo.

Coelho later met over lunch at union headquarters with Teamsters president Jackie Presser, who was about to be indicted by a federal grand jury in Cleveland and charged with embezzling $700,000 from the union to pay employees who did no work. The ghost employees were alleged to have Mafia connections.

The Teamsters had been run by a series of convicted criminals. A former president, Roy Williams, would testify that he felt compelled to do the bidding of mobsters out of fear they would kill him if he didn't. Williams spoke from a jail cell where he was serving a ten-year sentence for, among other things, conspiracy to bribe Democratic Sen. Howard Cannon of Nevada. He swore he had taken orders from Nick Civella, described in testimony as the boss of the Kansas City mob. "I made no bones about it," Williams testified. "I was controlled by Nick." He said two of Civella's henchmen told him that if he didn't follow orders, they would kill his family, then him. "They named my two children, my wife, and they said, 'You'll be last.' That's the threat I got." He also admitted getting $1,500 a month in payoffs from Civella.

Williams said Presser, too, was controlled by the mob. "He said that he could handle any problem through the group in Cleveland," Williams testified. "He had friends, ties, with the group in Cleveland." A former underboss of the Cleveland mob, Angelo Lonardo, would back up Williams's claim. He testified that Presser was controlled through Milton Rockman, a Mafia associate. Lonardo said Mafia boss Anthony "Fat Tony" Salerno had rigged the election in which Williams was chosen, then rigged the election of Presser, too.

A federal jury in New York eventually convicted Salerno of racketeering, but acquitted him of fixing Presser's election. The union quickly issued a press release, ignoring the testimony of its own ex-president Williams and saying Salerno's acquittal "forever shattered" the "myth" that Williams and Presser had been installed by mobsters. "The elections of Roy L. Williams and Jackie Presser were conducted in accordance with the high standards mandated by federal law," the union said.

Coelho saw the Teamsters as the largest single labor union, claiming 1.8 million members, and as a rich source of financial support. Its PAC would raise $4.4 million during the 1986 elections, and was shooting for $10 million in the 1987–88 cycle. It was using a payroll checkoff system, one of the most effective political fund-raising methods yet devised, through which participating members automatically donated one or two dollars from every paycheck.

The Teamsters were already members of Coelho's $15,000-a-year Speaker's Club, and his meeting with Presser produced some even bigger checks. Two weeks before the election the union's PAC gave $50,000 to Coelho's soft-money accounts, half to the "DCCC Non-Federal Account" and half to the "Democratic House Recount Fund." In December the Teamsters PAC donated $30,000 more to the non-federal fund, bringing its total support for the campaign committee's various accounts to $95,000. Here was a case of hard money turning soft. The Teamsters had raised it and reported it as hard money under the election law's requirements, but Coelho accepted it through soft-money accounts that allowed him to skirt the legal ceiling of $15,000 a year on gifts to the DCCC from PACs.

Presser's PAC also gave $5,000 to Coelho's Valley Education Fund. Coelho said Presser "had heard a lot about me, liked the fact that I was aggressive and wanted to make something out of the party." Presser was more interested in buying access to the highest reaches of the Democratic leadership of the House.

"His complaint about Democrats was that there was nobody to talk to when you wanted to talk to somebody about whatever your problem was. He said to me . . . 'I don't need to talk about legislation. We have lobbyists, and we contribute money, and we have members all over the place, and we're the largest union and we can get our members turned out to things. But when I have a concern, I don't feel there's anybody I can talk to that will listen, that will make the difference. And what I hear about you is good.' "

Presser didn't talk about drunk-driving legislation, Coelho said. But the union president soon had "a problem" of a very different sort, and the Teamsters called on Coelho and his colleagues for support. After Presser's indictment, the *New York Times* reported that the Department of Justice was considering filing a lawsuit under the Racketeer Influenced and Corrupt Organizations (RICO) Act to remove Presser and the entire twenty-one-member executive board from the union, installing a government trustee to run it. The Teamsters backed Ronald Reagan's election in 1980, took a formal part in his transition team before he was inaugurated, and supported him for re-election in 1984. But now the Republicans were turning on the union.

Coelho insisted that most of the union's members are Democrats and "deserve to be represented just like anybody else." He added, "And if [Presser] asked me to do him anything improper or illegal, I'd say no." He said that all

Presser asked him to do was speak to a Teamsters meeting. Later, Coelho joined more than half the members of the House, including many from both parties, in signing letters to the Justice Department trying to head off any attempt to replace the union leadership with a trustee. One letter was signed by Coelho and 263 other House members, who all told had received $1.2 million from the Teamsters PAC during the preceding five years. Nevertheless, in 1988 the government filed an anti-racketeering suit accusing the union's leadership of falling under the nearly total domination of organized crime.

In the use of soft money neither the Democrats nor the Republicans were really sure what the others were up to, because the money was by its nature largely hidden from view. But each party assumed the worst and acted accordingly. Coelho's appetite for soft money resulted indirectly from a probably inflated report of a Republican soft-money coup in 1980.

In her book *Politics and Money,* Elizabeth Drew said President Reagan's 1980 campaign got the benefit of $9 million in soft money from wealthy individuals and corporations. The figure came from Republican fund-raiser Robert Perkins, but senior GOP fund-raiser Rodney Smith called it "bullshit." Researchers for a Washington-based, bipartisan good-government group, the Center for Responsive Politics, later examined GOP disclosure reports filed in various states but found few traces of the fabled $9 million. Perkins himself admitted later that the money didn't flow through any national headquarters organization, that his program "mushroomed out of control," and that he kept no records that could support his claim. "The truth is that nobody really knows" how much was raised, Perkins conceded.

But accurate or not, the $9 million figure was believed by Democrats, who were determined not to be swamped by soft dollars in the 1984 presidential campaign. Former Vice President Walter Mondale began raising soft money almost as soon as he left office in 1981. He financed a good part of his own political activity with a secret soft-money account run by his personal political action committee. Later, as the Democratic nominee, he aggressively sought millions in soft money. With Charles Manatt as party chairman, the Democratic National Committee actually held a news conference to announce its soft-money goals. Mondale fundraiser Tim Finchem said in August 1984 that he aimed to raise between $4 million and $5 million this way.

Mondale's principal financial backer was Nathan Landow, a real-estate developer who had been given a ceremonial United Nations ambassadorship during the Carter administration as a reward for his money-raising efforts in the 1980 campaign. The Washington *Post* reported that Landow had been in line for an even more prestigious ambassadorship until it was discovered that he once had a brief business relationship with a notorious mob-connected bookmaker, whom he consulted about the gambling business while thinking about building a casino in Atlantic City, New Jersey. At one catered dinner at Landow's home, as Mondale and his running mate, Geraldine Ferraro, both circulated among the guests, Landow raised soft-money donations as large as $50,000.

Overall, the Mondale campaign spent $5.3 million in soft money, according to a one-page summary circulated privately by a Mondale aide. Much of it came from labor unions. No full public accounting was ever made, but the soft-money binge left abundant traces. One sizable fragment of the donations showed up in a report filed in Pennsylvania long after the election, where it was turned up by Edward Zuckerman, publisher of *PACS and Lobbies,* a newsletter. The report showed contributions as large as $100,000 from such individuals as Minneapolis department-store heir Mark Dayton and IBM Corp. chairman Thomas J. Watson.

As it turned out, there wasn't much of a soft-money operation for Reagan in 1984. There was hardly a need for one; the Republican National Committee spent more than $104 million in fully disclosed hard money during the 1983–84 election cycle, including millions to register Republican-leaning voters and to run generalized ads urging people to vote Republican. But the party's general counsel, Mark Braden, said that exclusive of the building fund, only $3.7 million ran through the GOP's soft-money accounts in 1984, not much more than the roughly $2 million taken in during a normal non-election year.

Democrats were inspired by Mondale's success at evading donation limits. Party chairman Manatt also turned to Landow for help, and Landow erected the party headquarters building. Landow also chaired the 1986 Senate-House fund-raising dinner, which produced much soft money for Coelho.

Shortly after the election, finance director McAuliffe produced a summary of funds received by the committee. Up to that point, on November 14, $1.7 million in soft money had been taken in. That amounted to 21.5 percent of the $8 million total up until that time.

The Capital Trust project pulled in $556,000 during 1986, according to McAuliffe. But Franks said donations continued to come in during 1987 and eventually totaled nearly $1.2 million, counting the $150,000 in leased computers from the seafarers. None of the money received in 1987 was disclosed. By that time the Federal Election Commission had issued a permissive opinion that allowed the campaign committee to cease reporting any of its building funds.

McAuliffe's accounting also showed the Speaker's Club got $301,500 in soft-money donations during 1985 and 1986, largely from lobbyists paying dues with business money rather than PAC funds. The annual Senate-House dinners produced $276,000 in soft money for the DCCC, which came to 42 percent of its total from those events. McAuliffe listed nine different categories of non-federal funds, including a gift of $150,000 from Pamela Harriman on the day the new media center opened.

Coelho liked to boast that half his money came through the mail, from small donations with no strings attached. In gross terms, that was true. But McAuliffe's numbers showed that after deducting the heavy expenses of postage, printing, list rental, and computer processing, the committee's net income from its small-donor program was only $900,000 in 1985 and $1.5 million during 1986. In practical terms, Coelho was netting several times as much from PACs, lobbyists, and soft-money donors than from the rank and file.

10

"You Sit Down with Your Buddies"

I've made a big fortune out of the game, and I'm gettin' richer every day, but I've not gone in for dishonest graft—blackmailin' gamblers, saloon-keepers, disorderly people. . . . There's honest graft, and I'm an example of how it works. I might sum up the whole thing by sayin' "I seen my opportunities and I took 'em."
—GEORGE WASHINGTON PLUNKITT

Tony Coelho vowed that not a single Democratic incumbent would be defeated in 1986. The pledge committed him to rescuing an old adversary, Fernand St Germain of Rhode Island, who had grown rich in the business of politics.

He was reared in a working-class family during the Depression in the grimy, industrial Blackstone Valley in southern Massachusetts and northern Rhode Island. Only a few miles away the yachts of the rich bobbed in the harbor at Newport, at the opposite end of the congressional district he would one day represent. But that millionaires' playground might as well have been on another planet.

One day the young St Germain visited a dye plant where his father worked as a foreman. "He brought me into that mill on a hot summer day, 110 degrees, 115 degrees," St Germain recalled. "His purpose was to say, 'Study hard.'" He hoped to become a dentist but signed up as an Army medic and later attended the Boston University Law School at night while working by day as a cloth spreader in a garment factory.

He found himself running for the state legislature on the side of insurgents challenging a corrupt Democratic machine in his hometown, Woonsocket. "They were trying to fill the slate and nobody would take the job," he said. He was swept into office when some of the opposition was indicted.

Still in his early twenties, he looked too young to be a legislator. On one of his first days in office, he recalled, "I was in the back of the chamber and a doorkeeper said, 'Run down and get me a cup of coffee.'" The doorkeeper had mistaken him for a page.

"I said, 'Run down and get your own cup of coffee.' He said, 'Whose patronage are you?' Well, I said, 'Whose patronage are *you?*'" More than thirty years later, St Germain still bristled at the insult. "You give a little man a little power, and he'll abuse it," he said.

Legislators were paid $5 a day and the legislature met for only a few months. St Germain made his living as a trial lawyer, defending American Mutual Liability Insurance against claims for compensation by workers injured on their jobs. The work provided a comfortable living but no more.

He came to Washington in 1960 after winning a backroom party struggle to become the Democratic nominee to succeed the retiring Rep. Aime Forand. St Germain argued that his French ancestry would provide ethnic strength to the ticket. He crushed a token Republican opponent in the general election, helped at the top of the ticket by John Kennedy, a fellow Roman Catholic from neighboring Massachusetts.

The newly elected congressman told a newspaper reporter at the time that he'd done "very well" financially, but when he moved to Washington with his wife Rachel and their twenty-month-old daughter, he looked in vain for "a home with a yard" that would fit into the family budget. They settled instead into a rented five-room apartment on upper Connecticut Avenue, a solidly middle-class enclave populated largely by civil servants.

Congressmen were paid $22,000 a year, but even after the stipend was raised to $30,000 in 1964, St Germain told an interviewer he doubted that any member of Congress could stay with the idea of making money. "Whatever you make you're going to spend," he said.

Congressional wages were kept low, compared to the sums corporations, labor unions, and trade associations paid their executives. Attorneys and lobbyists commonly earned several times as much as the senators and congressmen whose votes they sought to sway. But congressmen were reluctant to increase their own pay, fearing they would be attacked politically. In a town teeming with Mercedes-Benz dealerships, they drove Fords and Oldsmobiles. Some attempted to earn more than a salary from their political office. St Germain was one of those.

In 1971 he approached an old friend from Woonsocket, Roland Ferland, a carpenter's son who was rising to wealth as a builder. "I said, 'If something comes along, I hope you'll consider me,'" the congressman recalled. Ferland cut him in on a 192-apartment complex in East Providence. He was the only person outside the Ferland family allowed to invest, and he got the same terms as blood relatives. He paid $3,000 for a 15 percent share of the partnership, which the Ferland clan operated for the most part on borrowed money. It turned out to be a very good deal. St Germain cashed in most of his interest in 1980 for $184,798.90. His remaining 2 percent interst earned him an additional $2,400 in 1985 and $4,526 in 1986. Thus did $3,000 effortlessly grow to nearly $192,000, thanks to Ferland.

Here was a perfect example, updated to modern times, of the "honest graft" Boss Plunkitt had described eighty years earlier. St Germain could say he avoided the obviously illegal forms of graft, yet he asked for and received a favor that gained him $189,000 from a developer who in turn profited from housing subsidies that St Germain supported.

Ferland became one of the biggest developers and managers of federally subsidized housing in the Northeast. St Germain meanwhile used his growing influence over the Department of Housing and Urban Development, over which the Banking Committee had jurisdiction, to get a larger than normal share of subsidized apartments for Rhode Island.

Federal housing subsidies became a boondoggle for developers, but a questionable proposition for the poor. It was almost impossible for developers to lose money building and owning such apartments. Under the Section Eight program, which became the dominant subsidy method after 1974, the federal government encouraged the construction of apartments for moderately low-income people by agreeing to pay much of their rent. The government didn't quibble too much about what it paid to the owners, who realized rents for the low-income apartments that were actually higher in some cases than those for unsubsidized units.

Typically the subsidized apartments were rented to elderly whites. Poor black families generally had to look elsewhere for housing. Even by 1981, only one-quarter of poor renters received any form of subsidized housing.

Developers meanwhile often got a double subsidy. Besides federally guaranteed rent payments, in Rhode Island and other states they could obtain low-interest mortgages from an authority that raised the money selling bonds whose earnings were free of federal income tax. Their low-rate mortgages were thus indirectly subsidized by the loss of taxes to the U.S. Treasury. The tax code further provided bigger write-offs for low-income housing than for other types of real estate. With federally paid rent, federally subsidized mortgage money, and tax deductions, the Section Eight program for new apartments came close to a government guarantee of tax-free profits for developers. The system had all the economic inefficiencies of state socialism, but allowed favored capitalists to get rich.

Those developers recycled some of their profits as campaign donations. The National Association of Home Builders established a political action committee, BUILD-PAC, which dispensed campaign money to St Germain and other lawmakers who voted on the subsidies. Ferland was PAC chairman for a time. He also had helped raise the funds for St Germain's first House campaign.

By 1981 the federal government had run up a $130 billion bill for Section Eight housing, which taxpayers would be paying for thirty years. Even the cost-obsessed Reagan administration required almost its entire first term to halt this subsidy for developers. St Germain—by then chairman of the full Banking Committee—fought a rearguard action against the budget cutters.

The congressman didn't invest in any of the subsidized apartments but he enjoyed rewards indirectly, through Ferland's other, unsubsidized developments. In 1976 Ferland included him in a family partnership that developed a tract in Pawtucket. From a total investment of $7,500, the congressman received payments totaling $176,250 within ten years.

A third Ferland deal also made money, but so little that the developer apologized. For $2,000 St Germain in 1975 bought 20 percent of School Street Associates in Pawtucket. This partnership ran short of money and St Germain had to loan it a total of $16,000 more in 1980 and 1983. He got that money back in full when the property was sold in 1985, along with a second check for $20,000. Thus he realized an $18,000 gain on his original investment and the loans. In a letter accompanying the checks Ferland said, "This finally concludes one of our less profitable partnerships. I guess we can't have all winners."

St Germain was an extreme example of the way the political system encouraged waste, cheated the poor, and subsidized the rich, who in turn kept campaign funds and sometimes extra income flowing to the lawmakers who perpetuated the arrangement. He also benefited politically from the housing subsidies. His Rhode Island office became a referral center for low- and moderate-income people clamoring to get into one of the new apartment buildings where the federal government would pay part of their rent. The congressman had little incentive to question the rising cost of the subsidies, the limited number of needy families that benefited, or the profits realized by Ferland and other developers. The program provided him votes, campaign donations, and, indirectly, personal income.

St Germain found more honest graft in a string of pancake restaurants. He bought properties worth $1.3 million without putting up any of his own money, a feat made possible by friendly Rhode Island institutions that loaned him the money despite some extraordinary risks. In 1972 International Industries was trying to raise cash by selling off some of its International House of Pancakes restaurants at below-market prices. The congressman had few assets and had to stretch his $42,500 salary to cover both an apartment in Washington and a home in Rhode Island, where his wife had returned to live shortly after the birth of their second daughter. But he was by then chairman of a banking subcommittee overseeing federal regulation of financial institutions. Bankers were in no position to deny his insistent personal requests for financing.

Lenders had to overlook some big risks: the distinctive, orange-and-blue chalet-style buildings wouldn't be worth much if hard times struck the restaurant operators who leased them. Bank appraisals suggested that their value would drop by one-third if vacant. Rents were to be paid by International Industries, whose financial troubles made payment dubious. "The outlook for continued successful operation is in doubt," one of his lenders later said in an internal memorandum.

One federally regulated lender, Industrial National Bank, loaned him the entire purchase price of two Rhode Island restaurants. He bought three more restaurants in New York, Texas, and Maryland on similar terms from other lenders. The only institution that balked at his request for 100 percent financing was a state-regulated lender, Marquette Credit Union. But St Germain got around that by submitting a loan application listing a selling price $15,940 higher than the true figure.

St Germain soon began pressing his lenders for even more favorable terms. He induced them to lengthen the terms of the mortgages to reduce his monthly payments and increase the amount of cash he could realize from the rents. Meanwhile International Industries, just as feared, ran into further financial troubles and was tardy making its rent payments for a time. St Germain extracted $20,000 in late-payment penalties from the delinquent company in 1977. The episode underscored how risky the loans had been.

The congressman cleared a profit of $315,995 on the last day of 1984 when he sold one of the restaurants, in Providence. He was still holding the other four, which had all appreciated substantially, as the 1986 elections approached.

Meanwhile he kept Rhode Island voters ignorant of his appetite for honest graft. "People say I play my cards close to my vest," he once boasted. "They're imprinted on my chest." He put the restaurants in the name of an entity called the Crepe Trust, so his own name appeared nowhere on public records of the sales. His ownership remained hidden until 1978, when members of Congress were first required to make a reasonably complete public listing of their assets, debts, and outside income each year. Then St Germain was forced to state his ownership in the restaurants and the Ferland real-estate deals, but he still concealed their true value. His first disclosure was accompanied by a press release claiming his listed holdings were worth only $236,080, a gross undervaluation.

The deception continued for years. In 1978 he publicly listed the total value of the three Ferland deals at less than $3,000, even though he would receive a total of nearly $390,000 from them within a few years. In 1983 he publicly put the value of his restaurants at a maximum of $300,000, but in the same year he listed their true value at $1.8 million in a confidential loan application he gave to a financial institution.

St Germain's concealments helped him survive a 1978 re-election campaign in which his newly disclosed assets became an issue. John J. Slocum, Jr., a Republican, accused him of making his money under the table. "This man's a wheeler-dealer," the GOP candidate said. And Norman Jacques, a Democratic primary foe, called the connection to Ferland "improper" and said it shouldn't be allowed by law. But St Germain was re-elected easily.

After that, he lived a jet-set life, golfing in the winter in St. Petersburg and in the summer at Newport. In both places he bought waterfront condominium apartments at bargain prices from savings and loan associations that were foreclosing on developers. He junketed to financial-industry conventions in Puerto Rico, Boca Raton, Florida, and Hilton Head, South Carolina. Increasingly, he stayed at his St. Petersburg condominium when Congress wasn't in session, while his Rhode Island congressional staff took care of business back home.

St Germain reached for further honest graft with the help of a friend who was a major figure in the savings and loan industry, Raleigh Greene of St. Petersburg, chief executive of Florida Federal Savings and Loan. St Germain had come to know him when Greene was president of the National Savings and Loan League, a trade group representing large S&Ls. Early in 1979, only months after defeating Jacques and Slocum, St Germain flew aboard Greene's jet to St. Petersburg to inspect a six-room condominium overlooking Tampa Bay on the fifteenth floor of the new Bayfront Tower building. Greene was foreclosing on the developer. Florida Federal sold St Germain the apartment for $4,000 less than the appraised market price of $110,000. From then on St Germain made the apartment his Florida home as he set about buying up other real estate with Greene's help.

Greene arranged for St Germain to invest with him and others in three Florida real-estate partnerships starting in 1980: a tract near Gainesville, a lot in downtown Tampa, and a 160-acre parcel in the path of development not far from Tampa International Airport. Neither his nor Greene's name appeared anywhere on the public real-estate records. Later, when the financial links were finally uncovered, Greene explained the relationship nonchalantly: "It's like anything else," he said. "You sit down with your buddies and say, 'Do you want in?' And you either say yea or nay."

With Greene's help St Germain joined the city's two exclusive clubs, the St. Petersburg Yacht Club and the President's Club. In January 1983, as a result of yet another foreclosure by Florida Federal, St Germain acquired a beachfront condominium in the Sandpiper Key development in Englewood, Florida, south of St. Petersburg. He paid $174,000; Florida Federal lent him $173,000 to buy it.

St Germain then began reaching for honest graft that would, when exposed, trigger an official investigation. By this time he was chairman of the full Banking Committee and the undisputed godfather of the S&L industry. He tried to make a quick profit speculating in Florida Federal's stock.

It was the biggest S&L in Florida, but it was still a mutual association, legally owned by its depositors. Greene was pressing for permission to convert to a corporation. Newly issued S&L stocks usually provided fast money for those who got in on the ground floor. As a depositor, St Germain was entitled to buy stock at the issuing price. It looked as though he could make several thousand dollars quickly.

But there was a hitch. The Federal Home Loan Bank Board in Washington had to approve the sale first. The regulators generally favored stock conversions; they got more money into the S&Ls and relieved pressure on the badly weakened S&L insurance fund. But the board denied Florida Federal's first request for quick clearance under an emergency procedure. Greene applied again using normal procedures. As the process dragged on, St Germain's principal aide, Paul Nelson, chief of staff of the Banking Committee, contacted the chairman of the Bank Board and inquired about the pace of the Florida Federal application. The chairman, Richard Pratt, said Nelson called as many as three times about the matter. Nelson repeatedly contacted the Federal Home Loan Bank in Atlanta, which also had to approve the stock sale. Nelson's calls set off alarm bells within the Bank Board. Pratt said Florida Federal was the only institution St Germain's aide ever inquired about.

Though regulators later denied that Nelson's calls made them move any faster, Florida Federal got the regulatory clearance it wanted. St Germain bought 1,500 shares at the ground-floor price, paying $30,000 in May 1983. He didn't expect to hold the stock long. "The acquisition was intended to be temporary," he said later. But Florida Federal wasn't one of the hot ones; its stock price sank. St Germain sold it at a modest loss two years later, shortly after it became clear to him that an unflattering news story would appear. Later, Greene himself resigned.

St Germain concealed his conflict of interest as long as he could, reporting only an unspecified "holding" in Florida Federal without identifying it as common stock or giving the date of purchase, as required by law. On his report the stock appeared as nothing more sinister than an insured savings account.

When St Germain learned that reporters were investigating him, he filed an amended report showing his ownership of the S&L stock. It was a prudent move; a Republican member of the Banking Committee, George Hansen, was headed for jail because he had falsified his own personal disclosure forms. Hansen had concealed a risk-free $87,000 profit from a silver-futures trade arranged by conservative political backer Nelson Bunker Hunt, and $135,000 in loans from three men whom Hansen aided in an attempt to sell an experimental hydrogen-powered vehicle to the Army.

St Germain's new disclosure forms showed he, too, had been hiding embarrassing financial dealings. Besides his Florida Federal stock, some of his "investments" were now revealed as limited partnerships in Kentucky coal-mining ventures that the Internal Revenue Service said were abusive tax shelters. St Germain had been avoiding taxes on a grand scale.

The partnerships were a prime example of the need for

tax reform. Customers—they couldn't properly be called "investors"—wrote off $3 or more for every $1 they actually paid in. The deals produced big tax windfalls but hardly any coal. So little, in fact, that the IRS was considering bringing criminal charges against the sponsors. They eventually sought court protection from creditors under the bankruptcy law, and no criminal charges were issued.

St Germain had gotten more than $405,000 in tax deductions in return for a total cash "investment" of $120,000. The IRS eventually allowed him to settle the matter by paying the taxes he had avoided, plus interest.

On September 11, 1985, the *Wall Street Journal* published a front-page story about St Germain's wealth and tax avoidance under the headline "Making a Fortune." He suddenly was in a fight for political survival. And Tony Coelho came to his rescue.

A month after the *Journal* published its exposé, a Republican poll taker randomly quizzed 237 residents of St Germain's district, which constitutes the eastern half of the state. Just over two-thirds said they wanted St Germain to release his income-tax returns. This he was adamantly refusing to do, despite demands from his future opponent, Republican state party chairman John Holmes, and from the state's dominant newspaper, the Providence *Journal.*

St Germain had paid little or no federal income tax for many years. Besides his deduction-heavy real-estate partnerships and his coal-mining shelters, he had bought into cattle-feeding partnerships, cable-television deals, and other tax shelters. A television interviewer asked him point-blank: "You don't have one of those fancy-schmancy accountants who puts zero at the bottom line?" St Germain insisted he paid taxes but refused to say how much or in which years, or to provide proof.

Republicans drew additional encouragement from St Germain's poor performance on a television interview program following the *Wall Street Journal* story. The Providence *Journal*'s chief political reporter, Charles Bakst, and two other reporters asked him six times whether he was a millionaire. He rambled on unresponsively about the effects of inflation and the interest rates on his mortgages. An exasperated Bakst blurted out, "He asked you, 'Are you a millionaire?' and you give us interest rates from 1972." Finally, St Germain admitted his net worth was indeed over $1 million. If the interview had been a campaign debate, he would have been on the ropes.

Common Cause called for an investigation by the House ethics committee, as did the Washington *Post.* St Germain got little support from Democratic colleagues. A lobbyist said Speaker O'Neill remarked of St Germain, "I don't know a man with fewer friends in the House."

John Holmes hadn't yet raised any money or officially entered the race, while St Germain had a campaign fund of $676,470. GOP party strategists figured he would spend $1 million if necessary. Then the National Republican Congressional Committee decided it would try to soften up St Germain by attacking him with commercials that might not count as election spending. If the tactic succeeded, the Republican party could spend unlimited amounts against him.

A four-man television crew set up near a laundromat in a working-class neighborhood in the Newport area, and in a late-autumn snowfall they filmed interviews with Rhode Islanders. The ad began with a single word floating silently on the television screen: "Taxes."

Then came the voters:

"Congressman St Germain won't be out of trouble until he releases his income-tax forms," said Evelyn C. Green.

"If he doesn't have anything to hide, it doesn't do him any harm to release them," said Ezida M. Silva.

"I think he should open up his books. That way if he's clean, he's clean. . . . If not, 'We gotcha,' " said John J. O'Brien III.

"What he's done may not be illegal. It seems unethical,

but we won't know until he comes clean with the public," said Green.

The commercial closed with a picture of an IRS form 1040 and, in big type, the words: "Tell us the truth, Congressman St Germain." An announcer spoke those same words: "Tell us the truth . . ."

The ad blanketed the state for a week. Now it was St Germain who was calling for disclosure. "Where did the money really come from?" he demanded. "Fat-cat bankers? Fat-cat corporations?" But the $17,000 for the ad had come from rank-and-file party donors, and it clearly identified the Republican committee as sponsor.

Party lawyers screened each word of the "Taxes" commercial. It had only one ultimate purpose: to defeat St Germain. But as a legal matter it might not count as campaign spending: it contained no mention of an election, no call for voters to defeat St Germain or to elect John Holmes, no solicitation of money, no mention of any political party. The message wasn't much different from editorials in the Providence *Journal* or the Washington *Post* or the press releases of Common Cause.

The Republican committee also financed a group calling itself Rhode Island Citizens for Accountability in Government. It really wasn't a grass-roots movement; the only two Rhode Island citizens involved were Thomas Cashill, a friend of John Holmes, and Sandra Winslow, a Republican employee in the state legislature. With $10,000 from Washington they mailed more than 43,000 letters to Republican households in St Germain's district, echoing the theme of the television ad. "The people of Rhode Island have a right to know if our Congressman is telling the truth," it said. "Congressman St Germain must come clean by fully disclosing his taxes and finances."

Altogether the Republican campaign committee spent $27,000 attacking St Germain on television and through the mail. Soon after, a Republican poll showed only 41 percent said they would vote for St Germain over Holmes. The incumbent had lost 15 points since before the exposé. The $27,000 effort had dented the incumbent's armor. Winslow and Cashill said they would seek an additional $10,000 from Washington to sponsor radio ads if St Germain didn't release his tax returns. It began to look as though the Republicans would run endless follow-up ads.

Then Tony Coelho filed an official complaint with the Federal Election Commission challenging the spending as illegal. His official spokesman, Mark Johnson, called the GOP outlays "a felony," although the complaint alleged only a civil violation. One Rhode Island newspaper quoted a Coelho aide as saying, "We would hope that someone ends up in jail."

Coelho had to plug the Republicans' new loophole before it widened further, exposing other Democrats to similar attacks. The assault on St Germain seemed to be just the start of a multimillion-dollar "incumbent accountability" program, something Guy Vander Jagt had spoken of earlier in 1985. Although Vander Jagt trimmed back those early plans when direct-mail receipts proved to be disappointing, he still had vastly more dollars than Coelho.

In practice, limits on spending were as poorly enforced as those on contributions. Whenever limits began to pinch, clever lawyers found ways around, over, under, or through them. A vigorous and truly independent enforcement agency might have policed the limits zealously enough to keep them intact and respected, but the Federal Election Commission was hardly that. It refused to fight for the integrity of the election law the way the Internal Revenue Service battled loopholes in the tax code. It was more like the House Doorkeeper's office, a servant of the very incumbents whose re-election campaigns it was supposed to referee.

Neither party showed much allegiance to the restrictions. While Democrats chiseled on donation limits, Republicans cheated on the spending side, always looking for ways to use their abundant hard dollars. Actually, spending limits on parties made little sense. Congress enacted them along with restrictions on PACs. The special-interest groups were curbed to restrict vote buying, but the parties were subjected to limits because Democrats wrote the law and Republicans had deep pockets.

Party committees were restricted to giving $5,000 per election to their own House candidates, just as though they were PACs. At first that had little practical effect. Vander Jagt became Republican campaign committee chairman as the new law went into force in January 1975. Republican party finances were still withered from the shame of Nixon's resignation. "I never dreamed at that point that we would be able to do even $5,000," he said. The limit, he said, "might as well have been $10 million."

But $5,000 became a real barrier for Republicans after the 1976 election. By then party coffers were overflowing with small-donor money. As a practical matter, the limit amounted to $10,000 per candidate, counting both primary and general elections, or a total of $4.35 million if the party gave the maximum in every House race. Vander Jagt's committee raised $14 million in the 1978 election and nearly $29 million in the 1980 campaigns. What would it do with the money?

The committee exploited an obscure provision allowing political party committees to make an additional $10,000 in "coordinated expenditures" on behalf of candidates in the general election. GOP lawyers interpreted this as giving the party the right to pay bills run up by candidates, practically the same thing as giving them money outright. That effectively doubled the limit. There also was an automatic inflation adjustment for coordinated spending, and by 1986 that ceiling reached $21,810 for House candidates.

The Republican committee also claimed the right to spend in the place of any state party that would deputize it to do so. That doubled its allowance for coordinated spending. Democrats fought that stratagem to the Supreme Court, but lost in a unanimous decision in 1981. So by 1986 Republicans had expanded the $5,000 limit in practice to $53,620 for House candidates.

Republicans also supplied candidates with tactical advice based on expensive public-opinion polling, charging only a fraction of the cost as a contribution. In 1986 the committee would spend roughly $2 million tracking the final progress of their candidates in a few of the most keenly contested districts, including St Germain's. GOP aides would be instructed on how advertising campaigns should be tailored to sway wavering groups of voters. But because the candidates themselves wouldn't see the formal poll results, the money wouldn't be counted against the limits.

Each election brought new Republican spending gimmicks. Millions had been spent on national television advertising campaigns that escaped the limits. In 1980 the commercials said "Vote Republican, for a change." Two years later, faced with rising interest rates and high unemployment, Republicans ran commercials urging voters to "Stay the Course." They concentrated the messages in congressional districts where tight races were expected, to improve the chances of specific candidates. But the spending wasn't counted against limits because no candidates were named.

In 1984 the Republicans pushed such generic ads a step closer to outright campaign spending for particular candidates. Using a commercial titled "Elevator," they capitalized on Walter Mondale's statement that he would raise taxes if elected. The commercial showed a man trapped in a malfunctioning elevator with several voters.

"Say, aren't you our Democratic congressman?" one voter asked.

"It's him," said another.

"You're a Democrat, and your leaders are promising higher taxes," declared a voter. "Are you going to vote to raise taxes?"

As the captive congressman squirmed, the voters chanted, "Yes or no? Yes or no?" A narrator said, "We're stuck." He suggested that viewers question their real congressman, or "just vote Republican."

The GOP spent $3 million running that commercial in more than a hundred selected House districts. Coelho filed a complaint, and the Federal Election Commission's legal staff agreed with him that it constituted campaign spending subject to the limits in the House districts where it appeared. The law said limits applied to money spent by parties "in connection with the general election campaign of a candidate." That language needed no stretching to cover a commercial intended to weaken the chances of specific Democratic incumbents. But the three Republicans on the six-member commission refused to endorse the legal staff's view, forcing the FEC to drop Coelho's complaint.

Such partisan paralysis was common. Congress designed the FEC to be weak, requiring four votes from among the six commissioners for action. Congress also insisted on the appointment of partisan and less than zealous commissioners. As a result, the commission often refused even to investigate suspicious situations.

After the 1986 election the three GOP commissioners blocked a staff request to investigate an outlandish attempt by the American Medical Association's PAC—AMPAC—to unseat one of its sharpest House critics. AMPAC would spend $259,000 for a supposedly independent advertising campaign supporting the opponent of Pete Stark of California, who had insulted the AMA's leadership by calling them "troglodytes." Stark pointed to signs that the spending had really been coordinated with the campaign of the GOP candidate, David Williams. Legally, any coordination would make the spending a campaign donation, and thus a violation of the $5,000 limit. For one thing, Stark said, Williams had spent only $63,000 on his own, and much of that had been raised for him by AMPAC, which sent addressed envelopes to its members and urged them to give to Williams.

The FEC's legal staff agreed that the matter looked fishy, but their request for an investigation was blocked once again by the three Republican commissioners. Among them was Lee Ann Elliott, whose previous job had been assistant director of the American Medical Association's

PAC, from which she still drew a pension of $18,831 a year. She refused to step aside, telling Stark she participated "after deep introspection into my ability to fairly and impartially consider your complaint." Despite this episode, President Reagan then appointed Elliott to a second six-year term on the FEC. Stark testified against her, but the Senate confirmed her reappointment overwhelmingly. A Republican defender, Rep. Bill Frenzel of Minnesota, explained, "There isn't anyone we could put on the commission who doesn't carry baggage. In fact, we look for baggage because we want people with political experience."

Stark, who won re-election, unsuccessfully sued the commission to force the FEC to conduct an inquiry. The judge sympathized. "Stark observes, correctly, that the very ambiguity of the situation militates in favor of an investigation," he commented. But he said the law prevented him from substituting his own reasoning for the commissioners'. GOP commissioner Thomas Josefiak wrote that he couldn't favor an investigation "simply because the Commission does not understand or is uneasy about a particular situation."

Faced with such an attitude, Coelho was resigned to fighting the FEC in court. The commission's legal staff sided with Coelho on the $10,000 "come clean" mailing in Rhode Island, urging that it should be counted against the GOP's limits. But Republican commissioners refused to accept that advice. Josefiak, who had been a lawyer for the National Republican Congressional Committee, echoed the arguments presented by his ex-employer. "I don't see the electioneering case to be made here," he said. Commissioner Elliott said the Republican mailing was only demanding a House investigation of St Germain. "We see Common Cause doing just about the same thing," she said. Common Cause wasn't preparing to run a candidate against St Germain, however.

The "come clean" mailing was obviously intended to defeat St Germain, but Democratic commissioners could only protest impotently. "What else would be the purpose of this document?" demanded Democratic commissioner Danny McDonald.

When the FEC refused to act, Coelho sued and won a decision protecting St Germain. Federal judge Stanley Sporkin issued a ruling saying the FEC had "abdicated its statutory responsibility." He ordered it to reconsider what he called its "impermissible interpretation of the statute." That shielded St Germain against what would have been a damaging blow. The NRCC strongly considered running a new wave of its effective "tell the truth" TV ads late in the campaign, but dropped the idea because of Sporkin's order. "We didn't want to put the committee in the position of knowingly violating the law," said executive director Joseph Gaylord.

Coelho's victory was only temporary, however. After the election, the FEC appealed and won a decision validating its right to block the legal staff's advice on a deadlock if the dissenting commissioners give some reason in writing. The GOP commissioners did so retroactively in the St Germain case, cementing in place a precedent allowing parties to attack specific incumbents on issues without regard for spending limits. Yet another loophole had been opened, thanks to lax enforcement.

11

"Money Is What It's All About"

*The fact is that I was workin' for my district all
this time, and I wasn't bribed by nobody.*
—GEORGE WASHINGTON PLUNKITT

The headquarters of Fernand St Germain's opponent,
John Holmes, was in the rear of a little shopping plaza
several miles from Providence, under the same roof with a
beauty parlor, a butcher shop, and a Chinese restaurant.
Grass was growing through the cracks in the asphalt.

It was hard to see any magic political technology at work
in the Holmes headquarters one mid-August day in 1986. A
big fan pulled humid air through an open back door and
blew it into the weeds outside. The unisex toilet in the rear
was doubling as a broom closet. There was only one desktop
computer capable of communicating with the National Republican Congressional Committee's electronic bulletin
board in Washington, and it was inoperative, its keyboard
out for repair. In the candidate's private cubicle a tiny air-
filtering gadget strained gamely to clear the air of haze
from his eight-inch-long cigars. But the little machine, like

much else in the Holmes campaign, was overwhelmed by the demands put on it.

Holmes had encountered the challenger's paradox; he couldn't win without spending lots of money, but people wouldn't donate unless they thought he was going to win. Holmes said that even those who did give were telling him, "But, John, money is what it's all about. I'm going to help you out, but he's got a million."

Holmes had raised $114,000 but it was mostly gone. He had bought an early round of TV advertising in May, mainly to boost his rating in a local television-station poll in order to convince potential donors that he could win, so they in turn would give more money. The day-to-day overhead costs of even a modest campaign organization were considerable— rent and furnishings, a political consultant, catering and printing costs for fund-raising events, salaries for a campaign manager, press spokesman, fund-raising aide, and a driver to ferry him to personal appearances around the district. As of June 30, the cutoff date for his most recent disclosure report, he had only $20,139 in the bank and he owed a $4,422 bill for sending appeals for donations.

St Germain's campaign fund meanwhile continued to grow with special-interest checks. The incumbent's donations were running an average of more than $1,000 a day. He was spending for a public-opinion poll and for early television commercials, but still more money was coming in than going out. As of June 30 the total on hand had grown to $747,858.

Business PACs were helping him, not the Republican challenger. St Germain had received more than $210,000 from PACs, nearly all of them run by businesses or trade groups. Meanwhile Holmes received exactly two checks from business PACs, totaling $2,750.

A field representative from the biggest business PAC of all, run by the National Association of Realtors, had visited Holmes a few days earlier. The candidate grew irritated when the PAC man quizzed him about his campaign's secrets: "What do your polls look like? What have you been doing? What about money?"

Holmes said, "What the hell are you asking me these questions for? You've got a major investment in my opponent." The Realtors had given $4,500 to St Germain. "He proceeded to tell me that, number one, oftentimes they make contributions to both incumbents and challengers. Number two, that there was talk around town that Freddy was in real trouble, and they would like to give this particular race a good, hard look." As in the Salt Lake City race, the Realtors were thinking about giving to both sides. But in the end Holmes got nothing.

St Germain was now officially under investigation by the ethics committee, which began an inquiry on February 5 after months of delay. But that didn't deter the PACs. Merrill Lynch, which was keen on preventing banks from competing with stockbrokers, gave $4,000. The Independent Insurance Agents of America donated $5,000; they wanted to keep banks out of the insurance business. And, not surprisingly, the New York–based banking giant Citicorp sent $5,000, too; it wanted to get *into* the insurance and brokerage businesses. No faction in the turbulent financial-services industry wished to offend the chairman of the Banking Committee by failing to pay tribute.

Some of those who gave loathed St Germain personally. "He's as arrogant and pompous and as expectant a member as there is up there," said one senior official, whose association PAC gave thousands of dollars to his campaign. "He puts the arm on you," complained the head of another trade group that donated thousands. A third lobbyist said he resented having to "kiss the ring" of the chairman, but his group gave anyway. A lobbyist for a major bank said he treated the congressman like "a profit center." All of this, of course, was said behind the chairman's back.

St Germain sought money aggressively. In 1982 he became enraged at Tony Coelho for denying him a contribution from the Democratic campaign committee. Coelho was then trying to direct the committee's scarce resources to the expensive job of soliciting a reliable base of small donors and had cut back on gifts to incumbents who didn't need them. St Germain that year was so flush with money and so confident of victory that he finished the election with $240,000 unspent, after polling 61 percent of the vote against a lightly regarded opponent. But he flayed Coelho brutally, demanding a donation from the party. "Freddy got upset, went to Tip, and really put the heat on me," Coelho recalled. Speaker O'Neill upheld Coelho, however.

Despite that unpleasant history, Coelho aimed to save St Germain in his hour of need. St Germain had never had to run a modern political campaign before. Without polling or consultants, he had dispatched his opponents easily with the help of a local advertising agency and his smoothly functioning congressional office. Coelho insisted that he deploy the latest available political technology. To start, he furnished $5,000 worth of public-opinion polling, producing a report showing how vulnerable St Germain had become. "I said to him, 'The polls are not good,'" Coelho recalled. "I sat down with him and said, 'Freddy, what you need to do is . . . get out there right now with some bought media.'"

Coelho urged him to start spending money early to counteract the negative news coverage of St Germain's ethical problems. "Let this free press crucify you," he told St Germain. "You need to have the paid media saying certain things about you and the public will be all right."

St Germain began writing checks for an early round of advertising costing $80,000, nearly three times what the Republican campaign committee had spent against him on the "tell the truth" commercial and the "come clean" mailing. One of the incumbent's commercials portrayed him as a philanthropist, saying he had directed more than $38,000 in speaking fees to charitable causes. "Congressman St Germain—without him, we'd all be a lot poorer," the announcer concluded. The effect was only somewhat blunted when Republicans pointed out that St Germain had failed to report the $38,000 as required on his annual disclosures.

He was outspending Holmes better than two to one on early television advertising. The challenger was struggling just to introduce himself to voters, half of whom couldn't recall ever hearing his name. One Holmes ad featured his four-year-old son, John A. Holmes III, wearing a tee shirt bearing the words "I'm voting for my daddy, are you?"

Holmes found it difficult to raise money even in the wealthy enclave of Newport. He counted on collecting $75,000 at an August lawn party at a mansion where Senate Republican leader Bob Dole of Kansas had agreed to appear as the major attraction. But invitations had gone out late, reducing the response. Then, just an hour before guests began arriving, Dole sent word that he couldn't come because of Senate business. By then Holmes was flying to Washington to fetch him personally, aboard a chartered twin-engine plane that Dole required for such trips. The Newport event consumed the tiny campaign staff's time and energy for nearly three weeks, and netted only about $35,000, after deducting $5,000 for the plane.

Holmes had been startled in mid-June when a TV station released a poll showing that despite his advertising, only 25 percent said they would vote for him. He had dropped 5 percentage points since April. Holmes's private polling was showing that only 52 percent recognized his name. Among those who knew him, including many Republicans familiar with his work as state party chairman, Holmes actually seemed to be leading. But after five years in public life, $33,000 worth of advertising, and countless television and newspaper interviews, Holmes was still unknown to half the people he aspired to represent.

As a candidate, Holmes cast himself as a moralist, constantly demanding that St Germain disclose his taxes and detail his wealth. No other issue seemed to catch the attention of the "free media." He worked up safe, bland statements on arms control, South Africa, and drug treatment programs. But those weren't much different from St Germain's positions, and received just a few paragraphs deep inside the Providence newspapers.

Officially, St Germain was near the top of the GOP's list of Democratic incumbents to be defeated. But privately the Republican campaign committee's political director, Ed Goeas, said, "I think Holmes will run a fairly good campaign. But I think that if it's a fairly good campaign with no breaks, St Germain comes in at the end, dumps a bunch of money, and blows us out of the water, and we don't even get 45 percent."

Holmes got no break. He would have been helped had the ethics committee condemned St Germain's honest graft and deception of the voters, but the investigation dragged on past August and into September and it became apparent that the committee would remain silent until after election day. A new and more serious allegation surfaced at the end of August; a lawyer testified in a private lawsuit that his business partner once claimed to have paid $35,000 in bribes to St Germain in connection with federally subsidized apartments. But St Germain and the alleged bribe payer denied the story, which couldn't be substantiated and didn't help Holmes politically.

On the day the bribe story broke, Holmes had only $42,000 in campaign cash in the bank and St Germain had $677,000. Holmes wasn't mailing fund-raising solicitations on time, wasn't scheduling enough money-raising receptions, and wasn't getting anywhere near the amounts needed. From Washington, political director Ed Goeas pressured Holmes to replace his campaign manager with a woman trained at the party's Washington academy for political workers. Fund-raising efforts then began to go more smoothly, but there were only a few weeks left.

Polling on both sides indicated that Holmes still had a chance to win if—somehow—he came up with enough money. By mid-September a Republican campaign committee poll showed that 52 percent in St Germain's district said they favored a "new person" to represent them. St Germain's weakness was remarkable: 37 percent had an unfavorable opinion of him, a dangerously high index of negative feeling toward an incumbent who had represented the district for so long.

But Holmes hadn't been able to buy any television advertising since May, and in mid-September his name was still unfamiliar to nearly two voters of every five. St Germain would win by default unless Holmes could boost his name recognition. In mid-September he began broadcasting a thirty-second commercial that proved to be effective. A Republican campaign committee camera crew recorded Holmes standing before the Capitol saying:

"The future of Rhode Island and our country depends on what goes on in that building behind me. I hope to be working there in January. And if I do, you'll be reading about my legislation, and not my scandals.

"I'll be concerned about you, your parents, and your kids. Not my investments or the special interests. You'll always know what I own, because I'll continue to make my taxes public. But no one will ever own me.

"You may not always agree with me, but you'll *always* be able to trust me."

Holmes found enough money to run the ad for nearly two weeks, often enough so that a typical viewer saw it three times during each week. That was the least that political consultants considered necessary to register any impact on viewers, whose eyes and ears already were assaulted by a clutter of ads for hamburgers, cars, beer, and wine coolers. Some consultants urge candidates to buy their television time in blocks of 600 weekly gross rating points, so that the typical viewer will see the ad six times in a given week. St Germain was buying closer to the 600 level.

In the Providence television market, where thirty seconds of advertising on the top-rated *Cosby Show* cost $4,500, Holmes's minimalist advertising schedule would have to do. Even a challenger financed by Newport lawn parties couldn't afford a really heavy advertising budget. Holmes entered the final month with less than $21,000 in the bank.

His "trust me" ad was working. A new round of GOP polling showed that more voters had heard of Holmes, and his favorable rating was climbing. St Germain was still polling less than 50 percent.

Tom King, Coelho's political director, made the troubled St Germain campaign the lead topic on his weekly report for October 3. "The Republicans have Freddy under 50," he reported. The Republicans were spending $2 million on polling in selected House races, but Coelho's aides often got wind of the GOP's results within days, through PAC managers and political writers trading information. King reported that St Germain would respond with heavier advertising and begin attacking Holmes, whom he had ignored until then in his commercials. "They have agreed to go negative," King wrote.

"Freddy has agreed to up his TV buy so while it is going to be a very difficult race, I think Freddy wins," King concluded.

Holmes was spending an hour in the morning and another hour in the afternoon, every day, calling anyone who might be good for a contribution. It was too little; successful fund-raisers spend much more of their time personally soliciting donations. The campaign staff was getting fund-raising letters out more smoothly, but the mail would gross only about $7,500 in small donations by late October.

Holmes had to raise his money from his own constituents. His staff made a run at the PACs; his new campaign manager, Anna Mary Hoovler, had been a specialist in PAC solicitation at the Republican campaign committee in Washington. She tried to cash in on her old contacts. "We switched gears and began concentrating on PACs for about a week," she said. "By this time I had called up every PAC person I knew, begging." Some business PAC checks came in, including a few from brave banks. A PAC funded by imported-car dealers sent $2,500, showing dissatisfaction with the incumbent's vote for a protectionist trade bill. The American Medical Association, without any banking legislation to worry about, gave $3,500.

But mostly the PACs gave excuses. "They said, 'We don't have a plant in the district,' or 'We're out of money,' or 'What we have left is for debt retirement' [for winners, after the election], or 'We just can't get involved,' " said Hoovler.

In the end, Holmes got barely $40,000 from PACs, including less than $20,000 from business groups. St Germain eventually amassed a PAC total of more than $300,000, predominantly from business interests.

As a liberal Democrat, St Germain could take business PAC money without fear of reproach from consumer groups. He was one of their favorites because he often criticized bankers for charging high interest rates on credit cards and sponsored relatively trivial but crowd-pleasing bills to regulate unpopular commercial practices. In 1986 he was pushing a measure to force banks to credit deposits quickly, trimming the long "holds" they sometimes imposed while waiting for checks to clear. The check-hold problem was of much less import than such matters as the plundering of the savings and loan industry by unscrupulous operators who threatened to bankrupt the federal deposit insurance fund. But consumer groups generally stood by St Germain.

"We are less concerned about the chairman's private dealings than we are with his political stands," the chief lobbyist for the Consumer Federation of America, Gene Kimmelman, told the *American Banker*. Even Ralph Nader's camp stood up for him. "I don't think [questions about his personal finances] are likely to interfere with his banking work," said a spokesman for Congress Watch, a group usually critical of the influence of special-interest money on Congress.

One consumer group had to back down quickly after implying criticism. In late 1985 a Nader spin-off, the U.S. Public Interest Research Group, said it calculated that members of the Banking Committee had received $2.37 million from financial-industry PACs since 1981. St Germain led the list with $194,050. The group said the money was intended to buy votes. Staff attorney Michael Caudell-Feagan was quoted in Rhode Island news accounts as saying that St Germain's high total was "disturbing." St Germain called the release a "smear" and wrote an angry letter. "Let's go public," he insisted. "How many and who are they that have been bought off as the release implies?" Caudell-Feagan and his supervisor sent a reply that was nearly abject in its tone: "Not everyone who receives a large amount of PAC contributions will be anti-consumer," they said. "In particular, we applaud your leadership in putting the check-hold issue high on the agenda."

With St Germain monopolizing business money and escaping criticism for it, Holmes faced disaster. His money ran out and his campaign fell silent just at the time that Coelho's operatives were planning to redouble St Germain's advertising and "go negative." For several crucial days in early October, when the campaign should have been building momentum for the approaching election, Holmes had to withdraw his TV ads.

Holmes sank in the polls while his ads weren't appearing. Republican Gov. Edward DiPrete, polling daily for his own re-election campaign, added to his surveys an extra question asking voters whether they favored St Germain or Holmes. It showed Holmes's support was declining by about one percentage point every twenty-four hours that his commercials were off the air. It was as though his campaign no longer existed.

Holmes resumed advertising with help from Vice President George Bush. His presence enabled the campaign to sell $32,000 in tickets to a reception, although the event netted only $20,000 after paying expenses, including $7,500 for the Vice President's travel. The event was on a Monday and television stations were demanding $18,000 by Thursday to hold the time spots open. Holmes got the check delivered in time and bought another week's worth of television. By this time nearly every available dollar went into TV time.

Holmes couldn't afford to spend $1,500 for a professional coach to help him prepare to debate St Germain on television. But Coelho arranged for the congressman to get media training from Michael Sheehan, a leading Democratic consultant. Sheehan put St Germain through a session at the Democratic campaign committee's television studio in Washington, where he could watch replays of his practice performances. St Germain agreed to the exercise reluctantly. Coelho had to push him to do it. The campaign committee donated $450 worth of studio time and paid Sheehan's fee.

St Germain came in with a "Why am I here?" attitude, the consultant reported later. But by the time it was over, St Germain's administrative assistant told one of Coelho's aides, Andrew Spahn, that the results were "sensational." Spahn wrote in his weekly report: "Sheehan worked with him on three areas in particular: 1. 'Getting the chip off his shoulder' attitudinally. 2. Not looking guilty while answering hostile questions. 3. Being more 'calm' during aggressive questioning."

Coelho scribbled on the memo: "Excellent—he needed *all* three!"

Like any incumbent, St Germain was about as keen on facing a challenger in a public debate as he was on staring down a firing squad. Holmes stood only to win; he would introduce himself to voters who hadn't heard of him or formed an opinion, and if he could force St Germain into a blunder the undecided vote might begin to swing his way. Then money might come in from individuals and PACs who were sitting on the sidelines.

St Germain's media coaching paid off. He had to agree to at least one televised debate or risk giving Holmes an issue. So he followed a strategy his consultant often urged on incumbents: refusing invitations to debate on commercial television and agreeing instead to a single half-hour debate on a little-watched public television station. He also insisted on a format stacked entirely in his favor; none of the state's knowledgeable political reporters would be present to grill him about embarrassing topics. Media consultant Sheehan had often told clients in Holmes's position, "If there's dirty work to be done, let the press do it." Now the reverse applied. St Germain kept the press away.

Preparing for the debate, St Germain relied on Coelho's organization even to do research on his own voting record. "His staff called wanting to know how he could counter attacks by Holmes on being a big spender," Coelho's chief researcher reported. "So I found some votes where St Germain could say he had voted to hold the line on spending (though there weren't many)." Even so, St Germain used them to counter Holmes when the Republican accused him of being tied as "the number one biggest spender" in the House. St Germain said Holmes was using lines "spoon-fed by the National Republican Congressional Committee."

St Germain followed his media coach's advice; he smiled like a kindly uncle. He acted the part of a man falsely accused, but suffering his tormentors with patience and grace. He spoke softly and slowly, almost sighing. "Integrity? You bet I've got it," he said.

Holmes, lacking coaching, came off badly. He accused St Germain again and again of lying. "You owe it to the people, sir, to begin telling the truth. . . . Be an honorable man!" He was right; St Germain claimed he was no longer being investigated by the ethics committee when in fact the panel's chairman had said the inquiry was still pending. But Holmes appeared strident and unpleasant, a poor introduction to any voters looking for an embraceable alternative to the incumbent.

The Holmes campaign was all downhill from there. He fired his poll taker, Linda DiVall, and against her advice began airing a boisterous ad ridiculing St Germain's honest graft. It was intended to be hilarious, a send-up of television game shows like *Wheel of Fortune.* In a casino-like setting, a dealer wearing sleeve garters shuffled an odd-looking deck of oversize playing cards while a berserk announcer babbled away excitedly:

"Let's play . . . St Germain Rummy!

"See if you can become a millionaire on a small salary, just like our congressman, Fred St Germain."

The dealer laid out cards with pictures of restaurants on a green felt table.

"Wow!" the announcer gushed. "Just like Freddy, you bought *five* pancake houses with someone else's money! All you have to do is provide a few small favors."

More cards, this time with photos of condominiums.

"Look at this! Condos and houses worth millions! All for just a few small favors.

"Oh-oh!"

A card labeled "income tax" fell on the table, facedown. But hands reached down and ripped it quickly in half, discarding the pieces.

"Great! You're ignoring it, just like Freddy!"

Combative young staffers at the Republican campaign committee had urged that the ad be aired. But at an early preview Linda DiVall shook her head morosely. "I think very frankly that a spot like this could lose the race," she said. "You could redo the whole ad again, with a touch of humor. But not slapstick. This is amateurish."

When Holmes finally released the commercial, it had pretty much the effect DiVall predicted. St Germain's polling showed it fell flat, and his media handlers were amazed that Holmes kept it on day after day. But Holmes had too little money either to produce a new commercial or to buy the last-minute polling that might have told him that the "Rummy" ad wasn't working.

St Germain's ads ran more frequently and in better-watched time slots. He would have bought even more but several statewide candidates had already purchased all available television time. Instead, St Germain bought radio ads, sending his messages to nearly every car and kitchen in the district. Holmes had nothing to spare for radio, where it was as though St Germain was running without opposition.

The congressman attacked Holmes as a warmonger. Holmes had switched positions about aid to the Nicaraguan rebels. At first he opposed the Reagan administration's call for military aid, preferring only "non-lethal" assistance, such as medical supplies and clothing. But then Holmes emerged from a White House briefing and announced to a Providence *Journal* reporter, standing outside, that he had changed his mind. His flip-flop was just what St Germain needed.

Early in the campaign season Coelho had ordered up several ads that could be modified for use by any number of Democratic candidates. The instant commercials showed closed factory gates, abandoned farms, and soldiers slogging through Latin American jungles, all things for which Republicans were to be blamed. St Germain's media producer, Peter Fenn, took one that jumbled together shots of young American men playing basketball on a playground, shots of helicopters and jungle troops, and newspaper headlines reading "U.S. Troops Headed for Honduras" and "U.S. in Nicaragua: Another Vietnam?" Fenn excised a few frames showing a soldier's bloody corpse. He added a narrator saying that Holmes "gave in to pressure from Washington and changed his mind. Now he supports getting America involved in the war."

That was false; Holmes said from the start that he supported military aid to the rebels as an alternative to sending troops. But he didn't have money for an ad to counter the accusation.

Fenn was prepared to hit Holmes even harder. He wrote a radio ad implying that Holmes took a $25,000 payoff from the Republican party to change his position on military aid. Holmes did insist on receiving a $25,000 "severance pay" bonus when he quit the party chairman's job to run for the House, against the advice of strategists at the Republican campaign committee who saw what an inviting political target the money would make. Fenn's script said he took the money "just about the time he flip-flopped" on Nicaraguan military aid. "If $25,000 put in John Holmes's pocket buys his vote on the Contras, how much will it cost for him to oppose Social Security, or oppose help for veterans, or support cuts in student loans? Give the money back, John. Show Rhode Island you can't be bought."

That radio ad never ran; St Germain didn't need it. He had an endorsement from Sen. Claiborne Pell, the state's Democratic senator, who said, "I'd say to the critics of Fred St Germain, let's look at the record. It's a darn good one." Other commercials showed St Germain in a Rhode Island senior citizens center, on his parents' front porch in Woonsocket, visiting a drugstore where he had worked as a teenager, and eating, in shirt sleeves, in a blue-collar diner. There were, of course, no scenes of Florida golf courses, executive jets, or waterside condominiums. "Never forget your roots," St Germain said in one ad.

Despite the misgivings voters expressed to poll takers, St Germain won re-election easily, crushing Holmes by 57.7 to 42.3 percent. Political professionals faulted Holmes afterward as a candidate weak on personality, saying he gave voters little reason to support him. But St Germain wasn't very personable either. His strength lay in the federal money he had won for his district and in his special-interest campaign funds, which allowed him to dominate a contest fought largely on television and radio. Holmes lost, as nearly all challengers do, for lack of money.

After the election, Democrats chose St Germain to continue as chairman of the Banking Committee, and the ethics committee unanimously issued a report concluding he hadn't misused his office for personal gain.

The ethics committee, properly called the Committee on Standards of Official Conduct, cited St Germain for several infractions. It found he understated his assets by more than $1 million for several years, and it recited seven trips to Florida he took aboard Raleigh Greene's company jet, despite a House rule against taking gifts of more than $100 from anyone with an interest in legislation. But it minimized the violations and recommended no punishment, which the congressman accepted as vindication.

St Germain could hardly have hoped for a more accommodating jury than the twelve House members who made up the ethics committee, even though half of them were Republicans. They didn't question his income-tax avoidance, or even ask for a look at his tax returns. They never troubled St Germain by questioning him under oath, or even informally. In fact, investigators questioned nobody under oath. They failed to discover that St Germain's aide Paul Nelson had contacted Atlanta regulators as well as the Bank Board chairman about the Florida Federal merger, leaving them ignorant of the full extent of his inquiries, making it easier to pass them off as unremarkable. The committee accepted Nelson's word that he couldn't remember whether St Germain had asked him to make the calls.

The congressman kept up a relationship with at least one of his supposed inquisitors, Rep. George Wortley of New York. On May 15, ten days after the panel issued its first subpoena, St Germain appeared as a surprise guest at a Wortley fund-raising breakfast at the Mayflower Hotel in Washington. "I remember being surprised as hell when he walked in the door," one banking lobbyist recalled. Wortley was a Republican, and one that Coelho had targeted for defeat. The event realized about $15,000 from banking lobbyists and executives. St Germain later described the appearance as just a "courtesy" to Wortley, who was a member of the Banking Committee as well as the ethics panel.

Wortley meanwhile was telling other House colleagues that St Germain would be cleared (though he would later deny violating the committee's strict secrecy rules). The July 14 issue of the *Bank Letter,* an industry newsletter, said the ethics committee's investigators "have concluded they cannot make a case" against St Germain. It quoted an unnamed source as saying, "There is an awful lot of smoke. But St Germain is a former liability lawyer and every 'T' is crossed." Rhode Island GOP leader Leila Mahoney issued a press release predicting a whitewash. "They've ordered their paintbrush and their paint," she said.

The panel most likely would have absolved St Germain in time for the election if not for a surprise visit from the chief investigator for the Rhode Island attorney general's office,

Lee Blais. He told the ethics committee staff that a witness
was giving testimony about bribes. Thomas Broussard, a
California lawyer, swore that his business partner, Rhode
Island developer Ronald Picerne, claimed to have paid
bribes to St Germain. Broussard said Picerne told him on
two occasions in October of 1982 that he, Picerne, paid
money to the congressman for not blocking federal funds
for two of Picerne's federally subsidized apartment projects.

St Germain certainly was in a position to obstruct such
grants; no other member of Congress had more power over
the Department of Housing and Urban Development,
which administered them. Broussard told the bribe story
under oath, in pretrial testimony in a civil lawsuit in federal court in Providence. The testimony hadn't yet been
made public when Blais told the ethics committee about it.
Broussard swore that Picerne admitted making one cash
payment to St Germain of $15,000 and a second of $20,000.
He said that Picerne, his partner in the two housing projects, wanted him to reimburse the cost of the alleged bribes
and that he refused. "I told him that those payments were
illegal, that I had not approved or authorized them in any
way, [and] I would not participate in them in any way,"
Broussard testified.

Intensive investigation would be required to confirm or
refute such a story. Blais said later he expected the ethics
committee to pursue the bribe allegation. He miscal-
culated. The panel never questioned Broussard. Blais's visit
only slowed the rush to clear St Germain. The committee
did resume its own more narrow investigation after the
Providence *Journal* was given a copy of Broussard's testimony and headlined the story on August 20. Until then it
had been preparing to clear St Germain even though it
couldn't discover where he got $28,738 he had used as a
deposit when he bought his first two restaurants. St Germain said he couldn't recall the source. But eight days after
the *Journal* broke the bribe story, the committee issued four
new subpoenas for records. The additional investigation

established that the deposit money had been yet another loan from a federally regulated bank.

Besides ignoring the bribery allegation, the committee also made little attempt to look into St Germain's well-known penchant for running up bar and restaurant tabs at the expense of the savings and loan lobby. His wife had moved back to Rhode Island early in his House career, and he was seen night after night in Washington eating and drinking in the company of James "Snake" Freeman, lobbyist for the U.S. League of Savings Institutions. Rival banking lobbyists said Freeman's principal function at the S&L lobby was the care and feeding of his old friend St Germain.

The ethics committee's staff had called in Freeman for questioning early in its investigation, but quickly backed off when his employer raised objections. The final report contained not a word about free meals or liquor. But soon after it was issued the Department of Justice began a lengthy grand-jury investigation, seeking evidence that the S&L lobbyist's constant entertaining of the Banking Committee chairman constituted illegal gratuities under the bribery statute. Unlike the passive ethics committee investigators, prosecutors grilled Freeman extensively, under a promise that he himself wouldn't be charged. They issued subpoenas for his expense accounts and for records of some of the restaurants and night spots he and St Germain frequented together.

Prosecutors discovered that the chairman was accepting the lobbyist's expense-account hospitality two and three nights a week, running up big tabs at places such as the Prime Rib restaurant and Pisces, a disco club. Often the bills listed St Germain and female companions (as "staff"). The total cost to Freeman's employer ran between $10,000 and $20,000 a year. The subsidized revelry continued even as the ethics committee blindly went about its inquiry.

Some Justice Department officials were eager to indict St Germain, but career prosecutors cautiously recommended against pressing charges. For one thing, St Germain's attorney said he was able to prove that, possibly because of faulty record-keeping, Freeman had sometimes claimed reimbursement for entertaining the chairman on days when he was somewhere else. Also, permissive House rules seemed to allow members to accept unlimited meals and entertainment from lobbyists so long as the member's share of each bill didn't exceed $35. To win a conviction, prosecutors might have to call waiters to testify about which entrées and drinks were consumed by St Germain. In 1988 the department announced it wouldn't seek an indictment but would instead refer the matter back to the ethics committee.

The committee's 1987 report pleased St Germain. He said it "confirmed what my constituents, my friends, and I have known all along—that I adhere to the highest standards of conduct in both public office and private business affairs."

The committee could hardly afford to hold St Germain strictly to the rules, or to declare his honest graft to be improper. Any number of House members used tax shelters to avoid paying income tax and profited from deals with wealthy real-estate developers.

For example, William Boner of Tennessee, a Democrat, acquired a 5 percent interest in an $18 million Radisson Hotel project in Greenville, South Carolina, from Nashville real-estate developer Gary Price. Boner paid only $5 and didn't personally guarantee any of the partnership's debts. Price told the Nashville *Tennessean,* "I gave it to him as a gift because he is a close personal friend." Nevertheless, the House ethics committee's staff later concluded that the deal was an investment, not a present. Price also dealt Boner in for 5 percent of a $5.2 million Shoney's Inn and Restaurant in Richmond, Virginia, for which Boner paid $50. The ethics staff determined that wasn't a gift either.

The ethics investigators did fault Boner for using campaign funds to acquire $100,000 worth of computer equipment and other office machinery, a $17,000 Pontiac sedan with a mobile telephone, and an $80,000 office building. Boner leased them to his campaign committee for enough to cover financing costs, giving himself personal ownership and tax write-offs. The staff found that to be "conduct reflecting discreditably upon the House" and a violation.

The committee delayed its investigation of Boner for a year at the request of the Justice Department. Prosecutors were conducting a grand-jury investigation into a Pentagon supplier's claim that he had bribed Boner by paying his wife $25,000 a year for little or no work. James Wellham, who was convicted of selling inferior metal for missile-silo doors, turned out to be a poor witness; he flunked an FBI lie-detector test. Boner wasn't indicted, but the ethics staff later found "unconvincing" his claim that his wife had performed real work for Wellham. The staff said it required more proof to show that her salary wasn't a gift in violation of House rules. But by that time Boner had been elected mayor of Nashville and was no longer a congressman, and the panel closed the file on him without taking action.

Boner, whose financial dealings the *Tennessean* had detailed in an eighteen-month investigation, was endorsed by House Majority Leader Jim Wright during the 1986 primary election, which Boner was in some danger of losing because of the scandal. Wright denounced the newspaper for "journalistic arrogance" and praised Boner as "a man of character and courage and . . . integrity." Wright, before an audience of Boner's financial backers, said, "I know Bill Boner to be an honorable and honest man. I have no hesitation whatsoever in saying that."

Another case of honest graft, which the ethics committee never questioned, yielded Dan Rostenkowski a profit of more than $50,000 from a risk-free "investment" of $200 over a period of eighteen months. This was arranged for him by Daniel Shannon, a Chicago businessman whose stake in a forty-nine-story luxury apartment development, Presidential Towers, prospered with Rostenkowski's official help. Among other things, the congressman helped get Shannon's project low-interest federal mortgage money and an exemption from a law requiring that 20 percent of the apartments be set aside for low- and moderate-income people. The value of his holdings soared as affluent young professionals filled the 2,346 apartments, yielding him and his partners potential profits estimated at $40 million. Meanwhile Shannon, as administrator of some of the congressman's financial affairs, dealt him in for a portion of his own valuable stake in a small company that he and other investors were selling for a $1 million profit.

Rostenkowski's honest graft was at first obscured from public view by his misuse of a blind trust, a device designed—imperfectly, as it turned out—to prevent conflicts of interest. Such a trust allows public officials to place potentially troublesome holdings in the care of an independent trustee who has almost total discretion to buy, sell, or keep them, but who isn't supposed to reveal any of the transactions to the owner. In theory, officials can't be influenced, even subconsciously, by assets they don't know they hold. But everything depends on the integrity of the trustee, who is supposed to be a bank trust officer or someone else independent of the official's influence. Rostenkowski, however, chose Shannon to run his trust. The risk-free $50,000 profit never appeared on Rostenkowski's financial disclosure forms. Rather than preventing a conflict of interest, the blind trust obscured it from public view. Newspapers uncovered the arrangement anyway, after which Rostenkowski replaced Shannon with a certified public accountant from a major firm.

The longer congressmen served, the more vulnerable they seemed to be to the temptations of honest graft. Jim Wright had changed his attitude markedly over the years. Once he was an idealist, voluntarily making public his own federal income-tax returns at a time when the law required almost nothing in the way of financial disclosure from members of Congress. He wrote in 1975, "The damage suffered by the institution of Congress through the irresponsible conduct of a few of its members could be incalculable." But Wright himself became cynical and careless as he rose to power. As he prepared to run for Majority Leader in 1976, he had little to show financially for his years in the House. He had struggled along on a House member's salary, suffered through a divorce, and got married again, to a former secretary. He turned for help to a friend, J. D. Williams, a lobbyist. Williams was a former Senate aide who was amassing a personal fortune by winning lucrative tax concessions for wealthy clients, including Texas oil and gas drillers, insurance companies, and General Electric Co. Williams charged his clients a healthy hourly rate, plus a "success premium" if he won a reduction in their taxes. He realized enough such premiums to be able to keep a hunting preserve on the Eastern Shore of the Chesapeake Bay.

Williams suggested that Wright solicit donations from lobbyists and political supporters and use the money to improve his personal balance sheet. At a Washington dinner Wright cleared nearly $100,000, allowing him to retire some personal debts. Even years later Wright continued to convert lobbyists' funds to his own use, but through a more discreet route. An old political friend, Carlos Moore, who had once dispensed illegal campaign donations for Teamsters president Jimmy Hoffa and who went to jail for tax evasion rather than reveal the recipients, published in Fort Worth a small collection of Wright's old speeches and writings, titled *Reflections of a Public Man.* Wright earned more than $60,000 in royalties from sales made largely to lobbyists, labor unions, and other political supporters. The Teamsters PAC alone bought 2,000 copies in 1986, resulting in a $6,500 profit for Wright. Former Democratic Chairman John White, a lobbyist for the Chicago Mercantile Exchange and Coastal Corp., among others, said he also bought 1,000 copies to distribute as gifts.

The House applied to itself an ethical standard less strict than the rules for other government officials. On paper at least, executive branch employees were forbidden by presidential order from accepting even so much as a free lunch from anyone doing business with the government or even from news reporters seeking information. At the same time, House members allowed themselves to take free food, drink, and entertainment from lobbyists as often as they pleased, so long as the lawmaker's share of the tab didn't exceed $35. In 1987 that was raised to $50. Rules technically barred gifts of more than $100 from lobbyists or anyone with an interest in legislation, but that rule was interpreted so loosely that the ethics committee exempted six of St Germain's seven free flights to Florida aboard a corporate jet. It said commercial airlines were offering discounted fares of $99 on the same route. St Germain, of course, got first-class service.

The rare House member who urged an upright creed on his colleagues was shunned as a preachy eccentric. During the 1960s, Democratic Rep. Charles Bennett of Florida constantly pushed for creation of a permanent ethics committee, but when the House finally established one, his colleagues at first refused to make him chairman. When Bennett outlasted other Democrats on the panel and could no longer be denied the chairmanship, it was to preside over the expulsion from the House of Ozzie Meyers of Pennsylvania, for corruption. After that, House Democrats changed their rules to prevent Bennett from continuing to serve on the committee. Members were supposed to step off after four years. Later chairmen were more in line with the ethos of the House. In 1984 chairman Louis Stokes of Ohio was convicted of driving while under the influence of alcohol on his way home from a late session of the House. Later he used his campaign funds to pay his legal defense fees. The ethics committee permitted the practice under the reasoning that an acquittal would benefit a member's re-election.

Late in 1987 the ethics committee came under such intense criticism for its inaction in the St Germain and other cases that it abruptly recommended a reprimand for Austin Murphy, an obscure Democratic backbencher from Pennsylvania. His sins were allowing unauthorized use of official telephones and a copying machine, turning a blind eye while an aide whose mother was a cancer patient left work to tend to her, and allowing a colleague to vote "present" for him on three occasions years earlier. The reprimand had no practical effect, however.

House members relaxed their standards the longer they served. Only a rare few, like the pariah Bennett, seemed to escape the tendency entirely. The financial pressures were too great, the temptations too seductive, disclosure too casual, the press too somnolent, the culture of the House too forgiving, and the probability of rejection by the voters too remote for the beneficiaries to apply a refined code to their own behavior.

Indeed, a form of legalized bribery was flourishing openly. The federal bribery statute made it a felony punishable by up to two years' incarceration for any federal official to accept "anything of value . . . for or because of any official act," an offense commonly called an "illegal gratuity." An IRS agent who took a $50 tip from an accountant after an audit could be put in prison. Yet House and Senate members routinely accepted millions from lobbyists, military suppliers, and other federally regulated businesses. Lawmakers allowed themselves as much as $2,000 for a single appearance, for a total of up to 30 percent of salary for House members, 40 percent for senators. The House ceiling worked out to $22,530 in 1986.

Such "honoraria," as they were called, soared in the 1980s as PACs and lobbying groups proliferated. Moneyed interests set up regular programs to pay House members more to listen than to speak. The Chicago Mercantile Exchange and the Chicago Board of Trade flew House and Senate members to their city practically every week for tours of the trading floors and lunch with traders, who told the visitors why they should have special tax treatment and permissive regulation. Their standard fee was $1,000 for a House member, $2,000 for a senator. The Tobacco Institute, fighting against further increases in cigarette taxes, paid $1,000 for House members to spend an hour having breakfast with lobbyists. The American Trucking Associations, smarting from a failure to stave off economic deregulation and an increase in fuel taxes, paid a total of $97,500 in fees to House and Senate members in 1985 as part of what the truckers' chief lobbyist described as an "outreach program."

One of the worst abuses was uncovered in 1986, when the Washington *Post* reported that United Coal Co. flew fourteen Democratic House members to Virginia aboard a 727 jet with a wet bar, executive stateroom, and salon, for a tour of its mines and a discussion of legislation over dinner. The company offered them $2,000 each, although some declined the money and others returned it after the *Post* ran its story. Among the issues discussed was the pending tax bill, which contained repeal of capital-gains treatment for coal royalties and a change in the depletion allowance for coal. Rep. Frederick Boucher, who organized the trip, said: "Members of Congress, taking the time to do something like this, expect to get some compensation for it."

This explanation didn't sit well with the new head of the Justice Department's criminal division, William Weld. "Taking time out? This wasn't a dogsled to the Yukon," he said. The *Post* story sent Weld scrambling to the law books. He had just spent five years as U.S. Attorney in Massachusetts, where he and his staff had won convictions of 108 persons in public corruption cases. "This sounded to me, fresh from the hinterlands, like a *prima facie* criminal violation," he said. "I discovered to my surprise that in fact only members of the executive branch and the independent agencies are prohibited from supplementing their salaries with fees and honoraria for job-related activities."

Coelho himself was one of the most enthusiastic exploiters of honoraria. He logged thirty-nine paid appearances during 1986, for which he got nearly $60,000 from groups that lobbied him. He hung on to nearly all of the money until the last day of the year, allowing it to draw interest. Then he wrote ninety-two checks to charitable organizations, including the Epilepsy Foundation of America, to trim his net fees down to the allowable $22,530. The gross included $11,000 from tobacco interests alone. Grover Connell, the former Koreagate figure, paid him $2,000. Drexel Burnham Lambert gave $2,000 as well. Mobil Oil flew him to an oil-drilling platform in the Gulf of Mexico, a visit for which the company paid him yet another $2,000. When Coelho addressed the National Association of Beer Wholesalers, collecting $2,000 more, his speech was written by his press aide at the campaign committee, Mark Johnson, who cribbed ideas from the beer dealers' literature describing their goal of obtaining an exemption from antitrust laws to allow them regional monopolies.

Coelho defended these fees with gusto. "I believe that its good to be educated," he said. "I believe that if you're going to be in the United States Congress, you might not agree with the oil companies, but it's good for you to know about 'em. . . . I'm like a sponge, I *love* it, I love to be exposed."

Coelho acted as a kind of broker for colleagues who wanted fees for themselves. "People came to me with real serious financial trouble," Coelho said. "What I've done is, I've gone to people and said, 'I want you to have these people speak to you, or include them on a program, or do whatever you can to help them out.' " He arranged fees from labor unions, from the trucking industry, and from his friend Connell, the rice and sugar merchant. Coelho was the second-ranking Democrat on the Cotton, Rice, and Sugar Subcommittee, and his former administrative assistant, Archie Nahigian, landed a job high in Connell's business empire. Connell paid a total of $63,000 to House members during 1986. Coelho's referrals gained him gratitude from colleagues whose votes he was seeking in his campaign to rise in the leadership. "People said I did that for the Whip race," Coelho said. "Sure. Everything I did was for the Whip race."

Coelho and his colleagues also exploited another growing form of honest graft, free vacations paid for by lobbyists. Trade groups invited members, sometimes by the dozen, to address their conventions. Lobbyists staged golf tournaments in places such as Palm Springs with House and Senate members as the "celebrity" attractions, an excuse to entertain them at expensive country clubs. The Electronic Industries Association, the trade group for consumer electronics marketers, flew lawmakers and their wives to a week-long winter retreat at Florida's Captiva Island resort.

Coelho took his wife to the Hawaiian island of Maui for

seven days at the end of March 1986. In return for some appearances by Coelho, their air fare and most of their food and lodging were paid by Hawaiian sugar refiners and planters, who profited from Congress's refusal to allow more than a trickle of sugar to be imported from the economically depressed Caribbean. Hawaiian labor unions paid some of Coelho's hotel bills, too.

The House became more tolerant of such things each year. The total amount of honoraria paid to House members grew to nearly $5 million in 1986, up from barely $1 million only six years earlier. The value of the junkets and expense-account entertainment that House members also enjoyed probably was in the millions, but neither the members nor lobbyists were under any effective requirement to disclose the amounts.

In 1988 the committee took the extraordinary step of urging the expulsion of Mario Biaggi of New York, who had been convicted of accepting illegal gratuities the previous year and who was facing a second criminal trial. Biaggi's crime was taking free use of a Florida spa from an old political friend, the Brooklyn political boss Meade Esposito, who had an interest in a project Biaggi was aiding officially. That was hardly any different from the free vacations and cash payments that other members were constantly accepting from lobbyists. But Biaggi clumsily omitted the Florida gifts from his annual disclosure reports, perhaps because he was vacationing with a woman who wasn't his wife. That made him seem to be acting in a guilty fashion. Also, after the FBI questioned him, he was heard on a wiretap coaching Esposito to testify that the gifts had only been a token of friendship. That led to an obstruction-of-justice charge, of which he was also convicted.

Biaggi couldn't understand why his colleagues were turning on him for doing something that so many others did. He pointed out that the committee had in 1985 excused acceptance of $47,000 worth of free travel aboard the corporate aircraft of a Pentagon supplier by Dan Daniel of Virginia, who was allowed to repay the money and go unpunished, and who was later re-elected and died in office. Biaggi warned that others might be prosecuted. "We could all be vulnerable," he said. "All they need is a focus, whether it be a golf trip, whether it be a convention, whether it be a stay at a hotel. You are involved by someone who has a legislative interest."

Even though convicted of a felony, Biaggi insisted he had done nothing wrong. "I have an absolutely unblemished record," he said. "I am absolutely incorruptible." That was the mentality that prevailed in the Congress.

12

"We're Not Really Interested in Character"

A reformer can't last in politics. He can make a show of it for a while, but he always comes down like a rocket. . . . He hasn't been brought up in the difficult business of politics and he makes a mess of it every time.

—GEORGE WASHINGTON PLUNKITT

Democrats in 1984 had taken a drubbing in the South, especially in North Carolina, where Republicans defeated three incumbents. Coelho wanted to score some kind of comeback; otherwise Republicans would be seen as making irreversible gains, converting conservative Democratic voters permanently. PAC managers would start believing again that Republicans could one day rule the House. One of Coelho's best candidates in North Carolina, however, would insist on turning his election campaign into a crusade for good government, over Coelho's strong objection.

David Grier Martin, Jr., was born to the Southern academic gentry. His father was president of Davidson College while Martin was a student in the class of 1962. His basketball coach at Davidson, Lefty Driesell, once told a newspaper reporter that Martin was among the scrappiest players he ever taught. "He didn't have a lot of natural ability like some of the other kids," Driesell said, "but he was always such a competitor." Martin joined the Army's Green Berets, but didn't see combat. After Yale Law School he settled into a comfortable life as an expert in the federal law regulating interstate land sales.

To Coelho, the professional politician, the rise of PACs and money presented a threat to Democratic rule. To Martin, private citizen, special-interest money was becoming an affront to popular government. Coelho saw money as the key to power; Martin saw it as inimical to good government.

Martin learned how the PAC system functioned while running for the House in 1984, his first try for elective office. His eyes were opened while visiting what he called a "good PAC" in Washington, the National Committee for an Effective Congress, an old-line liberal group. Martin said NCEC officials told him the kind of candidates they liked included former congressman John Jenrette of South Carolina. Jenrette was among those headed for jail in the Abscam affair, in which the Federal Bureau of Investigation videotaped lawmakers taking bribes from an agent posing as an Arab sheik. Jenrette was enormously popular with his largely black constituency because he had been an unfailing supporter of civil rights even as a state legislator. He nearly won re-election in 1980 despite his conviction, getting 48 percent of the vote.

"They told me that he was one of their best candidates," Martin said. "I asked the question 'How could you support him so enthusiastically, given his character and the things that everybody knew about him?' And they said, 'Well, we're not really interested in character; we're interested in votes.'" Actually, the NCEC later said it would never support a convicted felon, but the words stuck in Martin's mind.

A couple of PAC donations showed up unbidden during Martin's 1984 primary campaign, but he returned them without saying anything publicly. When he won the nomination, just at the point where he could have expected some PAC support, he declared that he would accept none.

Refusing PAC money was an expensive decision. He was running for a vacant seat, and political handicappers rated the race as a toss-up. In such a contest a Democrat ordinarily could get $100,000 or so from labor and liberal PACs just by asking for money and avoiding positions offensive to them. But Martin didn't like the implied obligations that went with accepting such funds. "I just don't want to be obligated to either side," Martin said. "I'd just like to be in the middle and be as objective as possible."

Martin declined the money on principle. "Some people have suggested that this is naïve and idealistic," he told reporters. "It is not. It goes to the heart of practical politics for me. An election win that does not preserve and enhance my ability to represent the district with an open mind, independence and objectivity . . . that would be no victory for me."

He had enough money, even without PACs. His fund-raising efforts were headed by an old family friend, Hugh McColl, Jr., chairman of NCNB Corp., parent of the North Carolina National Bank and one of the South's largest banking concerns. Martin's wife, Harriet, from a wealthy South Carolina family, worked her own network for money. Martin spent nearly $700,000, part of it borrowed from banks using family assets as collateral. He would have to repay the loans personally if he lost. In essence, he made up for the missing PAC funds from his own pocket.

Martin had backing from poor as well as rich; blacks made up 21 percent of the voting-age population. He had for sixteen years attended the Siegle Avenue Presbyterian Church in Charlotte, near a formerly all-white housing project now populated by blacks. The congregation had become mostly black, but the Martin family remained. "We've always had white people come over to the black community to share talents and skills," a black church official, Smith Turner, told a newspaper reporter. "But D.G. is the one who stayed." The Charlotte *Observer* endorsed Martin, calling him "a man of compassion, common sense and intellectual depth." It saw in him the potential to be "a political figure of national stature."

But 1984 was a bad year for any Democrat; Ronald Reagan pulled 64 percent of the vote in the district. Meanwhile

PACs gave nearly $200,000 to the campaign of Martin's opponent, Alex McMillan, a former supermarket executive. And the National Rifle Association marked Martin as an enemy for refusing to respond to questionnaires asking how strongly he would oppose federal gun-control measures. Martin only wanted to remain independent of special-interest pressure, but objectivity wasn't what the PACs wanted.

The NRA's Washington-based political arm began attacking Martin in letters to its members in the district, calling him "unresponsive toward our firearms and hunting liberties." Its PAC donated $4,950 to Martin's Republican opponent. It distributed "Alex McMillan for Congress" bumper strips to its members and generated calls and letters to gun clubs and gun dealers around Charlotte denouncing Martin as soft on gun control.

Just before election day, the NRA began running a radio ad saying, "D. G. Martin . . . remains unresponsive to the concerns of North Carolina's sportsmen. North Carolina needs a voice in Congress to stand for the preservation of gun ownership, and our proud hunting heritage. That voice is Alex McMillan." Martin had no time to reply with a commercial of his own. The NRA ad ran only in the rural areas of the district, heavily populated with hunters. The NRA spent $16,942 on the radio ads and other pro-McMillan electioneering, in addition to the $4,950 donated directly.

Such shadow campaigns were becoming increasingly common, a tactic made possible by the Supreme Court in a 1976 decision, *Buckley* v. *Valeo.* The Court said that in politics money is equivalent to speech protected by the First Amendment. Limits on direct campaign donations were permissible to prevent vote bartering, but independent outlays like the NRA's couldn't be restricted.

However, lobbying organizations blended their own messages into election campaigns with such skill that they sometimes seemed to have been produced by the candidates themselves. Federal law required the true sponsors to identify themselves, but they satisfied this formality in their television ads with tiny letters displayed for a few seconds at the bottom of a screen. The announcer for the anti-Martin radio ads never mentioned the controversial sponsor's full name, saying only that the ads were "paid for by the NRA PVF," an acronym that sounded like a formula for plastic plumbing. (Actually, the letters stood for the National Rifle Association Political Victory Fund.) The Supreme Court's nice distinction between independent spending, which it equated with free speech, and direct donations, in which it saw the potential to seduce lawmakers, had all but vanished. As a practical matter the NRA might as well have given its money directly to McMillan and let him buy the commercial.

Harriet Martin said that people in rural areas who had been supporting her husband began calling her after hearing the ad, saying they would now vote for McMillan because Martin was soft on guns. Martin lost in 1984 by 321 votes, of nearly 220,000 cast.

He came so close, despite the Reagan landslide, that Coelho put him at the top of his list of challengers for 1986. "You lost, but you won," Coelho said. Challengers ordinarily have little hope of beating incumbents, but Martin never stopped campaigning. He wrote a weekly column that appeared in a widely circulated shopper, a free newspaper. He became the host of a weekly talk show, *One on One with D. G. Martin,* carried on a local cable-TV channel. Martin came across on television as warm, boyish, and friendly, while McMillan avoided the medium. Martin was practically a congressman-in-waiting.

The corrosion of ethics in Washington favored a candidate like Martin, with his reputation for personal integrity. A Senate debate over the PAC system was touching off a fresh wave of news stories and editorials critical of campaign money practices. *Time* magazine ran a lead story on influence peddling, with a cover photo of former Reagan aide Michael Deaver, who had become a high-paid lobbyist for corporations and foreign governments. A House inquiry on Deaver was underway; his sworn denials of impropriety would eventually cause him to be convicted of perjury.

In a widely discussed article assessing national prospects for 1986, Democratic poll takers Peter Hart and Geoffrey Garin wrote: "Deaver and the PACs represent voters' worst fears about the system—politicians who sell out and special interests that cash in, all at the expense of the average person.... Voters are trying to tell us something in 1986, and candidates who fail to get the message now will be sorry on Election Day. The message is simple: character counts. The voters do not want to be forgotten, and they do not want to take a back seat to the special interests."

Martin's own poll taker thought his chances were excellent. Hickman-Maslin Research reached a random sample of 456 registered voters in the congressional district by telephone during nine days in April 1986. That small sample provided a wealth of information, showing why such surveys had become standard in modern House campaigns. They probed for the underlying reasons voters favored one candidate over another and for hidden doubts about the opponent that might be exploited. Sometimes poll takers tested possible campaign themes to see which would work.

Martin's poll showed McMillan was in danger; only 47 percent said they would support him. Martin himself polled just 40 percent, with the rest undecided, but that was much higher than a lesser-known challenger would get at such an early stage. An astonishing 94 percent of the voters knew Martin's name, and more than half said they liked him. The poll taker's detailed cross-tabulations showed he was regarded favorably by 63 percent of blacks, 59 percent of upper-income whites, and 62 percent of women over age forty. But the poll also revealed Martin's weakness; too many voters saw him as indecisive. When asked which phrase better described him, 28 percent picked "seems a little wishy-washy." When asked to pick which candidate was "tough," only 27 percent chose Martin and 40 percent picked the incumbent.

The winning strategy was to be built around Martin's refusal to take PAC money. In the poll 68 percent agreed with the statement: "Even the most honest congressman's votes are swayed by the views of the persons or groups who give large contributions to their campaigns." And 72 percent said they would be more likely to trust a candidate whose money came in "small contributions from residents of North Carolina."

But how to exploit that public mistrust of special-interest money? Coelho favored attacking McMillan aggressively and personally for knuckling under to his donors.

The NRA was Coelho's first choice. He urged Martin to criticize the incumbent's support for NRA-backed legislation to relax federal rules on the interstate sale of rifles and shotguns, to ease record-keeping requirements for gun dealers, and to cut back authority for federal officials to inspect gun shops. He wanted Martin to say that the gun lobby had bought a vote for the nearly $22,000 it spent on McMillan in 1984.

But by that time Martin had quietly taken out membership in the rifle association himself. "I wanted to understand better the concerns my constituency were voicing," he said later. This time when the NRA's questionnaire arrived, he filled it out, expressing no strong views for or against gun controls. Martin wanted to avoid another confrontation with the big-spending gun lobby. "I don't think gun control or the lack of it goes to the heart of what's wrong with the country," he said. It seemed that even a man who couldn't be bought might still be intimidated.

Martin did attack McMillan on tax reform and trade votes, just as Coelho urged. In an early television interview he called McMillan an "accidental congressman" and suggested that money had influenced a vote he cast to prevent consideration of the tax-reform bill. Martin said the congressman accepted funds from "PACs and special-interest groups representing corporations that pay absolutely no income tax." Coelho had sent challengers lists of their opponents' donations from PACs of tax-avoiding corporations; McMillan's total was $17,500.

In the interview, Martin also reproved McMillan on foreign imports, another of Coelho's pet issues. Martin accused the incumbent of "buying foreign while he's preaching buying domestic," ridiculing him for driving a French-made 1983 Peugeot.

Coelho strongly approved Martin's attack, scribbling "Excellent!" on an aide's report of it. But many of Martin's closest supporters felt it was petty and out of character. A newspaper columnist joked that he could hear D. G. Martin stickers being ripped from foreign-made bumpers. Martin himself drove an old Ford station wagon, but the parking lot outside his campaign headquarters was filled with Toyotas, Datsuns, and Volkswagens. Coelho advised him to pay no attention, but Martin brooded over the unpleasant backlash.

Martin decided he couldn't impugn the character of an honest foe. He felt the worst he could truthfully say about McMillan was that he was a run-of-the-mill congressman who hadn't accomplished much. He resolved to attack not McMillan's character but the political system itself.

He figured that the PAC problem was simmering in the minds of voters, just ready to boil. "I believe that the people out there, including yourself, are worried about it," he told his cable-TV audience. He made a populist argument, saying PACs were taking power away from the home folks. "The focus is up to Washington, rather than what people are thinking about locally." he said. "Congress is almost an auction." He thought lawmakers shouldn't be just dispensers of patronage to cash-based constituencies, but ought to act like impartial mediators. That made PAC money seem sinister. "Some people say it's just like a judge taking money from a defendant," he said.

Martin developed a workable reform plan that would allow candidates to continue accepting money from PACs and Washington lobbyists if they wished, but would provide public funds for candidates who agreed to new strictures. They could get up to half their campaign financing from the U.S. Treasury if they would forswear PAC donations, take no more than $500 from any individual, accept no gifts from outside the congressional district, use no more than $10,000 of their own money, and spend no more than $400,000 overall. Martin also proposed to cut back on official mail and staff allowances for House members, to weaken the incumbent-protection system and also to save enough money to offset the cost of the new campaign subsidies. If any candidate exceeded the $400,000 limit, Martin's plan would provide his opponent enough from the government to match the extra spending dollar for dollar. That way a candidate who spent $1 million would achieve no advantage.

Coelho and his political director, Tom King, demanded that Martin shelve his proposal, however. Henry Doss, Martin's campaign manager, said King exploded when he first heard about it. "King said, 'You can't do that! Are you *crazy?* You'll just . . . Jesus Christ, are you *crazy?*' " King told Martin he would be attacked as a tax-and-spend Democrat for proposing public financing. "They're just going to beat you to death on that," he said.

Martin considered relenting. "We were about ready to back out," Doss recalled. "I was really worried. Then that night, I was lying there thinking, 'Twenty-four hours ago I was absolutely certain that what we were doing was right, in spite of the risks.' . . . I couldn't think of a good reason for not being certain anymore." They pushed ahead despite Coelho's continued opposition. King wrote in his weekly report: "They are adamant about releasing this 10-point cleanup elections program, including public financing. I think it is a dreadful mistake and I am going to continue working on them."

But Martin made the reform plan the centerpiece of his campaign, presenting it at a news conference for which he had rehearsed for days. "Yes, PACs are *bad,*" he said. He laid heavy stress on certain words, the better to get across on television. "They're bad because PACs most often are in pursuit of *power,* not *ideas* or *ideals,*" he said. "They're bad because they're tending to produce a *challenge-proof Congress,* where the incumbent, regardless of ability and leadership, entrenches himself and wins on the basis of his PAC finances rather than genuine popular support."

Coelho punished Martin for defying orders. "I still think matching funds is an awful idea," Tom King wrote in his next weekly report. "D.G. has requested a $5,000 general election contribution. . . . I don't recommend it at this time because we lose credibility by rewarding a candidate who is clearly not taking our advice." Coelho agreed; the campaign committee withheld the money, despite his earlier promise of maximum aid. King gave Coelho copies of the Martin plan. "This is a bunch of *crap!*" Coelho wrote on the memo.

PACs disliked Martin's plan as well. His race was being watched by lobbyists with much more intensity than an ordinary House contest. If Martin could stir up a popular revolt against special-interest money in Charlotte, there was no telling where it would stop. If Martin won by running against PACs, dozens of other challengers would soon be imitating him in other districts. PAC gifts could become a political liability.

In Washington a lobbyist for Mobil Oil Corp., Barney J. Skaladany, was selling $250 tickets to a "North Carolina Seafood Reception" that McMillan was holding for PAC managers and lobbyists. Skaladany sent a memo to fellow lobbyists saying, "You might be interested in the enclosed piece," a newspaper account of Martin's denunciation of McMillan's PAC gifts from companies paying no income tax. The seafood party raised about $14,000.

McMillan used Martin's public-financing proposal to wring even more donations from PACs. He hired his own PAC director, Pat Calhoun, whose job was to collect $250,000 in special-interest funds. Calhoun sent a solicitation:

"To: PAC administrators . . . Our opponent's PAC position has been widely publicized. . . . The Alex McMillan strategy has not changed. We need $700,000 to insure that Alex has every opportunity to return to Congress in 1987, and we initially budgeted $250,000 from the PAC community."

McMillan's campaign had received more than $150,000 from PACs by that time, but Calhoun's message urged: "We need to raise $100,000 from the PACs in the next twelve weeks. . . . We need your financial help and appreciate any consideration you would give to assisting us down the stretch."

McMillan spent nearly $200,000 during the first six months of the year, much of it for television ads, and still had a cash balance of $125,517 on July 1. Martin was almost indigent by contrast. He ran no early TV ads and spent half as much as the incumbent during the first six months, mostly to rent, equip, and staff his campaign headquarters. His cash balance on July 1 was $36,481.

McMillan was destined to outspend Martin by nearly two to one. The difference was almost purely PAC money. Eventually, PACs would donate more than $325,000 to the McMillan campaign, even more than it had hoped for. His ability to tap special-interest donations came partly from his seat on the House Banking Committee, which produced donations from bankers, savings and loan officials, and their PACs. "Bankers aren't obligated to me, and I'm not obligated to them," McMillan insisted. But at least one banker may have felt a compulsion. NCNB Corp. chairman Hugh McColl, Jr., Martin's main financial backer two years earlier, gave $500 to McMillan in 1986, a dramatic example of an incumbent's power to obtain tribute.

What McMillan's polls showed was hardly comforting; the congressman hadn't been able to get more than 48 percent against Martin since taking office. Martin was staying within striking distance, no more than 10 points behind, with the balance undecided. In an August poll McMillan reached 50 percent, but Martin had 41 percent. McMillan's surveys also showed that voters were suspicious of the very PAC money that was paying for them; in one poll 31 percent said they would vote against a candidate who took "a considerable amount of money from PACs" even if they liked the person in every other way.

Outwardly, the McMillan forces appeared unfazed. Lee Atwater, the congressman's political consultant, insisted that the issue was "too abstract" for voters to care much about. "It's not like interest rates or taxes," he said. But the McMillan forces were worried when Martin's PAC-bashing press conference attracted vigorous local news coverage. "It was the biggest press he had gotten since he announced," recalled Jay Timmons, McMillan's press secretary. "What concerned us most was, suddenly he looked like he knew what he was doing."

King's prediction of a backlash proved to be wrong. McMillan didn't try to paint Martin as a tax-and-spend liberal, and wasn't about to fight the PAC battle on the turf Martin had prepared. He had already tried defending PACs, with unpleasant results. Months earlier he criticized a Senate bill to limit the amount of PAC money that candidates could accept. "The liberals are raving," he said. But a Charlotte *Observer* columnist noted that Sen. Barry Goldwater of Arizona, the grand old man of traditional Republican conservatism, was co-sponsoring the bill.

In Washington, Coelho's aides were relieved at McMillan's silence. "D.G. went ahead with his complicated campaign reform bill press conference and so far he is getting away with it very well," reported field man Randy Johnston.

Coelho said he actually saw merit in Martin's plan. Indeed, the following year he would draft a spending-limit bill of his own. "I don't deny that it's good," he said. But he railed against Martin for what he saw as naïve tactics. "D.G.'s problem is that he's a boy scout," Coelho said. "I said, look here, you're in the major leagues. In triple-A ball they don't try to bean you. In the major leagues, if they think they have to bean you, they bean you." Because Martin couldn't abide by his own proposed donation limits and still run an effective campaign, Coelho thought he would be attacked for inconsistency.

But Martin suffered more damage from his allies than from McMillan. Trouble arose early when he tried to exploit the GOP "bundling party." McMillan was among the dozen House incumbents for whom the Republican campaign committee was raising PAC checks at a reception for President Reagan. Coelho encouraged Martin and other

Democratic challengers to attack those receiving bundled contributions. Martin issued a press release saying that the bundling "flagrantly violates the spirit of campaign laws now on the books." He added, "It's big money that's beginning more and more to call the shots in Washington."

Unfortunately for Martin, Coelho's own reliance on PAC money made McMillan's counterattack an easy task. The Democratic campaign committee itself had taken nearly $1.5 million from PACs during the 1983–84 campaign cycle and would receive more than $2 million during the 1986 campaign, not counting soft money. McMillan accused Martin of hypocrisy for accepting a $5,000 donation from the DCCC—financed in large part with PAC funds—while criticizing PAC gifts to others. Alluding to the attack on his Peugeot a month earlier, McMillan said, "You might call this Spitball II. First was the car, now we're on PACs."

Martin's decorous campaign irritated Coelho, who summoned him for consultations in mid-August. Reluctantly, Martin left Charlotte to attend a two-day training session in Washington for the party's best candidates. "The fact is, I needed to be back home, and I didn't need to spend $350 on plane fare," he complained. But Martin was struggling financially and Coelho was still withholding additional monetary aid.

The first evening, Coelho took his candidates for a dinner cruise aboard the *High Spirits,* which had been put at his disposal. As the yacht moved down the Potomac, Coelho criticized Martin for pushing a utopian scheme instead of an assault against the incumbent. "You had the guy by the balls," Coelho said. He told Martin that Lee Atwater, the McMillan consultant, was asking Democratic officials, "What is your guy in North Carolina doing? We can't figure it out, because he's not hurting us." The argument shook Martin; an hour after he reached the dock he said, "I didn't know how strongly Tony felt that the whole [public-financing] tactic was a mistake."

Nevertheless, Coelho was invoking Martin's name to raise money from his own rank-and-file donors. In an "urgent memorandum" to past givers, he was promoting Martin's contest as one of four North Carolina races in which Democrats had a chance to deliver a setback to the Republican right. "AT LAST . . . you and I have a wonderful chance to *beat* Jesse Helms. And beat him in his own backyard!" the letter said. He described McMillan as "a proponent of big business and special interest groups," brought up his National Rifle Association support, and said that "so far this year, almost 40 percent of McMillan's campaign funds have been from special interest groups."

Coelho's solicitation promised that donations would go into a "North Carolina Strategy Fund." There was, of course, no such fund. The mailing was merely a vehicle to invoke the name of Helms, whom liberal donors considered particularly odious and retrograde, to encourage them to part with money for Democratic candidates generally. Martin was getting very little of it.

Martin needed money because McMillan, as the incumbent, had a $1 million advantage before the first dollar of campaign funds was spent. Like any sensible incumbent, McMillan was using his official mailing privileges to foster political support. From House records, which are intentionally vague about such matters, Martin deduced that McMillan had mailed six district-wide newsletters to his constituents, a total of 1.8 million pieces. Additionally, McMillan sent hundreds of thousands of "meeting notices" inviting voters to attend his appearances around the district. Using taxpayers' money, he hired a computer firm to produce 213,975 letters on laser printers at a unit cost of 7.5 cents for printing and 22 cents for postage. He procured a mini-computer with four terminals, an IBM Personal Computer, and a Xerox Memorywriter typewriter. McMillan's office, like almost all others on Capitol Hill, was a factory for producing mail to voters.

McMillan wasn't just responding to the few constituents who might write about a particular bill or issue. He spent $1,304 from his official allowance for mailing lists of old people and farmers, so he could send them mass-produced letters about Social Security and farm subsidies. He also got lists of military veterans, who wanted to hear that their medical benefits were safe. In all, Martin calculated that McMillan spent $306,154 on "official" mail, much of which was self-generated, self-promoting, and geared mainly to promote re-election.

The free mail was getting votes. One citizen told the congressman's poll taker he would vote for McMillan because "he mails us questionnaires from time to time to get opinions on certain items. He is a good leader and a well-balanced man."

One newsletter arrived in September, just weeks before the election, containing a photo of McMillan shaking hands with President Reagan. Headlines said, "Tax Reform Cuts Rates . . . McMillan Works for Drought Aid . . . Congressman McMillan Introduces Bill to License Textile Imports." His name appeared eight times on the front page alone. The tax-reform article praised the final version of the bill, which McMillan supported, even though he tried to kill an earlier variation. Another article gave McMillan credit for getting free hay for local farmers during a summer drought. A third played up a textile-import bill he introduced after it became clear that Martin would portray him as a do-nothing.

Each report cost taxpayers more than $26,000 for printing and bulk-rate mailing. Not a dime had to come from McMillan's campaign funds. He didn't even have to affix address labels. To convert postal clerks to McMillan campaign workers, all he had to do was print on each one: "Postal Customer—Local, 9th Congressional District, North Carolina."

McMillan wasn't alone, of course. House members mailed a total of 461 million pieces during 1986, costing $60 million. The Senate spent $35.5 million to mail 298 million pieces. Costs were racing ahead of the rise in population and postal rates. During 1985–86 Congress appropriated seven times more money to cover its own postage than it did in 1971–72. Congressmen generated most of that volume and expense themselves, sending fifteen letters for every one they received.

Most Republicans and many Democrats attacked proposals for public financing of election campaigns as wasteful and wrong, saying it wouldn't be right to tax money away from citizens for use in propagating views with which they might disagree. Nevertheless, lawmakers had turned the franking privilege into an enormous system of public campaign financing, available only to incumbents and costing nearly $100 million a year for postage alone, plus additional millions for staff time, computers, and printing costs.

The expense of McMillan's official mail was nearly as large as the entire Martin campaign budget. Martin countered it the same way he fought McMillan's advantage in PAC money, calling a news conference to announce another reform plan. Standing before a Charlotte post office to provide a backdrop for TV cameras, he proposed to limit incumbents to spending $110,000 on mail. Coverage was lukewarm. "McMillan's Mail Privileges Irk D. G. Martin," read the headline on a story inside the Charlotte *Observer.* "His image as a whiner is becoming pretty apparent," said the congressman's campaign manager, Chris Henick.

Martin still resisted Coelho's urgings about "going negative." Too many of Martin's backers knew both men personally and would resent suggestions that McMillan was unethical. Martin explained: "We've got a base of 45 percent of the folks who will vote for me, regardless. And he's got a base of 45 percent who will vote for him, whatever he does. So we're competing for 10 percent. But I'll lose 5 percent of mine if I become a bad guy."

Martin rejected negative advertising even of the mildest sort. His staff proposed a jab at McMillan's astute refusal to debate Martin on television, a medium in which the boyish Martin inevitably made the incumbent look stiff. McMillan agreed only to a single TV debate, turning down fourteen invitations to other confrontations, by Martin's count. Martin's advisers wanted to run television ads implying that McMillan was a political coward. Martin rejected a script that called for him to sit on a stool next to an actor wearing a cloth hood over his head and fidgeting uncomfortably. "This is my opponent, the Phantom Congressman," Martin was to say. "Isn't *political courage* and a frank, open discussion of the *issues* something you *deserve* in deciding how you'll vote?" Martin was to lean close to the hooded "McMillan" and softly say "Boo!"—causing him to flinch and nearly fall off his perch.

The commercials that Martin did run were entirely positive. "He's fought special interests for three years," the announcer said in one. "Everyone's agreeing now: special interests are ruining the Congress." McMillan was being totally positive, too. His ads framed him as "our hardworking, effective congressman." North Carolina voters weren't accustomed to such gentlemanly sparring. "Are clean campaigns dull?" asked the Charlotte *Observer*'s editorial-page chief, Jerry Shinn, in a mid-September column. "Maybe we're too jaded to appreciate clean campaigns," he wrote.

Martin's message was getting through, however. "I like both men, but D. G. Martin has worked hard," one voter told McMillan's poll takers. "I just hate to see a hard worker like that not get elected." Said another, "He is intelligent and I like the way he conducted his campaign. . . . He has behaved as a perfect gentleman."

In mid-September, McMillan's own polling showed him leading Martin 52 to 42 percent, but Martin made steady progress during the closing weeks. On October 23, another McMillan survey showed him behind for the first time since taking office, trailing Martin 45 to 46 percent. A poll published the following day in the *Observer* gave the same numbers, except that McMillan led, 46 to 45 percent. With only two weeks to go, it was a dead-even race, and Martin was gaining.

This time, unlike 1984, Martin was being helped by the top of the ticket. The Republican candidate for the Senate, James Broyhill, was stumbling badly. Former governor Terry Sanford, despite his sixty-nine years, was coming off as livelier and more folksy. President Reagan came into

Charlotte on a rescue mission, but the polling results continued to worsen. "We watched Broyhill's numbers falling, and we were getting hit with the shrapnel," recalled McMillan's press secretary, Jay Timmons.

Coelho still wasn't spending party money to support Martin. "We believe that we have not been dealt with fairly and upfront," campaign manager Doss complained in a letter to Tom King. King wanted the campaign to spend more money on television. Doss said that without Coelho's funds the campaign would buy 1,100 gross rating points of TV time during the last five weeks before election day, enough so that the typical viewer would see a Martin commercial eleven times. If Coelho's money came through, he said the campaign would make a 2,200-point buy, costing $122,000. Coelho still hesitated, insisting that the campaign agree to a $6,000 poll; he wasn't going to waste money on Martin if he was too far behind. When Martin's poll showed him closing the gap to single digits, Coelho relented.

Even then, Coelho's support was considerably less than the full legal maximum he had promised. The law permitted him to spend $53,620 for Martin. He did buy $12,000 worth of broadcast time for Martin and spent $7,000 for a last-minute mailing to voters. In all, counting the cash contributions he had made in April and an in-kind donation of production time from his studio during September, he put $31,768 behind Martin's campaign, just 59 percent of the limit.

It was much the same with other challengers; Coelho's first priority was protecting incumbents. Frank McCloskey of Indiana, the man Coelho had saved in a controversial recount two years earlier, received $47,000 in aid. This time he won with 53 percent. Richard Stallings of Idaho, a freshman Democrat in a heavily Republican district, received $43,000 in aid and won narrowly. Coelho gave substantial help even to some incumbents who didn't need it. Rep. Les AuCoin of Oregon, who constantly pressed Coelho for aid, got nearly $42,000 although he faced a challenger who polled only 38 percent of the vote. Majority Leader Jim

Wright, who would receive 69 percent of the vote, got $10,000 worth of Coelho's off-the-shelf television ads.

McMillan had twice as much money as Martin overall, and spent four times as much on radio and television advertising through mid-October. He started his main barrage of advertising a full week before Martin had aired a single commercial. His advantage in early advertising probably kept him from sliding further and allowed him to go into the last week of the campaign even with Martin, rather than as an underdog.

The Republican's money also gave him better political intelligence. He had the benefit of ten polls, counting three paid for by the National Republican Congressional Committee. He took one per week during the last month, whereas Martin had only two.

McMillan's special-interest funding had one disadvantage; it made him a target for Martin's attacks. But Martin had trouble exploiting the incumbent's weakness for special-interest money because of his own party's dependence on PACs and soft money. Among the celebrities who came to Martin's aid was Jim Wright, who was taking in $630,970 from PACs for his own token re-election campaign, more than any other House member. Wright also ran a personal political action committee, Majority Congress Committee, through which he dispensed $392,000 to fellow Democrats during the 1986 elections to further his ambition to become Speaker. Wright thoughtlessly sent Martin an unsolicited $2,500 check from the PAC, despite Martin's well-publicized refusal of all PAC donations. The candidate returned the gift, and asked Wright to make a campaign appearance for him in Charlotte instead.

Similarly, Martin was hit by friendly fire from a liberal ally, the Committee for a Sane Nuclear Policy. SANE was a tax-exempt group lobbying to cut military spending, deny aid to anti-Communist rebels in Nicaragua, and stop U.S. production of nuclear weapons. It also ran a PAC, which endorsed Martin but, at his request, didn't give any money. SANE did, however, furnish Martin with help in registering voters, using tax-exempt, unreported money for electioneering in a way that was becoming increasingly common, especially in support of Democrats. Unfortunately for Martin, his supporters at SANE stumbled while attempting the intricate footwork required to make their maneuver legal.

SANE's executive director for North Carolina, Norris Frederick, sent invitations to an October 11 reception at his home for Martin. In it he said, "Charlotte SANE has employed two workers for this crucial race, Kimberly Reynolds and Joe Sistare. Kimberly and Joe have organized dozens of SANE volunteers who are working every day to win this election." He said the two employees had organized hundreds of hours of work by volunteers, recording information from voter files at the local Elections Bureau, knocking on doors to register voters, and calling SANE members urging them to volunteer for Martin's campaign.

Nationally, SANE functioned as part of the Democratic party's liberal wing. It endorsed 125 candidates for 1986, only 5 of them Republicans. Boasting that it "may be the smartest PAC going," SANE explained its strategy in its national newsletter: "The plan is elegant in its simplicity. First, SANE PAC identifies like-minded candidates in key districts. Then, instead of simply pouring money into a campaign, SANE PAC hires professional organizers to mobilize the local peace community behind the candidate. . . . The candidates also agree to make peace issues a part of their campaign and if they win, to establish a peace issues advisory council made up of local peace activists and meet with them regularly after taking office."

SANE sent money into campaigns in much the same way as business lobbyists and corporate PACs. A central element of its fund-raising and organizing strategy was what it called the "Adopt a District" program. "This provides an opportunity for SANE supporters in more liberal and progressive regions of the country to bring peace issues to the forefront in less progressive districts," said the group's literature. "Freeze activists in Massachusetts have already raised $10,000 to support peace work in Arkansas and North Carolina." This was exactly the sort of alien influence that Martin said his PAC-reform plan was designed to correct.

Because Martin refused PAC funds, SANE's PAC couldn't hire people to do purely campaign work as it did for other Democrats. Through its tax-exempt entity, however, it could still legally urge its own members to vote for Martin, and it could register blacks or nuclear-freeze advocates and urge them to vote, so long as it maintained a pose of non-partisanship and didn't ask whom the prospective voters would support. SANE workers also could be as partisan as they pleased on their own time, as volunteers. But these fine distinctions hadn't been scrupulously observed in Martin's case, as McMillan's aides learned when a copy of Frederick's letter fell into their hands.

McMillan's handlers brought two senior party officials from Washington to accuse Martin and SANE of breaking the law. Joseph Gaylord, executive director of the National Republican Congressional Committee, said, "D. G. Martin is a complete hypocrite. . . . He has stridently declared his opposition to and independence from special interest groups and PACs, yet he has been taking contributions from among the most liberal and dogmatic of them." Jan Baran, the GOP committee's top legal hand, outlined a complaint he was filing with the Federal Election Commission.

A year later SANE's Norris Frederick paid a $1,000 fine after admitting in an affidavit that the two employees worked twenty-one days registering voters and that one worked on SANE time to recruit precinct captains for Martin. The FEC closed the case without questioning any witnesses or going over SANE's books, although the legal staff said the matter warranted further investigation into where SANE obtained its funds. The commission quickly cleared Martin. He swore in an affidavit that he thought the SANE employees were volunteers like "thousands of others" who worked in his campaign. But the case wasn't closed until long after the election, and the matter caused him some painful political damage. It attracted attention to his liberal views, and even tarnished his clean-government image a bit. "I think D. G. Martin is crooked," one voter declared to McMillan's poll taker after the allegations were aired.

That was October 30. Martin's "favorable" rating had dropped sharply in the week since the previous poll, to 57 percent, from 64 percent, reflecting not only the SANE controversy but the effect of McMillan's heavy advertising schedule, in which he had begun attacking Martin personally. Voters with an unfavorable impression of Martin increased to 23 percent, from 17 percent. McMillan, who had been running a point behind Martin a week earlier, opened a one-point lead. Now 47 percent said they would vote for the incumbent, 46 percent for Martin.

Martin was learning the bitter truth of Boss Plunkitt's description of political reformers. "They were morning glories," the old pol said. "Looked lovely in the mornin' and withered up in a short time, while the regular machines went on flourishin' forever, like fine old oaks."

Martin lost, this time by 4,112 votes out of 156,592 cast, and didn't seek the office again.

13

"Wrestling with a Bunch of Bears"

The men who put through the primary law are the same crowd that stand up for the civil service blight and they have the same objects in view—the destruction of governments by party, the downfall of the constitution and hell generally.

—GEORGE WASHINGTON PLUNKITT

D. G. Martin wasn't the only Democratic reformer to give Coelho headaches. Senator David Boren of Oklahoma was advancing a proposal to put a modest limit on special-interest money in House and Senate elections.

Boren was living proof that reformers didn't always wilt; he had a flinty resolve to do something to cure a sick political system. But that was making him an unpopular man with PAC managers, with Republican party officials, and with leaders of his own party.

While Coelho had learned the business of politics as an apprentice, Boren had been born to it as the son of an Oklahoma congressman. He studied at Yale and was chosen for a Rhodes scholarship to Oxford. But with that cosmopolitan background he took a law degree at the University of Oklahoma and settled in Seminole, his eye on a career in politics. He was part professor, part practitioner. He won election to the Oklahoma legislature at age twenty-six, and then became chairman of the Department of Government at Oklahoma Baptist University.

Boren learned early that clean-government crusaders aren't always appreciated by their party. As a freshman state legislator he offered a bill to stop the practice of putting large, interest-free deposits of state money in banks managed by political allies of the incumbents. Hours after Boren introduced the bill, the state treasurer removed all state funds from the banks in Seminole County. He sent word that the free money would be redeposited when Boren left office.

Boren also sponsored a bill to force the legislature to conduct its business in public view. He had seen officials smash cameras of reform-minded citizens who tried to record vote results as they flashed briefly on an electronic tally board. The legislature didn't keep a record of those roll-call results, so citizens couldn't hold individual lawmakers accountable. For sponsoring the open-meeting bill Boren was stripped of a subcommittee chairmanship, removed from the influential Rules Committee, and exiled to an office on the attic-like fifth floor of the statehouse.

But Boren's crusading paid off. In 1974, just thirty-three years old, he ran for governor against a sitting incumbent. The nation was recoiling from the aroma of a political system being exposed by the Watergate hearings. In Oklahoma, Gov. David Hall was embroiled in another scandal, which eventually sent him to jail. Boren ran on a clean-government platform and won.

He remained a reformer when he ran for a vacant Senate seat in 1978. He refused to accept money from PACs. Unlike the more reticent D. G. Martin, Boren attacked his foes for their ties to outside bankrollers. In the primary runoff he faced Rep. Ed Edmondson, who took PAC donations. Boren ran a television commercial in which a list slowly rolled across the screen showing out-of-state PACs that had given to Edmondson. "We picked groups that looked like they had hostile interest to Oklahoma's farmers and oilmen," Boren recalled. One was described as "The Seafarers Union of

Brooklyn, N.Y." Oklahoma's farmers disliked New Yorkers, labor unions, and the maritime lobby's perennial efforts to require that American grain exports be hauled in high-cost, unionized U.S. ships.

Ironically, early in 1983 Boren found himself sitting in a seafarers' classroom listening to a seminar on techniques for raising money from PACs. The Democratic Senatorial Campaign Committee was holding a weekend retreat for senators at the union's seaman-training campus in rural southern Maryland. Senators up for re-election in 1984 were being briefed by their party's political experts on how to run successful campaigns. Things had changed since 1978, the experts said. Volunteers and hoopla were out; money and paid consultants were in. PACs had the money, and the lobbyists' pockets were ripe for picking.

That seminar floored Boren. He recalled toying with the idea of quietly dropping his anti-PAC policy. Watergate was a fading memory, campaigns were growing terribly expensive, and there wasn't likely to be much criticism from any Republican candidate, who would surely be taking PAC money, too. But Boren was repelled by the eager performance of a young party official who had raised PAC money for a Senate Democrat in the previous election. "This kid was incredible," Boren recalled. "I think he got contributions from 900 PACs."

The advice: Send polls showing you are ahead; PACs give to winners. Play one industry off against another. "You'd show the S&Ls that the banks had given." Bankers couldn't afford to be frozen out of your office when the next banking bill was up. Raising PAC donations was a matter of selling access.

"I was left feeling almost unclean," Boren recalled. "I wanted to go home and take a bath." His wife, Molly, was with him and was also sickened. "This wasn't what we got into politics for," he said. He stuck with his no-PAC policy.

That meant more work for Boren. As a member of the tax-writing Finance Committee, he knew that lobbyists would make PAC donations if he asked. But eventually he raised $1.2 million, all from individual donors. Much of it came from wealthy Oklahoma oil drillers whose tax advantages he had defended on the Finance Committee. But Boren also cast his net widely for small dollars, increasing his political popularity in the process. He held about 200 public meetings all over the state, asking both for votes and for funds at every stop. His person-to-person style proved so effective that he hardly needed the money. The Republicans fielded a token opponent who spent less than $7,000 and received 23 percent of the vote, even while Ronald Reagan was carrying the state with 69 percent.

Boren began his second Senate term determined to do more than merely represent Oklahoma's parochial interests. At the top of his legislative agenda was reform of the campaign-finance system. He had proposed a modest bill before, only to watch it die without a hearing. He introduced it again, vowing this time to make a fight.

It was a lonely struggle at first. Boren lacked support from any colleague or organized group. He didn't even have a seat on the Rules Committee, which had jurisdiction over campaign-finance bills. His proposal was modest, imposing some limits on the totals that candidates could accept from PACs and increasing the amount of money that individuals could give. Some senators had raised more than $1 million from PACs in their most recent elections, and not many House members were inclined to tinker with a system that guaranteed their re-election better than 90 percent of the time. Boren's anti-PAC legislation seemed like a political fantasy.

Still, House and Senate members complained constantly about the amount of time they spent calling donors and courting lobbyists for gifts. Hometown editorial pages were sniping at them for taking PAC money. Washington reporters kept asking questions about the parties' secret soft-money donors. Boren's tactic was to capitalize on the growing embarrassment by forcing the Senate to vote on his proposal. Opposing it would be seen as a vote in favor of PACs, and vice versa. In such a popularity contest, the PACs could well lose.

Boren wouldn't allow his bill to suffocate in the Rules Committee again. Instead, he offered his plan as an amendment to the unlikeliest of measures, the "Compact of Free Association," an obscure bill to ratify a settlement of claims by Marshall Islanders stemming from U.S. nuclear tests in the Pacific years earlier. Its virtue was that the Senate had to pass it; the bill would also extend an agreement allowing the United States to test missiles in the western Pacific range between California and Kwajalein. That agreement had already lapsed by a day when the Senate got to the bill on October 2. The Pentagon wanted it renewed, and quickly.

To satisfy Senate procedures, Boren inserted some otherwise pointless words in his PAC proposal to make it arguably relevant to the test-range bill. He rose on the Senate floor to announce that he would insist on a vote.

"It has some reference to Micronesia," he explained.

"Do they have a PAC?" asked GOP Majority Leader Bob Dole.

Boren's move startled fellow Democrats. Party leader Robert Byrd of West Virginia went directly to Boren on the Senate floor and said, "David, Senators Mitchell and I and others want to see you in my office about this rather quickly." He was glaring.

Byrd led Boren off the Senate floor to the Lyndon B. Johnson Room, where fellow Democrats grilled him for more than an hour about his anti-PAC bill. Present were George Mitchell of Maine, chairman of the Democratic Senatorial Campaign Committee, and two former chairmen of the campaign committee, Wendell Ford of Kentucky and Lloyd Bentsen of Texas. Their message, as Boren recalled it, boiled down to this:

"You're putting our guys, who are desperate to raise money, on the spot. They don't want to vote in favor of PACs. But on the other hand, they have to go and raise money from PACs."

Mitchell was particularly torn. He personally favored a combination of public financing and spending limits. But he thought such a measure had no chance of passage. Meanwhile the senatorial committee needed PAC money for itself and for its candidates. Mitchell's committee was even more dependent on PACs than Coelho's. It had done much less over the years to find small donors. Senate Republicans, on the other hand, were amassing the largest political war chest the nation had ever seen, $80 million, mainly from hundreds of thousands of small donors giving $50 and $100 at a time.

Boren emerged from the LBJ Room a bit shaken. "They were just pleading, 'Don't put us in this spot,'" he said. He told his aide, Greg Kubiak, "I feel like I've been wrestling with a bunch of bears."

Boren didn't get his vote that day. Dole had to pull the Micronesia compact off the floor because several other senators were trying to attach pet proposals as well. But Boren began to attract some surprising allies.

One co-sponsor he recruited was a mainstream Republican from Kansas, Nancy Kassebaum, daughter of Alf Landon, the GOP's presidential nominee against Franklin Roosevelt in 1936. Boren also landed two liberal Democrats, Gary Hart of Colorado and Carl Levin of Michigan.

The real prize, however, was Barry Goldwater of Arizona. Goldwater had been griping about the campaign-finance system for years, pushing ideas ranging from the impractical to the eccentric. Far from favoring public financing of congressional elections, he wanted to repeal it for presidential campaigns. One of his ideas was to legislate shorter presidential campaigns by forbidding candidates from raising or spending money before June 1 of an election year. Goldwater also favored imposing severe limits on spending by candidates—$100,000 total for a House campaign, regardless of the source. Goldwater's own bill was going nowhere, and he agreed to join forces with the Oklahoman.

Recruiting Goldwater was a coup; he was so conservative he was considered by many to be an extremist when he won

the party's 1964 presidential nomination. Now he was joining with the likes of Gary Hart in an assault on PAC money.
True, he was frail, old, cantankerous, and had announced
he was retiring from politics after 1986. In the twilight of his
career he found himself cut off politically from the younger
breed of New Right Republicans. But nobody dared say
Goldwater wasn't a conservative. Disgust with the PAC system was cutting across both party and ideological lines.

Common Cause joined as well. The liberal citizens group,
which then claimed about 250,000 dues-paying members,
had been pushing for public funding of House and Senate
campaigns for more than a decade. Boren didn't like public
financing and didn't provide for any in his bill, one of the
reasons that Goldwater was able to embrace it. But Common Cause was starved for a legislative victory. It hadn't
been able to force a floor vote on any campaign-finance bill
since an unsuccessful battle in 1978. Its president, Ar-
chibald Cox, praised Boren's bill nonetheless, saying it
"strikes at the heart of the evil" and is necessary "if we are
to save government by the people."

After the Common Cause press conference, Boren attracted another conservative ally, Democrat John Stennis
of Mississippi. He was the oldest of all the senators, and had
been in office longer than any of them, since 1947. He was
an unlikely reformer, having been among the few who
voted against public financing of presidential campaigns
after Watergate. But the courtly Stennis was growing dis-
mayed with the money-raising frenzy that gripped his
younger colleagues. Perhaps, too, he was shocked at how
money had allowed Republicans to challenge the one-party
system in Mississippi. GOP candidate Haley Barbour spent
$1.1 million against him in 1980, forcing the ex-segregation-
ist Stennis to campaign for black votes as never before.
Stennis won with 64 percent of the vote after spending
$944,000 himself, 24 percent of it from PACs.

"I feel that under the present law that we have now, we
are gradually moving the elections away from the people as
certain as night follows day," Stennis said. He said his own

people understood and distrusted this trend. "Those of us who have been around here for a while know that government does not come easy," he said. "It is perhaps getting more difficult. We had better stick to the fundamentals."

For all the grand talk, however, Boren's bill didn't really propose to do very much. It would for the first time limit the total amount of money congressional candidates could take from PACs: $100,000 for House candidates and between $175,000 and $750,000 for Senate candidates, depending on the size of the state, plus additional amounts in case of contested primaries or runoff elections. The maximum that any one PAC could give would be cut to $3,000 per election, from $5,000. But individuals would be allowed to give more, $1,500 per election, up from $1,000.

George Mitchell got Boren to include language to close the bundling loophole. But this was less out of zeal for reform than out of partisan self-interest. In the 1984 campaigns the National Republican Senatorial Committee had used bundling to funnel an extra $3.5 million to its Senate candidates, above and beyond the amounts it was allowed to spend for them directly. This hadn't attracted much public notice, but it was clear enough to Democratic party officials that unless the loophole was closed, Republicans could pump money to their candidates without limit.

Some of the most serious problems in the campaign-finance system received no attention at all in the Boren proposal. It did nothing about strengthening the Federal Election Commission's enforcement apparatus, making it likely that PACs and candidates would be evading the new limits as soon as they were enacted. The bill didn't restrict soft money or even require its disclosure. It left open loopholes allowing a whole range of abuses, everything from the pocketing of leftover campaign cash by retiring incumbents to financing with uncollateralized loans from friendly bankers. And Boren's proposal wouldn't take effect until after the 1986 elections.

But in its very modesty lay its genius. Because it would change so little, it was difficult to attack on substantive grounds. It became a symbol, mostly hollow but nevertheless powerful. If there were few strong reasons to vote for it, there were even fewer for opposing it. Even so, Boren assumed the proposal would be defeated, and so did nearly everybody else.

Republicans were mostly against it. They clung to the idea that the tide of PAC money favored their party. Their lawyers also saw that Mitchell's anti-bundling language would restrict their plans for evading limits on the use of party funds. Bob Dole, however, was preparing to run for President in 1988 and was reluctant to be depicted as a defender of special-interest money. Years earlier, he had been quoted by the *Wall Street Journal:* "When the political action committees give money, they expect something in return other than good government." That quote was cycled over and over by PAC critics as testimony to the insidious nature of special-interest money. But Dole also ran a PAC of his own, Campaign America, and was raising more than $1 million from PACs to finance his own re-election. Later he would raise nearly as much for his presidential effort as well.

Dole could have ruled the PAC proposal out of order on grounds that it had nothing to do with Micronesia. Boren was on soft parliamentary ground there. But Boren made it clear that he would try to tack his PAC amendment onto bill after bill until Dole relented. He called for negotiations, bringing in Stennis and Goldwater to help persuade the Majority Leader. Boren offered to let the Micronesia bill go through if Dole would allow a vote on the PAC measure as an amendment to another bill. Dole turned to an aide and said, "Find me a vehicle. We're going to get a vote."

Debate began December 2. By then Boren's amendment was attracting much more attention than the bill on which it would ride, a routine measure to ratify an agreement between several states on disposal of nuclear waste. Scores of editorials had appeared in newspapers around the country, inspired by a massive publicity campaign generated by Common Cause. "Cut Back on PAC Monies," said the Brookings (S.D.) *Daily Register.* "Limit PAC Receipts Now or Put Democracy at Risk," said the Bethlehem (Pa.) *Globe-Times.* "PAC Explosion Poses Dangers," said the Seattle *Post-Intelligencer.* "Time to Stop PACs," said the Kansas City *Times.* It seemed every senator had several home-state newspapers ready to denounce him if he voted down Boren's proposal.

Democratic leader Byrd, who two months earlier had asked Boren to holster his PAC proposal, now made a public display of requesting to be included as a co-sponsor. "I ... thank him for offering this legislation," Byrd said on the Senate floor. "I compliment him. I hope it will be adopted."

Opponents were hard to find on the floor of the Senate that day. Republican John Heinz of Pennsylvania carried the resistance practically alone. As the new chairman of the National Republican Senatorial Committee, he was planning a more aggressive bundling operation than the $3.5 million gambit of 1984; it would eventually send into Senate campaigns nearly $10 million in excess of the limits, according to an internal tally by chief fund-raiser Rodney Smith. More than $6 million of that would be apparent from the GOP committee's public reports. The GOP bundling effort would be one of the most massive and open circumventions of election law ever attempted, and would prompt an inquiry by the Federal Election Commission that would drag on, unresolved, well into 1988.

Even Heinz didn't attack the Boren plan directly. "What we are not talking about is campaign-finance reform," he said. "We are talking about PAC limitations." Heinz, not previously known as a reformer, offered an old Republican plan to remove all limits on party spending for candidates. This would clearly diminish the potency of PACs by expanding the influence of parties, but Democrats, unable to tap small donors the way Republicans could, refused to consider it. Heinz said that the Senate needed more time and that the Boren measure contained hidden flaws.

Boren was picking up strength, but counted no more than thirty-five senators in favor of his amendment. Indeed, on the morning of December 3, when debate resumed for the final two hours provided by Dole's agreement, the Washington *Post* unexpectedly editorialized against the PAC-limit bill, calling it unenforceable. "If the history of campaign spending regulation has provided any lesson it is that the politicians and their legal advisers and would-be purchasers never run out of ingenious ways to turn the new regulations to their advantage," the *Post* said. "Full disclosure and vigorous debate remain the best hope for an honest process." It was a surprising editorial because the *Post* was usually allied with liberal Democrats. Later it would begin crusading for even more stringent limits than those being proposed in Boren's bill. But for the moment it was siding with Heinz.

More setbacks followed. Goldwater's wife was dying, so he couldn't be present to speak for Boren's amendment. A leading Democrat, Alan Cranston of California, said the Boren measure would force senators to spend even more time raising money, to replace the missing PAC funds. Lowell Weicker, a liberal Republican who had served on the Senate Watergate committee, called Boren's plan "an independent expenditure proliferation amendment." He argued that PACs wouldn't dry up because of Boren's limits, but would merely spend their money in different ways, like the NRA's independent assault against D. G. Martin in 1984. "The only clear beneficiaries are the attorneys who will be paid to get around its restrictions," Weicker said.

For a time it seemed doubtful that Boren would even get the vote he had been promised. Just before debate resumed he heard a rumor that Dole might go back on his word by declaring that the PAC rider wasn't germane to the nuclear-waste bill. Dole previously had read the amendment without objection in the presence of Boren, Goldwater, and Stennis. "There was a gentleman's understanding," said Boren, "so I went boiling over to Dole's office." He left word with a Dole aide: "You tell him that if he tries to raise a point of order I intend to call Goldwater and Stennis on the floor as witnesses as to what the gentlemen's agreement was. And then I intend to give a speech several hours long about the meaning of the term 'gentleman.' "

The threat seemed to eliminate any idea of delaying a vote. Heinz announced to the Senate that he wouldn't raise such a challenge, "even though I think a point of order ... might technically be correct." But Boren still didn't have enough supporters. As he left the floor after the debate, he told a reporter he would be pleased to get forty votes.

Democrats and Republicans withdrew from the floor to meet at separate luncheons, where the debate continued behind closed doors. Boren found that many of his Democratic colleagues still resented being put on the spot. The *New York Times* had editorialized a day earlier: "The question tomorrow is one of principle. The PACs, with their deep pockets and narrow interests, wield a great power in politics. Which senators want to control it?" Boren said one colleague complained during the lunch: "I've had to be for this thing, but any of you that don't have to should vote to kill it, for the benefit of the rest of us."

But few volunteered. Boren said later, "I've never had so many votes for something and so much criticism at the same time." However sullenly, most Democrats were swinging to Boren's plan.

Among the Republicans, Heinz advanced a purely partisan argument. "He saw great dangers in the Boren amendment," said Rhode Island Republican John Chafee. "He felt very strongly that it was just the death knell for Republican candidates if the PAC contributions should be reduced." Publicly, Heinz was calling for broad reform. Privately, he argued that PAC money was good for his party.

Republicans were deferring to Heinz as their election-money expert. He had been chairman of the campaign committee during the victorious 1980 campaigns and was now heading it for the second time. "His voice had the voice of the oracle," Chafee recalled. "There seemed to be no objection to what he was saying." Chafee, however, warned that Republicans were making a serious mistake.

"I just think that we're nuts," he said. "Frankly, I think it's right. It's right to reduce the contributions from a single PAC down from $5,000 to $3,000. There's danger in these PACs getting too much of a say."

He pointed out the flaw in Heinz's argument. "It's all nonsense," he said. "It's the Democrats who receive most of the PAC contributions." And he reminded his colleagues that PACs are unpopular with voters. "Far better to be on the side of the angels," he said.

Chafee's argument routed Heinz in his own camp. Rather than risk defeat, Republicans chose delay. Dole announced that he would vote against the tabling motion, and said he was ready to enter negotiations on a broader bill that both parties could support. He called for hearings in the Rules Committee on both the Boren proposal and several other plans, including the GOP's perennial blueprint for unshackled political parties. Now he was talking like a crusader himself. "There is near-unanimous support for campaign-finance reform," he said. "The system cries for reform."

To Heinz now fell a most embarrassing task. "I am going to make a motion to table in a minute," he said. "And I am going to ask all my colleagues to vote against the motion." In the end only seven senators voted for Heinz's motion to kill Boren's amendment, including six Republicans and Democrat Edward Zorinsky of Nebraska. Eighty-four senators voted against Heinz's motion, including Heinz himself.

To some, the 84–7 vote showed that nearly every senator was fed up with the system and wanted reform. But in truth it meant that eighty-four senators were afraid to vote against even a weak, symbolic bill without any practical method of enforcement. Neither party was keen on altering the system if doing so could conceivably give the other party an edge. The true enemy of reform wasn't the special interests; it was narrow partisanship.

Even some of Boren's co-sponsors considered PACs to be little more than a public-relations problem. Arizona Democrat Dennis DeConcini added his name to the Boren bill two

days after Goldwater. But he said, "I do not believe that
PACs are insidious by their very nature. . . . I take PAC
money. In my last campaign, about 17 percent of the total
contributions I received came from PAC money. I received
money from labor PACs, from the Realtor PACs, from business PACs, and I am always pleased to have those dollars."
Another Boren co-sponsor, Democrat Carl Levin of Michigan, said that "the problem caused by the growing influence of PACs in Senate and House elections is principally
a problem of appearances."

The public-relations problem, however, was growing
worse, and an election year was coming up. Common Cause
continued to promote pro-Boren editorials around the country. By the end of March it had collected more than 150 of
them.

With Democrats controlling the House and Republicans
running the Senate and the White House, any real fix of the
system would require negotiations by leaders of both parties. No campaign-finance bill had ever been passed without two-party consensus. Leaders said they would try. "We
need to reform the system," Dole said after the 84–7 vote in
December. "I am certainly willing, if we can work out some
bipartisan way to approach it."

The outlines of a workable compromise were clear
enough. Republicans wanted parties to get much greater
freedom to finance their own candidates. That such a
move constituted reform was logically irrefutable; the
more a candidate got from the party, the less reliant on
PACs. The Holmes–St Germain contest would provide evidence enough that restricting the parties only strengthened the grip of moneyed interests. The only objection,
which would somehow have to be addressed, was that
Democrats had failed to attract much financial support
from their own rank and file and couldn't afford to let
Republicans use their money freely.

Democrats, too, had some appealing ideas. A strong Democratic faction favored incentives to encourage small donations from individuals. The House, in fact, passed a measure

in December 1985 to give a 100 percent tax credit for small donations—up to $100—to House and Senate candidates. The idea came from Richard Conlon, staff director of the Democratic Study Group, the in-house think tank for liberal House Democrats. He had worked on it for years, lining up enough moderate Republican allies to qualify the tax-credit plan as a genuine bipartisan effort. Coelho supported it too, figuring it would allow perhaps twenty to thirty more of his underfinanced challengers to raise enough money to mount credible threats to incumbent Republicans.

The possibility of a broader bipartisan bill, perhaps restraining PACs while encouraging political parties and small donors, seemed tantalizingly close. But the desire of incumbents for change was too weak, and partisan positions too hardened, to permit even a mild compromise to emerge. Democrats, concerned mostly about a mere image problem and dealing from financial weakness, wouldn't consider the GOP's arguments for deregulating political party finances. Liberal Democrats wanted public funding of House and Senate elections to negate the Republican advantage in party finances and the influence of business PACs. They were content to wait in hopes that a Democrat would capture the White House in 1988. Most Republicans remained emotionally wedded to business PACs, and opposed limits on them.

Two-party compromise got little more than lip service. Dole announced he would appoint a "task force" of Republicans to negotiate with a similar group of Democrats. Byrd chose a group of Democratic senators almost immediately, but they found no Republicans to talk to. Month after month, Dole delayed in selecting the GOP panel.

The Rules Committee held public hearings as promised, on January 22 and March 27, covering Boren's bill and six other campaign-finance measures ranging from public financing to unlimited party spending. But the chairman of the committee, Republican Charles Mathias of Maryland, couldn't round up the senators needed for a quorum. Not enough Republicans showed up, so nothing emerged.

Boren kept pressing Dole to bring his amendment back to the floor again. But it wasn't until the end of June that Dole agreed to allow two days of debate sometime before the Senate's scheduled recess for Labor Day. With that, Dole at last appointed Republican members of a task force to talk about a compromise, half a year after he first promised to do so.

As the head of that group he chose a senator who saw very little wrong with the campaign-finance system, Rudy Boschwitz of Minnesota. Boschwitz, like Coelho, was using fund-raising as his route upward. He had made millions in the lumber business in Minnesota, where he would appear in television commercials for his string of stores, wearing his trademark, a red-plaid lumberjack shirt. He named his own political fund Plaid PAC. For years before he got into politics he raised money for cancer and kidney foundations and the United Jewish Appeal. "I've given a lot of money," he said, "and I don't mind asking for it." He was aiming to succeed Heinz as head of the National Republican Senatorial Committee.

Boschwitz had written and circulated an exceptionally revealing fourteen-page memo on how he had raised and spent $6 million getting re-elected in 1984. The memo was supposed to be confidential, but extensive excerpts were published in the *Wall Street Journal*. It constituted a refreshingly honest, unstudied self-portrait of a successful practitioner of the modern business of politics.

Boschwitz's advice: Raise a million or two early. Don't release your income-tax returns if they might reveal a possible conflict of interest. Don't waste time giving speeches or debating the challenger, and especially beware of debates sponsored by such hostile groups as the League of Women Voters. "Mix in the Chamber of Commerce," he said. He recommended not talking to the press while buying lots of advertising. Hold your fund-raising events at a cheap hotel to save money, he said.

Boschwitz, who typed the document personally, said he gathered funds to avoid competition: "Nobody in politics (except me!) likes to raise money, so I thought the best way of discouraging the toughest opponents from running was to have a few dollars in the sock. *I believe it worked."* Boschwitz had raised $1.5 million before the start of 1984, and Minnesota's most electable Democrats stayed out of the race. He ran television commercials even before he had any opponent. "We bought TV time à la Budweiser," he said. *"From all forms of fund-raising I raised $6 million plus and got 3 or 4 (maybe even 5) stories and cartoons that irked me,"* he said. "In retrospect, I'm glad I had the money."

PACs helped the Republican Boschwitz win election and re-election in Hubert Humphrey's home state, the only one that voted against Ronald Reagan in 1984. To him, Boren's aversion to special-interest money was incomprehensible and his PAC-limit bill was as baffling as a glyph from some long-vanished race of scholars.

Even as Dole was appointing him to negotiate with Boren, Boschwitz was squeezing PACs for donations to fellow Republicans. He sent a letter to PACs saying, "I solicit your ideas and views. I urge you to stay in touch with me and my staff. Unfortunately, I know the pace of Senate activities makes it hard for me to be as totally accessible as I would like to be. So feel free to contact Steve Gordon, who . . . is my liaison to the PAC community."

In Boschwitz's office, sale of access was open and institutionalized. He was already raising money for a re-election race in 1990, five years away. Ever the innovative salesman, he invented special stamps for campaign donors to affix to their letters, which he promised to give preference over letters from non-donors. Members of his "Washington Club"—those who promised to give $1,000—got ten blue-colored stamps. "Skinnycats," givers of $99 per year or less, received access stamps with different markings. Boschwitz retained his enthusiasm for the access stamps even after reformers criticized him for the idea. Speaking to the Greater Minneapolis Chamber of Commerce, he said, "Common Cause says this is a way to buy a senator. You ought to try. My campaign needs the money."

Boschwitz later declared to the Senate, "I do not begin to buy the argument that senators and congressmen are for sale. I am certainly not for sale, and I think that I can speak for the rest of my colleagues when I say they are not for sale either." To him PACs were just good-government groups. His Minnesota colleague, Republican David Durenberger, called PACs "the United Way of politics."

Negotiations between Democrats and Republicans were perfunctory and failed to produce any compromise. But Dole had given his word that Boren's anti-PAC proposal would get two days' debate before Labor Day.

PAC managers began to take the offensive. The American Medical Association PAC dropped its plans to make a $5,000 contribution to Kassebaum, one of Boren's co-sponsors. It pointedly gave her only $3,000, the maximum that would be permitted under the bill. The U.S. Chamber of Commerce, a major source of influence among corporate PAC donors, sent a letter to every senator except Boren asking them to oppose his measure.

By late July, however, the tide was running strongly in Boren's direction. Republicans feared that if the bill came to a vote, it was likely to pass and be sent to the House, where Democrats ruled. "Our latest whip count shows we don't have the votes to beat Boren," a Heinz aide said privately. "If it comes out of the Senate, it's going to become law."

After all the months of delay, Republicans mounted a crash effort to produce their own bill. One early draft would have tried to outdo Boren by cutting the maximum allowable PAC donation in half, to $2,500. Some Republican strategists figured that would make Republicans look like reformers while hurting PAC-dependent Democrats more. The drafters proposed to trade tighter PAC limits for some items the party wanted, including a tripling of the amounts that parties could spend for their candidates. The GOP plan would also have preserved the bundling loophole for parties while abolishing it for PACs. "Nobody gave a rat's ass about PACs," the Heinz aide said. The main thing was to get a partisan advantage.

Eventually, Republicans settled on two "killer" amendments. One was a total ban on PAC donations to parties, which would hit Mitchell and Coelho much harder than the GOP committees. The other was a requirement for full disclosure of soft money to national party organizations. Soft-money disclosure was pure reform—there was no real argument against it—but it alarmed Coelho when it was proposed.

Boren's amendment was easily approved, 69–30. Very few senators defended PACs outright during the debate. Phil Gramm of Texas said they were in the tradition of Jeffersonian democracy, diffusing power into the hands of small businessmen. "Hardware dealers are too busy carrying buckets of nails and selling paintbrushes to be that active politically," he insisted. "What is wrong with them passing the hat and putting in a few dollars apiece and contributing to a candidate who believes in free enterprise?"

Boschwitz then offered his killer amendments, creating acute embarrassment for Democrats. An article in *U.S. News & World Report* had just alleged that $55 million had flowed into federal elections from labor-union and corporation treasuries. While it offered no source for that disputable figure, the idea that such huge sums of undisclosed money could be in the political system strongly buttressed the Republican proposal for disclosure. Even more damaging was a Washington *Post* article on the morning of the vote. It said the Democratic National Committee received 28 percent of its annual receipts in soft money, compared with less than 5 percent for the Republican National Committee.

Nobody argued publicly against disclosing soft money, and no Democrat openly defended the party's heavy reliance on PAC funds. But Democrats who had just voted to put a modest limit on PAC donations to candidates were now reduced to opposing a ban on PAC donations to their party. "This is a plainly, openly, cynically partisan attempt to increase an already embarrassingly one-sided advantage in the financing of congressional campaigns," said George Mitchell.

Boschwitz's package was approved by 58–42, mainly on party lines. That left a curious parliamentary situation. The two Senate votes approved the Boren and Boschwitz amendments as riders on a bill with nothing else in it. Dole had stripped out the main provisions of the nuclear-waste measure and arranged for their transfer to another bill, which had already been approved. Boren had allowed Dole to do that in return for a promise to permit a debate and a vote on his amendment. But Dole hadn't promised any vote on the bill itself, only the amendment. Technically, Dole had now fulfilled his pledge. He could easily let the nuclear-waste bill die, and the Boren amendment along with it. Many senators expected Dole to do just that, and figured they could safely satisfy their local editorial writers by voting for Boren's amendment, while privately assuring their PAC donors that it wouldn't become law.

But as the votes were still being counted for the Boschwitz amendment, Dole casually remarked to colleagues at the rear of the Senate chamber, "Maybe we ought to push this to final passage."

"Our jaws hit the floor," recalled a Senate aide. "It was totally out of left field."

Dole announced to the Senate that a final vote might even come that very day. "There is strong consensus we need campaign-financing reform," Dole said. "Maybe [we can] reach some agreement to permit us to complete action on this bill—if not today, sometime this week." Boren asked to proceed immediately to a final vote. "I may be willing to do that later on this afternoon," Dole said. It was already past 2:30 p.m. "I think we may want to work out one or two additional amendments."

Dole's remarks were televised live, as were all Senate floor proceedings, by cable television. Around Washington, lobbyists and PAC managers listened in amazement. Telephones began to light up at the National Republican Senatorial Committee as PAC managers called to protest.

Dole hadn't become an instant backer of PAC limits. He had just voted against the Boren amendment itself. He believed that moving for a final vote would unhinge Democrats who had voted for PAC limits with the idea that Republicans would kill them. "You'll see eleven heart attacks on the other side of the aisle," Dole remarked to fellow Republicans. A GOP aide explained: "We'd been getting beat up, at least in Dole's estimation, on the public-relations side. Boren had the high road and we had the low road. [Dole] wanted to capture a little bit of the high road."

Dole had heard that Coelho had already promised the managers of some large PACs, including the Realtors and the AMA, that he would personally kill the Boren measure if it got out of the Senate. Indeed, Coelho had met with a few top PAC managers and predicted that the Boren measure was doomed. He also offered some suggestions for improving the PACs' public image. He urged them, for example, to come up with a figure for how much of each donation they gave came from the recipient's own constituents. Candidates could then cite such numbers as a defense against the charge that outsiders were buying a local election. The PAC managers thought Coelho's public-relations idea was cockeyed and impractical, but they spread the word that he seemed willing to ambush the Boren bill if it ever escaped from the Senate. That suited Dole's purpose admirably. He would pass the bill and let Coelho take the heat for defeating it. Said a Republican aide, "He could be sanctimonious about how the House was controlled by the Democrats that really were opposing campaign-finance reform."

Dole wasn't able to get rid of the matter so easily, however. He couldn't schedule an instant vote on final passage that day because Boschwitz and a few other PAC supporters said they would object, blocking the unanimous consent required. Among the objectors was Alan Cranston, one of the few Democrats who had voted against the Boren measure. He wanted instead to impose limits on what candidates could spend.

Dole also found Coelho unwilling to take the blame for

killing reform. The two had become acquainted through their mutual interest in aiding the handicapped—Dole lost the use of his right hand from a World War II combat wound. But Coelho wouldn't help Dole this time.

"We're getting a lot of pressure over here," Dole said to Coelho. "What we'll do, we'll put the bill over there and you guys can kill it."

But Coelho responded, "You send that bill over here, we're sending it right back to you."

Coelho thought Senate Republicans were looking for a cheap vote for reform just before the election. His plan, which he said Speaker O'Neill approved, was to add killer amendments of his own before passing the bill back to a joint Senate-House conference to work out a final version. A conference could drag on for days, producing multiple news stories during the height of the re-election season. Unless the conference killed it, generating more of the political heat the senators hoped to avoid, there would follow yet another Senate vote on final passage, just before election day. That wasn't what Dole had in mind.

Coelho wasn't bothered by the Boren proposal itself, which didn't threaten Democratic dominance of the House. The Boschwitz amendments were another matter.

Coelho's committee was receiving $2 million from PACs during 1985–1986, which amounted to 16.8 percent of his hard-money receipts. The Republican campaign committee got only $302,462 from PACs, amounting to less than 0.8 percent of its receipts. Thus, Coelho got nearly seven times more PAC money in absolute terms, and in relative terms was twenty-two times more reliant on PAC donations than the Republicans. Outlawing PAC gifts to parties was a big threat.

Coelho also worried about Boschwitz's seemingly unassailable proposal to require disclosure of soft money. Nobody had argued against that on the Senate floor, but it was the main reason Coelho fought to scuttle the whole bill. He had been resisting restrictions on soft money for years. He once chewed out a Democratic member of the Federal Elec-

tion Commission, Danny McDonald, because he heard Mc-
Donald might be talking about outlawing soft money.

Coelho recalled that incident: "The Republican appoin-
tees [on the FEC] were trying to put through some regulations to go at us on soft. . . . On the street, the word was that
Danny had said that he didn't believe in soft dollars, that
was not the right thing to do, and that I was getting the party
in trouble."

Coelho summoned McDonald, an Oklahoman, to his office and told him, "You are a Boll Weevil Democrat, you
don't give a goddamn about where the party is going, that's
your problem. But I do. And I'm very uptight about what I
hear. We're in the middle of a war with these Republicans.
They are trying to stop us. . . . If you want to be a Republican,
if you want to side with the Republicans, get the hell off the
commission. We don't need another Republican."

McDonald denied to Coelho that he intended to side with
Republicans or move against Democratic soft-money operations. Indeed, long after the meeting, McDonald voted
with other commissioners—Democratic and Republican—
against any regulation to require soft-money disclosure.
Still, when he came up for reappointment in 1986, word
circulated that Coelho might try to block him, until the
congressman personally assured the Democratic leadership that the commissioner had his blessing.

With the FEC taking a permissive line on soft money, only
an act of Congress could force disclosure. Coelho didn't
want to let that happen either. Disclosure would dry up too
many donations. Publicity could also subject the party to
increased criticism for excessive reliance on labor unions,
lobbyists, and wealthy businessmen. *The New Republic* already had run a critical cover story: "The Millionaires Who
Own the Democratic Party."

Coelho's desire to kill the campaign-finance bill stemmed
from his awe of Republican political technology. "They've
got their building. They've got their media. They've got
their computers. They've got all their structure built," he
said. "Well, they're trying to stop us from doing it. . . . I'm

not going to idly sit back and let them destroy our ability to compete." Someday, he said, he wouldn't mind outlawing soft money entirely. But not until the Democrats caught up.

After talking with Coelho, Dole never again showed enthusiasm for pushing the campaign-finance bill to a vote. The Senate adjourned for its summer holiday without acting on it. By September, even Boren's zeal had waned. Passage would have satisfied no one. Liberal Democrats and lobbyists for Common Cause still wanted public financing and limits on overall spending. But weak as it was, the Boren-Boschwitz package was too much reform for either party to support. Republicans were intent on killing the anti-bundling provision. Mitchell couldn't afford to be without PAC money for the senatorial committee. And Coelho was determined to forestall restrictions on soft money.

Just as the old-line party bosses had once fought against civil-service laws, which ended the spoils system of handing out public jobs as political patronage, and against the primary laws, which took candidate selection out of the back rooms, party leaders were now fighting against changes in the modern, dollar-denominated system of political patronage. Partisan considerations remained paramount. Incumbents worried more about bad press than about bad government.

For a brief time it seemed possible that Boren's crusade might set in motion events that could lead to real reform. But this chance was killed by the shortsightedness of the reformers themselves. Boschwitz refused to agree to a final tally on the bill unless he could first get a vote on a widely supported proposal to create a blue-ribbon commission to propose a broad overhaul of the campaign-money system. Given the lack of bipartisan agreement, such a commission was exactly what was needed. The idea had been promoted for months by a widely respected liberal Democratic lawyer, Richard Moe, who had been Walter Mondale's chief of staff when he was Vice President. A bill to create a commission had been sponsored by Republican Warren Rudman of New Hampshire, who had lined up twenty-seven co-sponsors. It would have established a panel with a $1 million budget to conduct an eighteen-month study. The bill was sure to be approved if the Senate was allowed to vote on it.

Boren said he would accept a commission as an addition to the Boren-Boschwitz package. But he objected to Boschwitz's demand for a vote on the commission bill standing alone. Boren feared, with good reason, that the Senate would let the Boren-Boschwitz package die once it had approved a commission, reasoning that it should forgo any tinkering until the commission delivered a blueprint for a complete renovation of the system.

But there was another and more powerful reason that Boren recoiled from the commission proposal. It was opposed by some of the very reformers whose votes made up the core of support for his own PAC-limit bill. Boschwitz, in fact, was pushing a commission precisely because any academically respectable panel wasn't likely to endorse public financing of House and Senate candidates, the pet proposal of Common Cause and liberal Democrats. The unspoken assumption was that a commission would be more likely to endorse a strengthened party system than one of public subsidies for candidates.

"You wouldn't get public financing out of there, because most of the academics who were studying this issue just didn't think that would necessarily work," said Dan Meyer, Boschwitz's legislative aide at the time. "Once a commission came out there would be a great deal of political pressure to support the recommendations. But [Republicans] were willing to do that because they thought their viewpoint would be favorably received by the folks that are considered to be the unbiased experts."

The same thought had occurred to Fred Wertheimer, president of Common Cause, who had been crusading for public financing for fifteen years. In his mailings, Wertheimer called the PAC system "the most troubling scandal to hit our federal government since Watergate," and said the Boren measure was a "historic opportunity." Common Cause was running a fund-raising campaign keyed to the

Boren bill. It was called "People Against PACs." Computer-addressed mailings, more elaborate than anything Coelho could afford for the Democratic party, asked recipients to petition Congress and send in dues to Common Cause. Such mailings were adding thousands of new, dues-paying members to the organization's rolls. The longer the debate dragged on in Congress, the more money it produced for the reform lobby.

Privately, Wertheimer saw little chance that the Boren measure could become law. He had already been negotiating with Coelho, who was spreading word that he would be supporting a public-financing bill in the next Congress, when he expected to be Majority Whip. That would improve chances for getting the House to pass it. If Democrats captured the Senate in the November elections, Wertheimer calculated, prospects for achieving a public-financing bill would be better than they had been for a decade. True, Ronald Reagan was almost certain to veto anything containing public subsidies for congressional candidates, but he would be gone by 1989. With political prospects for public financing improving, however glacially, why risk everything by setting up a commission that would probably have other ideas? Wertheimer rejected the commission idea and Boren followed suit, removing any chance of action and ensuring that the debate would continue into the new Congress.

Both the Boren-Boschwitz package and the commission bill died without a final vote when the 99th Congress adjourned. PACs would hold even greater sway in the 100th Congress. Soft money from corporations, labor unions, and millionaires would continue to flow in secret. The decaying, abuse-ridden system would grow even worse. Tony Coelho would co-sponsor a bill to restrict spending by congressional candidates and to subsidize their campaigns with public funds. And Common Cause's membership would continue to grow.

14

"The Party
of Entrepreneurs"

*The politicians who make a lastin' success in
politics are the men who are always loyal to
their friends, even up to the gate of State prison,
if necessary; men who keep their promises and
never lie.*

—GEORGE WASHINGTON PLUNKITT

"Look around you," Jim Wright instructed the newly
elected Democratic members of the House, "and be thankful for the generosity."

The elections of 1986 produced a smaller victory than Coelho had hoped for, but it would do. Democrats scored a net
gain of five House seats, less than the pickup of ten to fifteen
seats Coelho had been predicting earlier. But only one Democratic incumbent was defeated, and Democrats won just
over half the open seats.

Wright's words echoed slightly in the Great Hall of the
Library of Congress, the grandest public room in Washington. Coelho picked this place, with its carved stone staircase
and towering colonnades of polished marble, for a "New
Members Dinner," a sort of coming-out party for twenty-
seven newly elected Democrats. Wright found it a fitting
metaphor, this gathering of moneyed interests amid one of

the world's great collections of books: "the two bases of our party, intellectual and financial wherewithal."

The party truly was now based largely on money, more than ever before. The elections produced no evidence that voters cared enough about the growing dependency on special-interest funds to defeat anyone on that account. The losses of John Holmes and D. G. Martin showed that incumbents won elections by taking PAC money, and challengers lost without it.

Indeed, here was the Majority Leader of the House, soon to be elevated to Speaker, telling the newest members of his flock to be thankful for the money given by the lobbyists and wealthy donors Tony Coelho had placed at their tables. Seated with the new lawmakers-to-be were dozens of PAC managers, lobbyists, and rich individuals who had financed Coelho's political machine. Their money paid for the lobster bisque and veal on which the victorious candidates dined, for the string quartet that serenaded them, and for the waiters that filled their glasses with wine. Their money would help retire debts of those incoming freshmen who borrowed heavily to win, and would contribute to financing the next campaign, already less than two years away.

One of those donors was a multimillionaire from Dallas, Thomas Gaubert; Coelho and Wright both had special reason to be thankful to him. Gaubert had become rich renovating slum properties; he described himself as a sort of "junk dealer" in real estate, and claimed a net worth of nearly $21 million. He was a major donor to the Democratic Congressional Campaign Committee. Coelho had made him the DCCC's Finance Chairman, and Gaubert expressed an ambition to rise from that post to Finance Chairman of the Democratic National Committee, and from there to national party chairman. Democrats honored him like a prodigal son; he had flirted with the GOP before returning to Coelho's fold. He had been a lifelong Democrat, but in 1980 he voted for Ronald Reagan, like most other Texans. One week after the 1980 election he gave $750 to the National

Republican Senatorial Committee. Later he attended special briefings the GOP staged for its donors, and received a Ronald Reagan plaque. But he felt unsatisfied. "It didn't take me long to find out all they wanted was my money, and they didn't want my input," Gaubert said. Then he met Coelho.

"Coelho made a speech, talked about how the Democratic party was the party of entrepreneurs," Gaubert said. "I just liked him and I walked up to him . . . and I said, 'I'm ready to put my money where my mouth is.' " Gaubert began to write out a check for $500, but Coelho asked for more. "Can you write a check for five grand?" he asked. So Gaubert filled in an extra zero, and became a member of the Speaker's Club.

That was March of 1983. In the months that followed, Coelho drew Gaubert more deeply into the campaign committee's affairs. He gave $7,500 more in July, and wrote a flurry of checks to House, Senate, and presidential candidates. He began traveling to Washington regularly, attending Democratic party briefings, dinners, and fund-raisers. This time he got more than a plaque. "I started being able to have a dialogue with different members of Congress," Gaubert recalled. He gave $1,000 to Fernand St Germain, who was often at Speaker's Club events. Eventually, Coelho took Gaubert along on a mule-pack trip in the High Sierras, a yearly expedition to which he invited only an especially honored few. Gaubert found himself sitting around a mountain campfire with Charles Manatt, the chairman of the Democratic party.

Coelho encouraged Gaubert to take a second look at his hometown congressman, Jim Wright, whom Gaubert had previously considered too liberal. With Coelho as matchmaker, Gaubert warmed to Wright and became one of the Majority Leader's principal financial backers. In 1985 Wright and Coelho found themselves faced with a political shoot-out in Texarkana, and Gaubert came to their side.

The Reagan avalanche of 1984 had Republicans talking once again of political realignment. The national GOP staged a $750,000 campaign called "Operation Open Door" to get 100,000 conservative Democrats to re-register as Republicans in Pennsylvania, North Carolina, Louisiana, and Florida. And in Texas, the GOP arranged for a raid on a congressional seat that Democrats had held for a century. GOP Sen. Phil Gramm, a former Democrat himself, persuaded Reagan to open the seat for a special election by appointing the incumbent, Democratic Rep. Sam Hall, to be a federal judge shortly after the 1984 election.

Gramm's candidate was Edd Hargett. He had never before run for public office, but he was still remembered fondly in Texas as the quarterback who led the Texas A&M football team to a Cotton Bowl victory in 1968. He played professional football in New Orleans and Houston for seven years after that. And he had plenty of money. Republican donors from all over Texas and around the country sent more than $1 million to his campaign. If the GOP won the special election it would be concrete evidence that realignment was really happening, and political psychology would begin working in favor of Republicans. They would find good candidates easier to recruit for 1986 races. Business lobbyists and PAC managers would be less timid about giving money to defeat entrenched Democrats. Gramm brought in Lee Atwater, the GOP political consultant, to supervise the Hargett effort. "This is a long shot," he told Atwater, "but we've really got nothing to lose."

Coelho and Wright, however, had plenty to lose. A Democratic defeat would turn the momentum of the 1986 races against Coelho, damaging his campaign to become Whip. And a GOP victory in Wright's backyard would be especially difficult for him. "One of the issues in this race," said Lt. Gov. Bill Hobby a month before the election, "is whether Jim Wright of Fort Worth, Texas, will be the next Speaker of the House of Representatives." Coelho's campaign committee staff worked on little else for several months, and Wright became heavily involved in the race. Gaubert meanwhile set up a political action committee called East Texas First, headquartered in the Texarkana branch of a

savings and loan association he owned. It was a curious sort
of PAC, in that it supported only one candidate in one House
race, then dissolved. Gaubert described himself as the
PAC's "informal chairman." Later it would be reported that
some of the money may have been given illegally. A *Wall
Street Journal* story quoted a person familiar with the fund-
raising drive as saying that directors of the Sunbelt Savings
Association were summoned to a special directors' meeting
for which they received fees intended to subsidize $1,000
contributions. Several donations from officials of that S&L
showed up at Gaubert's PAC the same day.

No PAC could legally spend more than $5,000 on the spe-
cial election unless it did so entirely independently of any
of the candidates or their agents. Gaubert's PAC was even
more limited; because it supported only a single candidate
the donation limit was $1,000. Yet Gaubert's effort spent
nearly a hundred times that much, meanwhile touching
base with the staff of the DCCC, which was trying to direct
overall strategy in the race. "I talked to the D-triple-C about
ideas and so on and so forth," Gaubert recalled. Such contacts could be construed as destroying the independence of
his PAC and making his spending illegal. The briefings
Gaubert received may have been unauthorized. Once, at a
senior staff meeting, when an aide began reciting what
Gaubert was doing, Martin Franks cut him off and forbade
further discussion. As he recalled it later, Franks said,
"Goddamnit, we can't talk about this. We cannot be collud-
ing with them in any way, shape or form."

In all, Gaubert's PAC spent $99,121 in support of Jim Chap-
man, a Democratic state senator who faced Hargett in the
election held August 3, 1985. The money went for mailings
to old people, attacking Hargett as a Republican pension-
cutter. It also paid for a get-out-the-vote drive on election
day, designed to move Chapman supporters to the polls.
Gaubert claimed his spending made Chapman a congressman. "I think in the long run he would say that we made the
difference," Gaubert said. Chapman won by only 1,933 votes
out of 103,407 cast. He was actually trailing 44 to 43 percent

in a poll taken barely a week before election day. Republicans said later they were swamped by an influx of election-day organizers. Gaubert's PAC paid thousands of dollars for telephone callers who contacted voters on election eve. The PAC chartered a bus to bring in workers from Wright's district on election day and kept them fed with doughnuts and fried chicken. The supposedly independent operation meshed perfectly with Chapman's campaign and the efforts of Wright's organization.

The Democratic victory was a sweet one for Coelho. "Texas, What Realignment?" read the headline in *Newsweek*. Talk of a Republican revolution was put to bed once again, this time with no small thanks to Gaubert.

Gaubert became a fixture at the DCCC. He would invite staff members to visit him on what he called "my boat," the *High Spirits*. Gaubert stayed aboard when in Washington, giving cruises and dockside parties for Coelho's staff and political donors, for alumni of Coelho's mule-pack trips, and for Coelho himself. He said later that his guests included some of the Democratic party's most glamorous celebrities, including Edward Kennedy and John Glenn. There were some less celebrated figures too, including Fernand St Germain of Rhode Island. Gaubert said he found St Germain aloof at first, but "not such a bad guy once you got a couple of drinks in him." He invited St Germain to Texas and paid his expenses for the trip.

Gaubert was wrangling with federal investigators who saw him, not as an "entrepreneur," but as a crook. Both the Federal Home Loan Bank Board and a federal grand jury were investigating a Gaubert real-estate deal involving a shaky savings and loan association that later became insolvent. Gaubert walked away from the deal with several million dollars in profits on forty-four acres of land in Dallas he had bought for $1.1 million. But the deal left Capitol S&L of Mount Pleasant, Iowa, stuck with $8 million in loans to a friend of Gaubert, a Dallas developer who ceased making payments.

The Capitol deal was later detailed in an extraordinary

182-page report by an independent counsel the Bank Board hired to assess the wreckage. It said Gaubert presented the lender with an appraisal valuing the land at more than eighteen times what he paid for it just three months earlier. He pushed the complex arrangement through with only four days between his proposal and a chaotic closing. Gaubert and his colleagues "essentially made up the deal as they went along," according to a title-company official quoted in the independent counsel's report. Long after the closing, the lender discovered to its dismay that the lawyers who were supposed to be representing the S&L's interests were also working for Gaubert.

Less than two weeks after Gaubert pocketed his millions, he lent $150,000 to a Capitol S&L official who approved the deal and who continued to act as his advocate during much of the controversy that followed. The S&L official didn't even have to sign an IOU and, so far as the independent counsel could find, didn't repay the money. Gaubert later said he got some stock in a lumberyard as security, but the shares were practically worthless. When the man later confessed to getting money from Gaubert, federal regulators referred the matter to the United States attorney in Des Moines for possible prosecution. An official in the Dallas office of the Federal Home Loan Bank Board wrote an internal letter accusing Gaubert of "possible bribery or pay-offs" and "personal dishonesty" in the Iowa matter.

Gaubert denied doing anything wrong. He claimed he never read the allegedly inflated appraisal, but merely delivered it to Capitol among two boxes of other documents, as a favor to the buyers. He also denied covering up his own enormous profit from the transaction, which Capitol executives said they were shocked to discover after the deal went sour. He denied that the $150,000 loan was a bribe.

Gaubert had big ambitions. He had bought a tiny S&L in Grand Prairie, Texas, for $1 million cash. In the reckless and permissive atmosphere that Congress had created in the industry, Gaubert was able to increase the S&L's assets from $40 million to $223 million in less than a year, attracting short-term deposits by paying exceptionally high interest rates. Now he was asking federal regulators for permission to absorb another S&L and to take over twenty-two branches of a third, moves that would suddenly give him control of $1.3 billion in federally insured deposits. It was a brassy request, considering the fact that he was under grand-jury investigation on suspicion of having swindled another S&L out of millions. Indeed, Gaubert said his own attorneys at one point advised him that he was dead in the industry and should get out to save himself time and money, according to the Bank Board report. But with help from his newfound friends in Washington, Gaubert fought to stay in the business and expand his empire. Here was the modern patronage system in its fullest flower, a political donor profiting from a system of federal subsidies and permissive regulation arranged by the politicans he financed.

Gaubert's ambition to control a financial empire was made possible in the first place only because of favors St Germain and his colleagues had done for friends in the S&Ls. For years they had been a conservatively managed source of mortgage money for families, one of the engines of the housing boom that followed World War II, allowing millions to move from city rentals to homes in the suburbs. S&Ls and their cousins, the mutual savings banks common in the Northeast, made up what was called the thrift industry. For years it earned that name by encouraging families to save their money in government-insured accounts that paid a bit higher interest than banks, and lending it back to them on the solid collateral of their homes. But under St Germain's dominion the industry became a paradise for fast-buck operators and high rollers.

Years of unwise decisions by Congress had made it possible for unscrupulous operators to achieve enormous profits. Some were looting their federally insured deposits for private benefit in ways that federal regulators, when they realized what was going on, would charge were illegal. While two-thirds of the industry was piling up billions in profits, the remainder was failing so badly that the federal deposit insurance fund first ran dry, then went into the red. In 1986 the Reagan administration requested a $15 billion bailout to cover the losses of the worst cases. Even that would prove to be inadequate; the true shortfall was by some estimates approaching something closer to $50 billion.

Congress had come to govern more for the benefit of industry executives than for the public. In 1980, for example, St Germain pulled off a coup that increased to $100,000, from $40,000, the amount of any single S&L savings deposit insured by the federal government. The Senate had voted to raise the level only modestly, to $50,000, and the House hadn't approved any change at all. But with St Germain taking the lead, the Senate-House conferees "compromised" at $100,000. Banking regulators cautioned that such a radical move was unwise. But the S&L lobby wanted the higher level, and St Germain slipped it into the large and complex banking bill.

The rise to $100,000 was a perversion of the consumer-protection ethic that deposit insurance once embodied. At $40,000, insurance had been more than adequate to protect unsophisticated savers, the people Congress originally intended to shield when deposit insurance was enacted during a wave of banking failures in the Depression. St Germain pushed it up, not to protect depositors, but to aid S&L owners. With their deposits insured up to $100,000, the associations no longer had to rely on the savings of citizens in their own communities. A huge, unregulated national market in brokered deposits developed. Corporations and wealthy individuals found they could split up their spare millions into convenient $100,000 bundles and park them as federally insured certificates of deposit in S&Ls all over the country. So long as they kept no more than one such CD in any single S&L, they were protected almost as completely as though their money was in Treasury bills. With St Germain's help, Congress had passed resolutions declaring that the full faith and credit of the United States government stood behind the deposit insurance fund, putting taxpayers morally, if not legally on the hook for future losses that couldn't be covered by the insurance premiums of the S&L industry itself. Gaubert and other ambitious S&L operators found they could get their hands on hundreds of millions of government-insured dollars, quickly, by advertising high interest rates through the network of deposit brokers.

S&Ls had new freedom to speculate with those easily gained deposits. No longer were they restricted mainly to making home-mortgage loans. Everything changed in 1982. The industry was losing billions of dollars because of high interest rates that drove up the cost of its deposits faster than its income from long-term mortgages. St Germain and his Senate counterpart, Republican Jake Garn of Utah, ushered through the Garn–St Germain Act, giving S&Ls new powers that, it was hoped, would produce new sources of profit. The bill allowed S&Ls to enter new and unfamiliar lines of business, including car loans, equipment leasing, securities, land sales, and real-estate development. The associations were permitted to buy land and erect buildings directly, rather than merely making loans to seasoned developers. Owners could also borrow depositors' money to finance their personal projects. In Texas, which had lax regulations for state-chartered S&Ls, they could loan more than the purchase price for speculative land deals.

The new rules gave immense financial leverage to aggressive S&L operators. Federal regulators required owners to have only $3 of their own capital invested in an S&L for every $100 of deposits taken in. That was half what was required for banks. In practice, the S&Ls often had $1 or less invested for every $100, because Congress and the regulators allowed them to depart from generally accepted accounting procedures and to legally cook their books, claiming more capital than truly existed. It was called "regulatory accounting." The idea was to help weak, traditional, home-lender S&Ls get over the rough times of 1981–82. The practical effect was to turn the industry into a playground for speculators who were gambling with billions of dollars in federally insured money.

The Garn–St Germain legislation created conditions in

which speculation and swindles were sure to flourish. At
the same time, Congress allowed enforcement to deterio-
rate practically to the vanishing point. Congress confirmed
only persons approved by the S&L lobby to sit as members
of the governing Bank Board, and wouldn't consider any
suggestion that S&Ls be placed under the stricter and more
independent rule of federal banking regulators. Worse,
Congress and the Reagan administration kept federal S&L
regulators on starvation budgets. S&Ls could go for two
years without a visit from examiners. In Texas the situation
approached anarchy; federal regulators were uprooting
their offices for the region from Little Rock to Dallas, causing a turnover of all but a dozen of the forty original employees.

Understandably, developers began taking over small
thrift institutions or starting new ones. They typically
pumped up deposits by offering high rates for what were
called "jumbo" certificates, using the money to finance
their own deals or those of friends. Borrowers could get the
full purchase price plus enough to cover interest payments
for a couple of years. From the money loaned, the S&L
would book the fees and interest "payments" as profits, appearing to increase its capital and allowing it to take in
even more depositors' funds to make more such reckless
loans. For the lucky borrower, who had nothing of his own
invested in the deal, there could be a big profit when the
property was sold, but only if inflation continued to push up
land prices at a rapid clip. If the deal went sour, the borrower could merely walk away, leaving the S&L to foreclose
on land worth much less than what it had lent. Sometimes,
such unsuccessful deals were hidden in "trash-for-cash"
arrangements in which another borrower took over the ailing property in return for a generous new loan, some of
which he could keep for himself.

Gaubert was only one of the wheeler-dealers taking over
S&Ls. In Texas it was as though the oil-boom days of a
bygone generation had returned. One of Gaubert's friends,
Donald Dixon, got control of an S&L in Vernon, sixty miles

west of Wichita Falls, Texas. Before long Dixon's S&L owned a fleet of aircraft, including a helicopter and a baby-blue Falcon 50 jet so large it looked like a downsized Boeing 727.

With the help of a $6 million loan from Sunbelt, the S&L whose executives made allegedly illegal donations to the East Texas First PAC, Gaubert bought a controlling 27.8 percent interest in Telecom Corporation and installed himself as chairman, president, and chief executive. The $43 million holding company owned, among other things, an air-conditioning distributorship, a souvenir manufacturing company, and a maker of pecan-processing equipment.

Gaubert loved to tell a story about his son Mike, who played football at Southern Methodist University, notorious for providing lavish perquisites for star players. "When the weight coach took him in, he said, 'This guy's an ideal candidate. He's already got his own Porsche, and he's also got his own condominium.' " Gaubert was finding no reason to regret that first $5,000 check to the Democratic Congressional Campaign Committee. Coelho surely had been right when he said Democrats were the "party of entrepreneurs."

Ironically, Gaubert gained control of his $1 billion institution because regulators were already overburdened by the excesses of other S&L operators. The Federal Savings and Loan Insurance Corp. was in poor financial shape and getting worse. Gaubert, even though under grand-jury investigation, was offering a deal to regulators. He proposed to take over and "rescue" a troubled S&L, Investex, that otherwise was going to cost the FSLIC somewhere between $40 million and $50 million to fix. The regulators couldn't resist; they allowed Gaubert's S&L—which he had renamed Independent American—to absorb Investex. They also permitted it to buy up twenty-two branches and $600 million in deposits from another S&L, on the theory that Independent American would have to grow much larger to make a success of the troubled Investex. Gaubert himself was asked, and agreed, to step aside from day-to-day management of

Independent American while the grand jury and the regulators investigated his activities at Capitol. But regulators allowed Gaubert's brother Jack, another stockholder, to run the S&L in the meantime.

The grand-jury investigation stopped when Gaubert agreed to buy back the forty-four acres from Capitol, which had foreclosed, for the amount it had loaned. That settled a civil lawsuit brought against him by the association, and seemed to end the threat of criminal charges. But to regain personal control of his own $1 billion S&L, he needed Bank Board investigators to clear him as well. The investigators soon learned that Gaubert had powerful friends in Washington.

In March 1985, St Germain asked Bank Board officials about the status of the Gaubert investigation. He wanted to know if it would be appropriate for him to attend one of Gaubert's political fund-raising events. The board's general counsel sent the request to the attorneys handling the case, and they subsequently stepped up the pace of their investigation. They called in Gaubert for three days of questioning, under oath, about the Capitol loan and other matters. During a break in the proceedings Gaubert told one of the investigating lawyers that he was thinking about contacting his friends in Washington to ask them to set up a meeting with Edwin Gray, the chairman of the Bank Board. The attorney wrote a memo about the conversation, saying that she believed Gaubert would use whatever political influence he had to prevent the inquiry from going against him.

Gaubert pressed constantly to regain control of his S&L and its cash reservoir. During this same time he was putting together his $99,000 effort to help Wright and Coelho with the Texas special election. Gaubert and his family contributed $4,000 personally; the rest came almost exclusively from officers, employees, and borrowers of his and other S&Ls. He collected $13,000 from Dixon, his wife, and various officials of Vernon. There was $21,000 from Ed McBirney's Sunbelt S&L, the one that reportedly reimbursed donors from corporate funds. The PAC was a Democratic war chest funded by some of the most reckless S&L operators in Texas.

Nevertheless, the lawyers investigating Gaubert recommended that he be forced out of the S&L industry permanently. At a stormy meeting on August 22, 1985, the head of enforcement of the Bank Board, Rosemary Stewart, called Gaubert a crook to his face. Her office pressed him to withdraw from the industry voluntarily, rather than face mandatory expulsion proceedings. After protracted haggling, Gaubert finally signed a settlement on January 9, 1986, agreeing not to serve as an officer or director in any federally insured S&L, or to vote the stock in his own association, Independent American. Gaubert got to keep his stock in Independent American. He also voided an agreement he had made to put his own money into the association if the institution's capital fell below required levels. To get him to go quietly, the Bank Board relieved Gaubert of obligations that could have wiped him out financially, and it allowed him to retain his majority interest in the S&L.

Shortly afterward, the Bank Board also removed Gaubert's brother Jack from the management. Regulators began to uncover what they called a pattern of unsafe and unsound lending and conflicts of interest, and a deteriorating financial condition. According to a report prepared by regulators, the S&L was selling shopping centers at inflated prices supported by appraisals made by one of Independent American's own subsidiaries. Buyers were lured by the prospect of no-money-down loans from the S&L, secured only by the real estate, for enough to cover not only the purchase price but also fees, sales commissions, and several years of interest "payments" to Independent American entities. The S&L was claiming big profits from the land sales, interest income, and fees, while in reality, according to regulators, it was wasting hundreds of millions of dollars of depositors' money.

Horrified examiners said there were almost no accurate records or books to examine. Even so, they determined that the Gaubert brothers had rendered their S&L hopelessly insolvent. New managers, approved by the regulators, began to learn the full story of what had gone on under the Gaubert regime, and how much the fiasco was going to cost the deposit insurance fund.

Alarmed at seeing his empire slipping away, Gaubert complained to Wright. The Majority Leader meanwhile began crusading for Gaubert and other S&L operators and borrowers in Texas. He asked the chairman of the Bank Board, Edwin Gray, to his office at the Capitol. When Gray arrived he found several other House members from Texas present. Wright made a little speech, as Gray recalled it, about "these deep concerns . . . how we were mistreating these S&Ls." Wright told Gray he had friends both in the S&L industry and in real-estate development, and those friends were accusing the chairman's subordinates of "Gestapo tactics." To show he meant business, Wright blocked passage of an emergency bill Gray was seeking to infuse $15 billion into the deposit insurance fund, which was nearly broke. Texas S&Ls were hemorrhaging millions of dollars a day in additional losses, yet here was the House Majority Leader pressuring regulators to go easy.

Wright had been hearing complaints from other Texas real-estate developers who felt pinched by the regulators. Craig Hall, a Dallas promoter of real-estate tax shelters, had financed his troubled empire largely with money borrowed from two California S&Ls that became insolvent and were taken over by regulators. When one threatened to foreclose, Hall complained to Wright and regulators relented.

Wright also received advice from Fort Worth developer George Mallick, a close friend and business partner who had helped him financially for years. Wright asked Mallick for financial help the first time the two met, cutting the ribbon at a shopping center that Mallick had developed. "He was a young congressman and I was a young developer," Mallick said. "We went out to have a cup of coffee together, and we found that we liked each other. . . . He asked me if I knew of any business opportunities, and about a year later about ten of us got together and bought a piece of land. We did very well on that. That was in about 1963."

Other deals followed. "We just became very close," Mallick said. Wright, Mallick, and their wives formed a company they named Mallightco, blending the two family names. Another joint venture was called BMW Drilling, which held a one-thirty-second interest in sixteen oil and gas wells. Wright's wife, Betty, drew a salary from Mallightco, which Mallick said was for services in planning some condominium developments that never materialized. The Wrights got rent-free use of a two-bedroom apartment owned by Mallick, which they used as their Fort Worth residence. Mallightco invested in stocks, and even speculated in rubies and other gemstones imported by one of Mallick's sons. In 1986 Wright drew more than $15,000 from Mallightco in dividends.

When he began hearing complaints about savings and loan regulators, Wright asked Mallick to arrange a meeting with unhappy Texas S&L operators and their borrowers. "I was going to have a luncheon for fifteen or twenty people," Mallick recalled. "Well, it got all over the state . . . and we ended up with more than a hundred and fifty people there." The gripe session was at the Ridglea Country Club in Fort Worth and Gaubert was among the participants.

At the meeting, developers complained of "Gestapo" regulators. Privately, some went so far as to tell Wright that a homosexual ring was at work, with certain regulators referring legal business from S&L foreclosures to friends in private law firms. Wright later echoed those charges to Bank Board chairman Gray. Wright said he didn't know whether they were true but was disturbed to hear them.

The Ridglea group claimed their woes were due to bad luck: the price of oil had plunged, putting the Texas economy into a tailspin and reversing the run-up in land values on which many of the speculators had bet their money and that of their depositors. If federal regulators moved aggressively to protect taxpayers against the mounting losses, it would mean wiping out S&L stockholders, foreclosing on their borrowers, and selling off their holdings. So overheated had been the building boom in Texas that the state was full of empty office buildings. Even conscientious developers feared that their holdings would be hurt if the government held a fire sale of land and buildings taken over from busted S&Ls.

"They were just trying to foreclose, foreclose, foreclose," Mallick complained. "Texas was overbuilt, and [the regulators' attitude] was just making the property values fall." Mallick himself owned an office building in Fort Worth and so had a personal financial interest in preventing foreclosure sales. Wright, nevertheless, asked Mallick to prepare a formal report advising him. Mallick turned in a twenty-five-page document accusing regulators of taking far too hard a line. He argued that they should show more forbearance, giving borrowers additional time and even lending them more funds in the hope that real-estate prices would bounce back. Wright adopted that line as his own. His policy, which became that of the Democrats, was being influenced by Gaubert, on whom he and his party relied for campaign donations, and Mallick, on whom he relied for personal income.

Gray, then only vaguely aware of the Mallick and Gaubert connections, tried to explain that the deposit insurance fund was facing a crisis. "We as regulators need your support," he told Wright. "We beg for your support. We can't do our job without your support." Not long after that, in November, the Majority Leader asked Gray to give Gaubert an audience. Gray felt he had to say yes, even though his attorneys advised him against such a meeting and Gaubert supposedly had agreed to withdraw from the S&L industry months before. The meeting in Gray's Washington office lasted more than two hours. "It was a diatribe," Gray recalled. "He was almost ready to cry." Gaubert claimed he had been whipsawed by regulators. He said they led him on so he would take the troubled Investex S&L off their hands, then froze him out. He made an astonishing accusation: he said the managers picked by the regulators had bankrupted his S&L while he had been locked out.

Gray was flabbergasted. "Your story is so different from what I've heard from my people," he said. Indeed, the regulator-backed managers at the S&L were lodging civil fraud and racketeering charges against Gaubert, his brother Jack, and others from the old management. The lawsuit accused Gaubert and the others of looting the S&L of $5.2 million by selling some of their stock back to the association at an inflated price based on "false and misleading" information. Gaubert claimed the S&L had a net worth of $40 million, but the lawsuit said it really had a negative net worth of $87 million. Even that turned out to be an optimistic view, compared to what followed. The new managers soon concluded that in reality Gaubert's S&L was in the red by $550 million.

But Gray, feeling pressure from Wright, promised Gaubert he would conduct an inquiry into the actions of his investigators. Never before had the Bank Board done such a thing. Gaubert had turned the tables; the regulators who got a grand-jury probe going against him would now come under investigation themselves. Wright told Gray he approved of the arrangement, repeating that he had heard charges about a network of homosexual lawyers supposedly victimizing Texas S&L owners. Gray even chose the independent investigator, Nashville lawyer Aubrey Harwell, from a list of acceptable choices supplied by Gaubert's attorney.

Nevertheless, it went badly for Gaubert. Harwell spent three months interviewing forty-five witnesses and examining 15,000 pages of documents. He concluded that Gaubert's main claim was groundless. "Neither the evidence nor common sense supports Gaubert's allegations," Harwell wrote. He said regulators made some mistakes in dealing with Gaubert, chiefly letting his S&L take over Investex in the first place. But Harwell said they "certainly" didn't set out to ruin Independent American as Gaubert claimed. Nevertheless, Gaubert later filed a lawsuit seeking damages from the Bank Board.

Meanwhile Independent American shareholders voted to throw out the regulator-backed managers and reinstall some of the old management. According to the Dallas *Morning News,* which quoted an unnamed S&L official, Gaubert was present at the stockholders' meeting and, after the vote, personally directed security guards to escort the deposed management out of the building. The reinstated executives sought the protection of Texas state regulators, who were notoriously close to the industry. This was possible because the S&L was under dual state-federal regulation, operating under a state charter and federal insurance. Wright, who had been Speaker of the House for less than three weeks, denied any involvement in the coup. "I have discussed these concerns on several occasions with agency officials here [in Texas] and in Washington," Wright said. "But I had no role whatever in actions this week involving Mr. Gaubert."

Gaubert's victory was short-lived. In May 1987 federal authorities finally declared Independent American to be insolvent, placed it in receivership, and transferred all assets to a new, depositor-owned entity with a federal charter. Gaubert's stake was wiped out. In all, nearly 40 percent of loans had gone so sour that borrowers weren't even making interest payments, the Bank Board said. Gaubert found himself in the midst of another criminal investigation, as the Justice Department and the FBI moved teams of prosecutors, agents, and accountants into Texas to focus on allegations of massive S&L fraud in the state. Gaubert filed lawsuits blaming regulators and their managers for the collapse of his S&L. His argument came down to this: the regulators tricked him into the merger, froze him out, and conspired with the new executives to mismanage and loot the S&L. It was the same argument that Harwell, the special investigator, had dismissed as nonsense.

Wright was unable to protect Gaubert this time. Furious at the Speaker's past intervention, government officials were taking their case to the press. Columnist Jack Anderson ran a series of articles charging that Wright had interfered on behalf of Gaubert and others. William Black, deputy director of the Federal Savings and Loan Insurance

Corp., the Bank Board's deposit insurance fund, criticized Wright—without naming him—in remarks quoted by the *New York Times.* "We are seeing recurrent attempts to use political influence to prevent FSLIC from taking effective enforcement action against hopelessly insolvent thrifts," Black said. "Such interference from influential, powerful members of Congress will increase FSLIC's losses. Somebody's going to have to pay for the losses."

Regulators were eager to get fresh money into the insurance fund. Wright allowed the $15 billion bill to go through the House shortly before the 1986 election, but it died in the Senate because of an unrelated issue. Now Wright was rallying Democrats to oppose the $15 billion measure in the 100th Congress. Wright appeared at a special meeting of the House Banking Committee's Democrats to plead for a watered-down bill being pushed by his S&L friends, who feared the money would give regulators the wherewithal to move more aggressively. Shaky S&Ls believed they would be closed down. Even solid associations rebelled at the idea of paying higher fees to the insurance fund. Most of the $15 billion would be borrowed by floating bonds on Wall Street, but eventually it would all come from fees from surviving S&Ls unless Congress appropriated general revenues for the insurance fund.

A direct taxpayer bailout was becoming all but inevitable. One study estimated that the entire S&L industry was already about $50 billion in the red. Even worse, this deficit was occurring during economic conditions that were producing healthy profits for those S&Ls that had stuck to the home-lending business. Low interest rates, brisk home sales, and a demand for refinancing of existing home mortgages were generating so much business that many lenders were swamped. If the industry was tens of billions in the red during such times, what would an economic downturn bring? The seeds Congress had sown with the permissive Garn–St Germain Act and St Germain's $100,000 deposit insurance maneuver were leading to a fiscal calamity.

Coelho and Wright, nevertheless, pushed to keep regulators on a short leash. They wanted only a $5 billion infusion. The bill they backed also included "forbearance" provisions requiring regulators to go easier on troubled S&Ls. Coelho said later he was working, not to help Gaubert, but to aid California S&Ls. "They wanted $2 billion," Coelho said. "The $5 billion was a compromise, if you can believe that." Californians were incensed that Gray, who had been a public-relations man for a big California S&L before joining the Reagan administration, would turn on them. Gray the industry speechwriter had become Gray the zealous regulator, disliked and feared by his ex-colleagues. Coelho recalled appearing at a meeting of the U.S. League of Savings Institutions, the S&L's main lobbying arm. "A guy said, 'Don't give Gray his $15 billion to keep harassing us and helping his friends.' I said, 'I'm not for giving Gray any more money to run amok.' The place went wild, it went absolutely wild."

Coelho carried on even after Wright ceased lobbying for a weakened insurance bill. Wright switched amid more bad publicity about another Democratic benefactor, Donald Dixon, for whom he had interceded with S&L regulators. Dixon had contributed to Gaubert's $99,000 spending effort in the Texas special election. Court records revealed later that Dixon's S&L had paid expenses for Coelho's cruises and dockside parties, an apparent violation of federal law prohibiting corporate campaign contributions. Gaubert, it turned out, didn't have even partial ownership of the *High Spirits.* One of Dixon's corporate aircraft also took Wright on a 1984 trip that stopped in Dallas, Shreveport, Louisiana, and Los Angeles. Coelho arranged for that trip through Gaubert. Dixon's S&L didn't send Coelho any bills for use of the yacht or the airplane, and the campaign committee didn't ask for any.

Dixon's grandiose S&L, like Gaubert's, had bought brokered $100,000 CDs. Then it collapsed in an orgy of spending, business gambles, and, according to federal regulators, outright thievery. Before Dixon gained control in 1982, Vernon Savings and Loan Association was a local institution with $83 million in assets, serving the northern Texas oil town of Vernon. But within five years it had $1.7 billion in assets of highly dubious value. Its offices were as far away as California and Switzerland. Federal regulators said Dixon skimmed off $40 million in dividends and bonuses for himself and six top officers of the thrift, and used Vernon's money to finance an expense-account lifestyle on a royal scale, including the yacht, planes, a Ferrari sports car, a hunting club, and a $2 million beach house in Del Mar, California, where Dixon and his wife billed the S&L $100 a day for flowers. In October 1983, the couple toured the finest restaurants and wine cellars of France, Switzerland, and Spain, supposedly a business trip. His wife kept a diary recording, among other things, a marathon lunch with champagne and truffle soup, at which master chef Paul Bocuse lined up his twelve subordinate chefs in a Lyons courtyard for the Dixons to review. Dana Dixon wrote that she left France "with visions of those 27 Michelin Stars forever in our heads, and a dearth of adjectives to ever describe it all adequately!" Vernon paid $68,000 for that trip and four others, examiners later calculated.

Wright might never have embroiled himself in Dixon's messy affairs if it hadn't been for Coelho. He said he had never met or spoken to Dixon. There is no record of Dixon's ever making a campaign contribution to Wright's own reelection campaign or to Wright's personal PAC. But in November of 1986 Coelho asked Wright to listen to Dixon's regulatory problems. Wright took Dixon's call because he was told it was urgent.

Coelho took this indirect approach to avoid criticism of himself; congressmen's contacts with federal regulatory agencies are legally a matter of public record under the Freedom of Information Act, so Coelho studiously avoided making calls for donors himself. "I was very careful not to get involved in their particular problems," he later told the

Washington *Post.* "No agency logged me in with a letter or call."

Dixon claimed that he had a buyer willing to put additional money into his S&L and needed an additional week to close the deal, but that regulators were threatening to close Vernon the following day. Wright called Gray and asked him to accommodate Dixon's request by keeping Vernon open a while longer.

Gray assured Wright that Vernon couldn't be closed without his permission, which was true as far as it went. But within hours Vernon's managers had been forced out and the S&L was being run by new executives picked by regulators. The S&L was still open, as promised, and depositors were protected, but Dixon and other Vernon stockholders were wiped out. Wright was enraged at Gray; he never spoke to him again after that. Months later, former party chairman Robert Strauss, a Texan and one of Wright's strong supporters, arranged what was supposed to be a peacemaking session between Wright and senior regulators from the Dallas region. The meeting was in April 1987, after Wright had become Speaker. Gray was pointedly not invited. But the session went sour when William Black insisted on coming and tried to explain to Wright that Gray hadn't deceived him; ousting Vernon's board wasn't the same as closing the institution, he pointed out. According to Wright's friend George Mallick, who was present, Wright erupted: "Goddamnit, you're using semantics on me."

Not long after that, Secretary of the Treasury James Baker called Wright in Fort Worth to tell him the President would replace Gray with a Bank Board chairman acceptable to the S&L lobby and to Congress: Danny Wall, chief Republican aide to the Senate Banking Committee. Baker implored Wright to accept the administration's $15 billion bill. Wright said he promised Baker during that conversation that he would back off his opposition.

But Wright didn't announce a switch until a few days later, amid great embarrassment. Regulators filed a lawsuit formally accusing Vernon's managers of having "looted, dissipated and wasted" the S&L's assets. By that time the government had closed Vernon. Regulators said 96 percent of Vernon's loans were in default and its net worth was at least $350 million in the red, and sinking. Bank Board officials went out of their way to put documents onto the court record giving the first public glimpse of what Dixon and his colleagues had been doing. Newspapers carried accounts of the jets, the beach house, and Dixon's lavish lifestyle. The day after the lawsuit was filed, Wright at last said publicly he would support the $15 billion bill the regulators wanted.

Meanwhile, Coelho battled on, rounding up votes for the weaker measure the S&L lobby wanted. The House passed it despite Wright's change of position. The Senate voted for a slightly stronger rescue measure, but the final bill still provided only $10.8 billion for the tapped-out insurance fund, less than requested and far too little to deal with the known casualties. The fund had to pledge $1.3 billion to deal with Vernon alone, making it the most costly single action to that point. Many other such rescues were looming. Vernon was only the third worst, in terms of losses, on the insurance fund's list of terminal cases. Independent American was sixth.

Authorities estimated that fraud and insider abuse were contributing to half of all S&L failures. Dixon invoked the Fifth Amendment, refusing to testify on grounds of possible self-incrimination, as FBI agents and federal prosecutors looked for the causes of Vernon's collapse. Gaubert himself would eventually be indicted for his role in the Capitol deal. A new federal grand jury in Iowa charged him in early 1988 with five felony counts of fraud and false statements, all of which he denied.

Wright, criticized for interfering with the regulatory process, said he had only asked Bank Board officials to look into the complaints of his Texas constituents. "It is the kind of thing most congressmen do almost every day for some private citizen or another," he said. He said he never again spoke to Dixon after the single telephone conversation in which Dixon called for help. But he continued his relationship with Gaubert, who served as finance chairman of a fund-raising reception in Fort Worth that realized nearly $1 million for Wright in late 1987.

Meanwhile, regulators predicted that they would more than double the number of S&Ls they would be forced to liquidate. They reported that 345 insolvent S&Ls lost $9.5 billion during 1987 and that many others were also operating in the red. By passing a weak insurance bill requiring regulators to go easier on failing S&Ls, Congress had only made the problem worse.

In December 1986 Coelho was elected Majority Whip, ranking him third in the Democratic leadership. He easily defeated his closest rival, Charles Rangel, on the first ballot. The race was actually decided months before the vote, as Coelho canvassed every House Democrat who wasn't a sworn enemy, pressing them to support him. His ear was tuned to all the equivocating phrases that House members use to avoid giving a solid promise of support: " 'You'd make a great Whip.' 'You're doing a tremendous job.' 'I've always admired the way you worked.' Those are all 'No,' " Coelho explained.

He campaigned compulsively, and as methodically as he had once gone about milking 250 cows starting at 2:30 each morning. As his wife, Phyllis, told it, "He's almost a fanatic. He loves to have things in order. His closets, his shirts. Everything has to be in place. He would come into the kitchen; he would see things weren't in order, and he would start rearranging—the cans on the shelves, the spices. He likes all the green beans lined up, all the olives. He wants to know when we have more than one of anything. My sister-in-law used to say, 'Send him over to *my* house!' "

Campaigning, he carried a list of all the Democratic members' names in his coat pocket, jotting coded notations beside each to indicate those pledged to him on the first ballot, those leaning in his direction, those pledged to him on a second ballot if their first choice failed, even those who promised to vote for him as their third choice. House members are notorious for promising support to more than one colleague in such internal contests, so Coelho took nothing for granted; he sent thank-you notes to those who said they would vote for him, less as a courtesy than to create a written record of the pledge. He had been stung bitterly years earlier when his boss, B. F. Sisk, fell short in a bid to replace the ailing Hale Boggs of Louisiana as Majority Leader. "Sisk depended on others for his vote counts," Coelho recalled. "He depended on Wilbur Mills and others to bring in votes for him." Coelho made it what he called an "eyeball-to-eyeball campaign," waving aside offers of help from outsiders. "No labor unions. No lobbyists. No former colleagues. Nothing," he said. "It was like running for student body president."

Coelho worked harder and longer than his rivals. When William Alexander dropped out of the race during a congressional recess, Coelho's aides had already prepared a list of telephone numbers where he could reach Alexander's supporters, scattered all over the country for the recess. Coelho dialed first from a San Francisco hotel room and later from a political consultant's Jaguar sedan as they motored to a meeting in Palo Alto. By Coelho's count, Alexander had only eleven supporters when he abandoned the race, far fewer than he was claiming. By nightfall, Coelho had promises of support from seven of them. Some got their first word of Alexander's withdrawal from Coelho. When Rangel went to the Far East for ten days, Coelho was contacting his own supporters, just to make sure they weren't wavering. His campaign manager, Rep. Vic Fazio of California, thought Coelho was joking when he called. He wasn't. "Well, how about it?" Coelho asked. "Tony, I'm *with* you," his campaign manager said.

Coelho's hard work, personal charm, and meticulous organization resulted in victory, but what made him a contender in the first place was money. His reputation was built upon his talent and skill at running a modern, money-based political machine. Coelho was a good legislative tactician; he pushed through bills for the wine industry, dairy farmers, and veterans, among others. But his reputation didn't rest on that. He was the undisputed Democratic champion of campaign funds. He was a partisan warrior, battling to preserve the power of Democratic barons like St Germain, and he fought his battles with dollars. No other House Democrat pursued special-interest money with Coelho's energy, or his unconcern for appearances, his "inner peace." Older members regarded him as a young magician who could beat the Republican fund-raisers and political technicians at their own game. Many of the newest members thought of him as a mentor, the man who in many cases had recruited them to run initially and who provided them with advice, technical support, and money. In remarks to the newly elected freshmen a few days before the vote for Whip, he told them, "I know you, and understand your districts and your issues, what you can and can't do for the leadership."

Coelho insisted that the hundreds of thousands of dollars he disbursed from his own PAC were much more useful in the Whip race than the millions he controlled from the campaign committee. "The people you just give [campaign committee] money to don't appreciate it, because they think that's what you are supposed to do anyway," Coelho said. Furthermore, "if you do your job right, you say no to a lot of people." But without the Democratic Congressional Campaign Committee, Coelho would be only the tenth-ranking Democrat on the Agriculture Committee.

During his six years as head of the campaign committee Coelho transformed it, creating a permanent institution where before there had been little more than an annual fund-raising dinner. But for all his talk about imitating the Republican small-donor success, he couldn't wean the committee or his colleagues from their addiction to special-interest money. He built a better television studio than the Republicans, but found that while paying for it he was catering to labor-union demands more than ever. He craved computers and arranged for a labor union to buy them for him, but had little idea what to do with the new machines. On election night a computer terminal was on his desk ready to flash the latest results from any House district, but he never touched the keyboard, relying instead on a team of runners who brought in results on slips of paper.

Coelho's great accomplishment, the thing for which his colleagues mostly regarded him as a hero, was that he made the House safe for Democratic incumbents. He provided protection from the threat of Republican "political technology," which had so panicked his colleagues. Guy Vander Jagt's Republican campaign committee, for all its small-donor money, was only effective so long as it was unopposed. Coelho provided the counterbalance.

He still couldn't match the Republican effort dollar for dollar, even though Vander Jagt's money began slipping in 1984 and declined so badly that he was forced to borrow $2 million from banks to meet his spending budget for the 1986 campaign. Vander Jagt sent $5.7 million of direct financial aid to GOP candidates, while Coelho managed only $2.1 million to his.

Coelho also had less success at the polls in 1986 than he had predicted, but few people noticed. Most public attention on election night focused on a turnover in the Senate, where Democrats reclaimed control after six years of GOP rule, and did it by a 55–45 margin, larger than any party official had predicted. Incredibly, more seats changed hands in the Senate than in the House. When news accounts mentioned the House results, it was usually to give Coelho credit for a modest gain of perhaps eight seats. Even that turned out to be overstated. What was historic about the House election was the very lack of change. Only six incumbents were defeated in the general election, a rate of less than 2 percent, the lowest in history.

Out of the eight seats that Coelho claimed he gained, three, in Indiana, Minnesota, and North Carolina, were close contests where Democrats were disputing election-night totals that showed Republican incumbents ahead. Coelho contributed money from a recount fund, made up largely of donations from the Teamsters and undisclosed gifts from AFL-CIO unions, to legal battles trying to reverse those apparent GOP victories. Even a month after election day, Coelho was declaring the Democrats to be provisional winners in all three, placing their names in the program he printed for the dinner for new members. Asterisks indicated they had been elected "subject to recount." But in the end, none of the recounts succeeded. Coelho had to settle for a net gain of five seats, increasing the Democratic margin in the House to 258 Democrats and 177 Republicans. During six years with Ronald Reagan in the White House, Republicans had been unable to bring about much political realignment. Coelho's Democrats had regained more than half the seats lost in 1980.

Coelho came close to fulfilling his promise to save every single sitting Democrat. Besides St Germain, he rescued George Brown of California. Hearing that Republicans were taking aim at Brown, Coelho conducted a $7,500 poll that showed him well below 50 percent of the vote with only weeks to go before election day. Republicans later gave Coelho credit for saving Brown by rushing money and a seasoned campaign strategist to the district. The only incumbent Coelho lost was Robert Young of Missouri. Young had always allowed his wife to run his campaigns for him, and Coelho insisted that she step aside. "I said, 'Look, I don't care. You can continue to handle his campaign. You can handle this one. But the day after the election, you better remember, you're going to be responsible, nobody else. Not even Bob.'" But Young lost even with Coelho calling strategy. The Republican challenger attacked him as a big-spending labor flunky and pork-barrel politician.

The House elections earned a small place in history because of the high re-election rate. The power of incumbency, augmented by PAC money and the well-financed new party organizations, had succeeded in making the House something approaching an American peerage, with tenure almost guaranteed for life. Competition was withering rapidly. In the 1980 general elections thirty-four incumbents lost and thirty-three others won with precarious vote totals of less than 55 percent. But in 1986, six incumbents lost and only twenty-three were held to 55 percent or less. Of the incumbents who ran in 1986, only 16 percent failed to get more than 60 percent of the vote. Six years earlier that figure was 30 percent.

Coelho's machine was only one ingredient in the mix that kept incumbents in office. House members were being insulated from competition mainly by their taxpayer-financed staff and franked mail, the rapidly rising cost of campaigning, and their PAC money. David Price, a former political science professor who was one of Coelho's victorious challengers for a North Carolina seat, said he received some advice from a senior colleague who said, "The two best friends an incumbent could have [are] Mr. Frank and Mr. PAC." More and more, House elections were being decided long before voters entered the polling booth. Funds from special-interest donors frightened away challengers. Two elections were being held, one in the districts where the voters still pulled the levers, and another in the lobbyists' offices in Washington, D.C., where donors wrote the checks.

When the bills were counted from the 1986 elections, House incumbents were left with nearly $48 million in campaign cash, gathering interest for the 1988 races. Democrats held $28 million of that. And almost instantly, incumbents began raising even more PAC funds for the election two years in the future.

Coelho continued to press business PACS to support Democratic incumbents. A few days after the election he appeared before a lobbying workshop held by the National Association of Realtors, whose PAC spent $6 million during the campaign. He spoke for the new patronage system, the new business of politics. He advised the Realtors to shun broad philosophical issues, to concentrate their lobbying on housing subsidies affecting their pocketbooks directly, and to give their money accordingly. Otherwise, he said, "you're making a big mistake as business men and women."

" 'Special interest' is not a nasty word," Coelho told the Realtors. He warned the Republican-leaning group against too much partisanship. "If the perception is there that you're one-party-oriented, then [you will] suffer the consequences," he said.

Coelho's special-interest ties would soon cause him more embarrassment and legal trouble than he had ever envisioned. As the Texas savings and loan scandal unfolded in court, regulators made public documents indicating that some of the money allegedly dissipated by Dixon had gone to subsidize Coelho and the Democratic Congressional Campaign Committee. Billings sent by the captain of the yacht *High Spirits* showed that Dixon's savings association absorbed the expense for several dockside parties and cruises for Coelho. Coelho had sponsored eleven events aboard the yacht during 1985 and 1986, mostly entertaining donors. Court records also revealed the free trip Wright took on one of Vernon's airplanes in 1984. Accepting such in-kind donations from a business corporation was almost certainly a violation of federal law. Martin Franks blamed a clerical lapse, saying that aides should have asked for bills when none arrived. "We screwed up," he said. "It was an error of omission." Coelho accepted responsibility. The campaign committee and his own re-election fund paid a total of $48,451 to reimburse the insolvent savings association. Coelho issued a one-page statement saying, "Oversights were made in these instances which I genuinely regret."

But that humiliation was still months in the future when Coelho was elected Majority Whip by his colleagues on December 8, 1986. He received 167 votes, almost as many as he had predicted. He suspected that St Germain, who had been incommunicado in Florida for several days following the election, was among the few who had reneged on their promises. It was a decisive win; Rangel polled 78 votes and the third man remaining in the race, Bill Hefner of North Carolina, had so little support that officials announced his total as "fewer votes," mercifully withholding the number. Phyllis Coelho watched her husband's triumph from the gallery.

In accepting, he said, "There's one person who would be my great friend even if she weren't my wife." Members of the Democratic Caucus rose, applauding. They rose and clapped again when Coelho singled out Martin Franks for praise. Franks was leaving to become a lobbyist.

The next evening Coelho celebrated with members of the Speaker's Club in a private dining room a few blocks from the Capitol.

"We owe our victory yesterday to you people," Coelho told his donors. "Somebody in the press yesterday asked me, 'Do you owe your success in the Whip race to your success at the D-triple-C?' And I said, 'Is the Pope Catholic?' "

Coelho kept defending his integrity, though nobody present was questioning it. "We have been able not to be tainted in any way these past years," he said.

No longer was Coelho the "young and gallant monk without an order," the alter ego of the saintly, fictional Mr. Blue. No longer did he regard all wealth-seeking businessmen as selfish. The Portuguese-American farm kid, with his small-town Hoosier bride, had risen to political power on a tide of money.

"We are products of the American system," he said of himself and Phyllis. And to his donors he said, "You are products of the American system as well."

Afterword:
Toward Real Reform

Nearly everyone complains that something is wrong with the American political system. Liberals see a Congress bought by business interests, while PAC managers complain they are being shaken down by money-hungry legislators. Lawmakers detest the rising cost of campaigning, the inconvenience and indignity of asking for money, and the criticism they endure for accepting it. Democrats envy the Republican party's financial strength and decry the sinister influence of big money and expensive political technology while trying to get as much of both for themselves as possible. Republicans, betrayed by the business PACs they nourished, seethe at their inability to dislodge Democratic incumbents. Critics of various leanings deplore lawmakers who use their office to help themselves or moneyed benefactors. Liberal and conservative commentators alike are calling the system "corrupt."

The problem isn't corruption; it is more serious than that.

If unprincipled buying and selling of official favors was at fault, then the solution would be simple; honest legislators would refuse to participate, and prosecutors or voters would deal with the rest. To be sure, corruption does exist; it is hard to imagine any other community of 535 souls where felonies are so often proven. But those illegalities are only symptoms of the underlying sickness.

The true predicament is that perverse incentives twist the behavior of ordinary legislators. The system of money-based elections and lobbying rewards those who cater to well-funded interests, both by keeping them in office and by allowing men like Fernand St Germain to enrich themselves while they serve. It also punishes those who challenge the status quo, as D. G. Martin discovered. And it bends even the best of intentions, like Tony Coelho's priestly instincts, toward the courtship of moneyed cliques. As Coelho himself says, "the process buys you out." The system doesn't require bad motives to produce bad government.

America is becoming a special-interest nation where money is displacing votes. Congress commands less and less support among the electorate as it panders increasingly to groups with money, yet its members cling to office like barnacles on the hull of a broken-down steamer.

Voters seem to sense their diminished influence. The more money the politicians spend, ostensibly to get supporters to the polls, the more people just stay home. In 1986 only 33.4 percent of those old enough to cast ballots actually did so for House candidates, the lowest turnout since 1930. Congressional candidates spent a record $450 million in the 1986 elections, not counting additional millions in both hard and soft money raised by political parties and the independent electioneering of PACs. That represented an increase of 20 percent over the previous election and a rise of 131 percent from 1978. But the money served mostly to protect incumbents, especially in the House, where sitting members outspent challengers three to one.

The inverse relationship between spending and turnout

doesn't mean that too much money is being spent: quite the opposite. In races where both incumbents and challengers spend freely, turnout generally goes up, for the obvious reason that voters are more aware of the contest and the candidates. The problem is that the outcome of most races is being determined in advance, largely because fewer challengers can raise the ever-larger sums necessary to mount a credible campaign. Fifty-one House members had no opposition at all in the 1986 election, and more than 98 percent of the incumbents who ran were re-elected. For too many constituents, voting is becoming a waste of time.

Parties are losing their competition with the growing influence of special interests. Coelho's energetic "party-building" efforts have actually encouraged House Democrats to become more reliant on special-interest money. The campaign committee gets its own funds increasingly from lobbyists, PACs, and businessmen, and committee officials constantly push candidates to raise PAC money for themselves. House Democrats are drawing nearly half their re-election funds from PACs and a minuscule portion from the party. More than ever, members of Congress are political freebooters, financially beholden not to their party but to scores of favor-seeking groups.

Some political scientists are using the term "ungovernable" to describe such a society, marked by the increasing power of narrow factions. As cash-based constituencies proliferate, lawmakers are tugged and hauled in all directions. Defending particular spending programs, tax breaks, and permissive economic regulations keeps needed campaign funds flowing. But such measures collectively contribute to intractable federal budget deficits and a malfunctioning economy.

Individual lawmakers manage to escape their share of the blame for deficits and economic calamities. They win re-election regularly by attending ribbon-cuttings, announcing federal grants and contracts, sending out district-wide mailings, keeping their large staffs busy chasing passports and wayward Social Security checks, and accumulating enough money from PACs and lobbyists to make the strongest potential challengers seek alternative careers.

This is what Gary Jacobson, a political scientist and a scholar of the electoral system, has called "the fundamental flaw" in our political system: "great individual *responsiveness,* equally great collective *irresponsibility.*"

The United States isn't alone; all industrial democracies suffer from the special-interest malady. Britain, the oldest, had such an advanced case that the disorder was first called the "British disease." Political economist Mancur Olson, in his book *The Rise and Decline of Nations* and in other writings, shows that the longer a society enjoys stability, the more special-interest groups it accumulates and, not coincidentally, the slower its economy grows. He calls the illness "institutional sclerosis." His theory helps explain the puzzle of "stagflation," the combination of stagnant economic growth and rapid inflation of prices and wages in the 1970s and early 1980s that seemed to confound classic economic theory. Olson's thesis also provides a reason why the United States is losing its competitive edge to Japan, West Germany, Taiwan, and South Korea. They all began after World War II with clean slates, politically as well as industrially.

Olson's basic principle is that small groups have more incentive to take a larger share of the pie for themselves than they do to work toward enlarging the pie for everyone. Furthermore, narrow organizations such as labor unions, trade associations, or cartels are more likely to form than large, encompassing groups representing the interests of all citizens. In time, self-serving combinations proliferate and society becomes, as Olson puts it, "like a china shop filled with wrestlers battling over the china and breaking far more than they can carry away."

Washington looks very much like Olson's china shop, full of muscular groups clamoring for favors at the expense of the majority of citizens. Dairy farmers have large cooperatives and well-financed PACs to push for expensive federal subsidies and government-sanctioned cartels that push up prices for milk drinkers, cheese eaters, and ice-cream lovers, who themselves have no organized representation. Textile companies and the garment workers' union ask for protection from inexpensive imports, but shoppers have no spokesman in Washington. Construction unions demand government protection from non-union contractors, pushing up the price of apartments, factories, shops, and offices. Gun manufacturers and owners have the National Rifle Association, while people who wish to avoid being machine-gunned are on their own. The *Washington Representatives* directory lists more than 8,500 groups with agents in the capital. Even the lobbyists have lobbies: the American Society of Association Executives represents trade-association officials, the American League of Lobbyists serves the growing number of independent practitioners, and the National Association of Business Political Action Committees consists mainly of corporation-sponsored PACs.

The pernicious effect of narrow factions can be seen clearly in the way Congress set up housing-subsidy programs that aid wealthy developers more than they help poor families. It showed itself in a tax code that allowed "investors" to profit from coal-mining ventures that mined no coal. It was at work as tax-shelter syndicators grew rich through deals that drained the Treasury without producing any tangible product. It was working when Fernand St Germain engineered passage of an increase in federal deposit insurance for the benefit of the operators of savings associations rather than for the great majority of unsophisticated savers. It was apparent when Jim Wright interceded with federal regulators for the benefit of men like Tom Gaubert and Donald Dixon, and when he and Coelho pushed through legislation denying regulators the wherewithal to cut the insurance fund's losses. It is functioning as Washington fails year after year to eliminate colossal federal budget deficits that nearly every lawmaker agrees are a fiscal cancer.

The paralysis is especially severe when one party holds

the White House and the other retains control of one or both chambers of Congress, as has been the case for all but four years since Richard Nixon took office in 1969. This creates yet another perverse incentive; when a Republican is President, bad economic times are good politically for Democrats. Their electoral prospects soared in 1982 when the unemployment rate topped 10 percent the month before election day. In 1986, Coelho's media center produced ads dwelling on lost factory jobs and hard times on the farm. One poignant commercial used in distressed agricultural states showed scenes of an empty farmhouse accompanied by the ghostly voices of a departed mother, father, and children. "It wasn't just a farm, it was a family," the announcer said. The final frame showed two words: "Vote Democratic." Nothing was said about what more Democrats could do for farmers, who were already collecting $26 billion in annual subsidies accounting for 35 percent of their net income.

The campaign-finance laws make a bad situation worse. The reforms of the 1970s malfunctioned. No longer is political cash being passed around in brown paper bags; the money is mostly out in the open now, flowing through legally sanctioned channels that give it official approval. The reforms turned what had once been a subterranean trickle of special-interest money into a roaring cascade.

New reforms are being proposed, but the leading plan is at best cosmetic, and perhaps even harmful. After regaining control of the Senate, Democrats abandoned David Boren's bipartisan strategy for obtaining modest limits on PAC financing and began pushing a bill designed to induce candidates to accept quasi-voluntary spending caps. Common Cause backed the new Democratic spending-limit bill, but Republicans saw it as a threat to their own capital-intensive campaigns, especially in traditionally Democratic Southern states, where the GOP hoped to spend its way to parity. They blocked the bill with a filibuster that survived eight cloture attempts, a record.

There is no denying the good intentions of many who

favor spending limits, an understandable but superficial response to the rising cost of elections and the growth of PACs. However, limits won't do anything to provide more abundant funds for challengers or less troublesome sources of financing for incumbents. If lawmakers set limits too low, as it is in their narrow self-interest to do, challengers will be prevented from spending the sums necessary to match the built-in advantages of incumbents. Voters will have even fewer choices, and less influence.

Furthermore, limits are unlikely to be enacted so long as a Republican President holds veto power. And even if Democrats capture the White House and then push through spending limits, they will find ceilings unenforceable. Such a partisan law would inspire a host of new loopholes and evasions. Special-interest funds would be driven underground, where much soft money is already flowing. The best that can be said for spending caps is that if they are high enough they probably won't do much harm.

A promising opportunity is being missed. Many Republicans are becoming disenchanted with the PAC system as it dawns on them that most of the special-interest money continues to flow to Democrats. A bill offered by several GOP senators in 1987 proposed to eliminate PAC donations entirely. Even many PAC officials are disgusted with the unceasing pressure to contribute. Few in Washington would mourn the passing of the present system, if only it could be replaced by something more appealing. But spending limits can't cure the true illness; imposing them would be like commanding a fever patient to stop shivering. A better bill could earn the bipartisan support that spending limits have failed to attract.

True reform will require a program endorsed by both parties, one potent enough to return power to voters and to cure the paralysis that grips Congress. To arouse the interest of a skeptical public, it needs to be as progressive and exciting as the tax-reform bill of 1986. To work, it will require much stronger enforcement.

What is proposed here is an attempt at just such a com-

pact. Political parties would get both new freedom and
abundant funds to finance candidates. Incumbents would
turn over their fund-raising chores largely to their parties.
PACs would be forbidden to contribute to candidates, but
would be allowed to take on a new and more constructive
role. Voters would get more well-financed candidates to
choose from. Also, the dilution of the voter's influence
would be reversed by banning out-of-state campaign contributions altogether. Tax credits would promote more small
donations, the healthiest form of political money. A rejuve-
nated Federal Election Commission would begin strict enforcement of fewer and simpler regulations, including total
disclosure of all sources of party money. Tighter financial
ethics rules would govern House and Senate members.

Strengthening parties: To rein in the irresponsibility of
lawmakers and the undue influence of PACs and lobbyists,
authority needs to be returned to party leaders. As Gary
Jacobson writes in *The Politics of Congressional Elections:*
"Political parties are the only instruments we have
managed to develop for imposing collective responsibility
on legislators. There is nothing original about this observa-
tion: it is a home truth to which students of congressional
politics are inevitably drawn." The current campaign-finance laws weaken parties by limiting what they can spend
to support their own candidates. All such limits should be
lifted.

The limits, after annual upward adjustments for inflation, allowed the party campaign committees in 1988 to furnish financial aid of only $56,100 for a House candidate,
amounting to little more than one-tenth of what a typical
contestant needs to win a disputed election. The limit for
Senate candidates is between $109,700 and $1.9 million, de-
pending on the size of the state. These sums are but a minor
part of what nominees must spend to transmit their message to voters in the television age. Candidates ought to get
most of what they need from their parties, not from special-

interest donors. Most will turn to their parties gladly if the funds are there. The common complaint of incumbents is that they must spend too much time raising money themselves. If parties supplied the funds, party leaders would naturally have greater influence.

Scuttling limits on parties, a long-sought goal of Republicans, is not enough, however. Parties will have to get the money somewhere, and so far only Republicans raise anywhere near enough. Even they are finding that money is drying up as the Reagan era closes; the income of national GOP committees dropped 29 percent between 1985 and 1987. Furthermore, Coelho's experience shows that parties, when desperate for money, can themselves become too dependent on special-interest donors. Indeed, Republicans are already stepping up solicitations of PACs and lobbyists to replace their dwindling income from small donors. Removing limits on party spending without providing for income would almost guarantee that parties would once again become money laundries, merely passing through special-interest donations to candidates in a way that defeats limits on donors and conceals vital information from the voters. To some extent, that is already happening.

The solution is to provide massive public subsidies for the major political parties, enough to provide a minimally adequate campaign budget in every House and Senate race. It would cost just under $109 million per party during each two-year election cycle to provide $250,000 campaign allowances for candidates in all 435 House districts. Funding competitive Senate races in each of the 33 or 34 states that have seats up for election in a given year would cost roughly $60 million per party, given current rates of spending by successful candidates.

Federal funds should merely provide a minimum level of support. Parties also need new tools to gather private financial support from rank-and-file donors. They shouldn't become mere dispensaries of federal grants; they should be encouraged to recruit dues-paying memberships much larger than they have now. Direct mail is proving expensive and inefficient. The answer comes from PACs themselves, which developed a far more effective way to raise money—the payroll checkoff.

The Teamsters' union was raising about $10 million during the 1987–88 election cycle through aggressive use of the checkoff. Under collective bargaining contracts, employers agree to withhold voluntary PAC donations from union members' paychecks in the same way they do for dues. Union officials make their pitch once, and after that the dollars flow in automatically, week after week. Dairy-farmer cooperatives employ a similar device, building sizable PACs by withholding political donations from checks they send to farmers to pay for collectively marketed milk. The United Auto Workers, the National Education Association, and other unions also use the checkoff with great success.

A payroll scheme could work even better for parties, which have tens of millions of potential donors. Congress could require employers to give workers an option of having, say, $1 a week set aside to finance their party, or to be divided between both. Employers would forward the money with their regular Social Security and federal income-tax withholding, with almost no additional paperwork required. The IRS would then send the pooled donations to the party organizations designated by the workers. To prevent coercion, employees shouldn't have to disclose their party preference to their boss, only to the government and the party.

Party-based public financing would be controversial; lawmakers would resist giving up the autonomy that their PAC-based financing now gives them. It would also require the party organizations to adapt: who, exactly, should decide which candidates receive funds, and how much? And any number of tough decisions would have to be made about important details, such as when, or even whether, to subsidize splinter parties. Should Lyndon LaRouche's party qualify? What about the next John Anderson? The next George Wallace?

These, however, are questions of tactics. The strategic goal should be to strengthen parties through steady, dependable income from paycheck withholding and federal subsidies. With ample funds and the freedom to deploy them, the parties would gain strength and greatly offset the influence of PACs and lobbyists. And with money flowing exclusively from the Treasury and from voluntary paycheck withholdings of ordinary citizens, party leaders would no longer be forced to court moneyed factions the way Tony Coelho did.

Curbing special interests: Congress should outlaw PAC donations outright, just as past reforms have forbidden the use of corporate money and funds from labor-union treasuries. It should also banish out-of-state donations. The legal lines that lawyers have smudged and blurred over the years should be redrawn crisply and brightly; candidates ought to accept money only from their party or from individuals who live in their home state.

Limits on individual donations to candidates should remain at $1,000 per election. But parties ought to be forbidden to accept PAC donations, and the annual limit on gifts to parties should be reduced to $1,000 per person, from the present $20,000. Otherwise, operations like the Speaker's Club will continue, and candidates will have too great an opportunity to launder big gifts through the party.

PACs can't be eliminated, but they should be reformed. Most smaller PACs would probably vanish if forbidden to donate, their lobbyist masters glad to be off the fund-raising treadmill. But larger PACs, with permanent political staffs and income in the millions, won't go away, nor should they. Instead, they should put their money to worthwhile ends.

Congress should create strong inducements for PACs to spend their money on grass-roots action, rather than trying to buy influence with Congress. They should be encouraged to turn their efforts to registering and turning out voters sympathetic to their aims and promoting their views on issues widely through the electorate. PACs that engage only in such healthy activities ought to be given freedom to raise funds from almost any source, including corporate or union treasuries, and in any amount. For those that do not, the limit on what they may collect from individuals should be reduced to $1,000 per year, from the present $5,000.

Reformed PACs would be doing the same sort of thing already being undertaken by many political groups that currently abuse their tax-exempt status through electioneering. Such groups now conduct voter drives and "educational" activities intended to help specific candidates in specific states or congressional districts, often in concert with the parties or candidates they are helping, as SANE did for D. G. Martin, and the A. Philip Randolph Institute did for Mike Espy. Voter drives aren't inherently bad, quite the contrary. But the tax-exempt groups become, in effect, conduits for disguised political donations. The money can come from any source, in any amount, and need not be disclosed. This situation is ripe for abuse.

Such tax-exempt entities should also reform. Grass-roots voter activity should be allowed only if it is wholly independent of any candidate's campaign. The same rules should apply here as now apply to independent spending by PACs; otherwise the money becomes just like a direct donation. Also, all such activity should be disclosed fully, with a breakdown of the states and congressional districts the outlays are intended to affect.

Indeed, reformed PACs and reformed tax-exempt groups should be merged into a single new class of political organization. Eligibility to receive tax-deductible donations would be another powerful inducement for PACs to adopt a new, more positive role. PAC defenders, a diminishing class, say the special-interest funds "involve people in the political process." PACs should be stimulated to make good on that claim.

Unreformed PACs will still be able to conduct independent political campaigns attacking specific candidates. This is unavoidable in a free society. But such spending is overrated. The NRA's effort against D. G. Martin seemed to work in 1984, but more ambitious efforts, like the American Medical Association's campaign against Pete Stark, have failed spectacularly.

The best restraint on independent spending is a natural one, already available. The narrower and more self-interested the group doing the spending, the more its endorsement is likely to backfire. During 1986 a PAC called Auto Dealers and Drivers for Free Trade conducted polling to learn where they might launch independent campaigns to support candidates opposed to protectionist legislation, but found that many voters resented the idea that Japanese car dealers would try to influence them. Congress should require that any independent political ads carry both video and audio disclaimers saying clearly that "this advertisement is paid for by and expresses the opinions of" the sponsoring group. Printed or mailed material should contain similar disclaimers in large type. Voters can then assess the messenger with the message.

Unreformed PACs might also turn to bundling, but this would become only a slight problem with the outlawing of donations from outside the candidate's state. This is a fundamental reform that ought to be undertaken regardless of what is done about PACs. Most of the ills of the current system stem from the way in which donors become a second constituency, with interests often alien to those of the local voters. Texas developers and Wall Street tax-shelter syndicators should have no role in Georgia politics; nor should wealthy life-insurance salesmen around the country be able to use their money to limit the choices of Oregon voters. If a workable enforcement mechanism could be devised, Congress probably ought to limit House candidates to accepting funds from within their own district as well.

An additional reform would benefit even primary candidates, who would get little of the plentiful new party funds. Congress should enact a 100 percent tax credit for small contributions to House or Senate candidates or to political parties. This is another form of public financing, but one that doesn't rely on a cumbersome and potentially unfair federal bureaucracy to dispense the money. Candidates who have qualified for a place on the primary ballot would be authorized to give standardized receipts to their donors, like a W-2 form. Donors could submit them with their income-tax returns to claim a dollar-for-dollar tax reduction, up to a limit of perhaps $100 per taxpayer. Candidates could say, "Loan me $100 until next year."

Tax credits and party subsidies would cost perhaps $500 million every two years, maybe more. But that is a pittance by comparison with the economic waste and annual federal deficits that the current system is producing. The money should come straight from general revenues. Congress already spends about that much for its mailings and personal staffs, a form of campaign subsidy that is now denied to challengers.

Less costly, but urgently needed, is an overhaul of disclosure rules. Nearly everyone now agrees that political parties should fully reveal all receipts and expenditures, regardless of their purpose. Building funds, recount funds, "non-federal" accounts—all should be thrown open to public view. Federal disclosure rules should be extended to state and local parties that participate in elections with a federal candidate on the ballot. The Federal Election Commission should be required to computerize all receipts and expenditures by parties, candidates, and other political committees within thirty days of receiving reports. Parties, candidates, and political committees should also be given incentives to file reports directly on computer tape or discs, easing their own paperwork burden and making computerized information available instantly. A basic principle of campaign finance is that dirty money always goes where it can hide. The dark places must be fully illuminated.

Restoring competition: A resurgence of competition in House and Senate elections would occur once PAC donations and out-of-state money were banished and parties given ample funds and the freedom to finance promising challengers. But even more should be done. In economic terms, the goal should be to lower the entry barriers to politics, giving consumers more choices.

Public debates should be required and encouraged. One reason money provides incumbents with such an advantage is that it allows them to avoid face-to-face appearances with their opponents while campaigning instead by purchasing broadcast commercials and mass mailings. Public debates give a challenger free opportunities to communicate with voters.

A reform package should require, by amending House and Senate rules, that lawmakers debate their election opponents in mutually agreeable settings open to news coverage, including live broadcasts. The number of debates should be specified; three should be a minimum, five or six would be better.

An impartial authority is needed to sanction and promote debates. Such a body has been created with the support of the Democratic and Republican parties to oversee debates between the 1988 presidential nominees. The National Commission on Presidential Debates should be made a permanent body, and expanded to include congressional debates as well.

Challengers should enjoy one of the great advantages of incumbents: the franking privilege. Major-party nominees should be allowed to send two or three free mailings to every home in the district during the campaign. There should be no restriction on the political content of the mailings or the timing. For incumbents these campaign mailings should count against the limits that currently apply to their "official," quasi-campaign mailings.

Making laws work: The Federal Election Commission doesn't do its job, and any serious reform plan must overhaul it or replace it.

Congress designed the commission to fail, building in the

propensity for partisan deadlocks, insisting on the appointment of pliant commissioners, and creating a morass of procedural defenses for suspected wrongdoers. Enforcement is so weak that political professionals often calculate that the benefits of taking money in violation of the rules far outweigh the slim risk of being caught and fined. "People take the attitude that the commission is never going to get four votes, and so they can do anything they want," says Daniel Swillinger, a lawyer who once was an assistant general counsel at the FEC.

The commission needs a strong chairman. Unlike that of most other regulatory agencies, the FEC's leadership is largely ceremonial and rotates among its six members. Each serves a year at a time, presiding at meetings and signing documents, but lacks authority to hire or fire staff or exert more than a trivial influence on the agenda. In all important matters, each commissioner has an equal say, making drift and deadlock inevitable.

A reform plan should give the chairman a four-year term and the power to hire and fire staff, to authorize routine inquiries into alleged violations, and to issue warning letters or citations for the minor violations that make up the bulk of enforcement cases. The other commission members should vote only to set policies, to authorize subpoenas in the most serious investigations, and to act as a court of appeal.

Commission procedures also need streamlining; it currently requires several months and cumbersome legal analysis before the FEC can extract a fine for a tardy disclosure report. For such common offenses, the equivalent of a traffic ticket would do. The laws need simplifying; the unenforceable state-by-state spending limits for presidential candidates should be abolished, for example. The FEC also should hire a cadre of trained investigators skilled in following the paper trails that money leaves. Presently its lawyers take a passive role, mainly evaluating statements sent in by complainants and accused violators. The commission also needs a secure budget that can't be held hostage by members of Congress who are displeased when their own campaign violations are uncovered. It should have what California's election-law agency has—a yearly, inflation-adjusted budget that the legislature can increase, but can't legally cut.

Ideally, the present commissioners should be removed and a new, five-member panel installed. The current members, with one or two exceptions, are too closely identified with the PACs, parties, and incumbent lawmakers they are supposed to be regulating. A new slate of commissioners would allow a fresh start and help restore public trust. Reducing the size to five would also get rid of the built-in tendency for the commission to deadlock. The structural bias should be in favor of enforcement, not against.

Without safeguards, a strong chairman might abuse his or her position for partisan advantage. That danger can be reduced by requiring that the chairman be chosen from outside the President's political party, subject, of course, to confirmation by Congress. The appointment should run until two years after the following presidential election, so that the chairman will handle any violations by the winner.

Nothing can guarantee perfect justice, naturally. A President still might install a chairman who is accommodating or even corrupt. But unjust enforcement actions could still be appealed to the federal courts. The law also ought to be changed to make it easier for victims of serious violations to take perpetrators to court if the commission refuses to act.

Structural changes alone aren't enough. The FEC's institutional culture has decayed, and a new spirit must be instilled. Commissioners spend their time haggling over legal technicalities, drafting ever more permissive interpretations of increasingly complicated rules, and maneuvering for partisan advantage. They see their constituency as the members of Congress and the parties, not the voting public.

The FEC's performance has been so poor, and its friends are so few, that an overhaul might be the easiest of all reforms to get through Congress. Coelho, for one, seemed ready as he pushed his lawsuit in the St Germain case. "Do away with the whole damn thing. It's a farce what happens," he said. "It's used for cover when you want it, and you abuse it when you want to. The public is not benefiting from the damn thing at all. . . . I think you go back to the law of the jungle and the public would demand that something else be put in its place."

Improving congressional ethics: The special-interest malady has inflamed a chronic sore spot—the financial ethics of lawmakers. With Washington awash in political money, lawmakers face an ever-diminishing chance of being evicted from office. At the same time, they find increasingly tempting opportunities to benefit financially from their offices. For too many the enticements are overwhelming. This only tightens the bonds between the favor-seeking groups and the legislators.

Congress should abolish honoraria payments to lawmakers, recognizing that this form of honest graft is morally indistinguishable from the illegal gratuities forbidden by the bribery statute. For the same reason, Congress should also outlaw free vacations from special-interest groups. Travel and entertainment for members of Congress should be paid by the government if it is truly official, by their party or campaign committee if it is political, or out of their own pockets.

Executive branch officials are under such tight rules that they are forbidden to accept a free lunch from a contractor, a lobbyist, or even a newspaper reporter. But House members allow themselves practically unlimited free travel, food, and drink from lobbyists. This ethical double standard must be ended.

At the same time, House and Senate salaries should be increased substantially, to a range at least comparable to that of a junior vice president of a mid-size corporation—say, $150,000 a year. Demagogic arguments aside, skimping on congressional pay only encourages honest graft.

A reform plan should also close the loophole that allows senior members—those elected before 1980—to pocket leftover campaign funds after they leave office. After the 1986 elections thirty-eight House members each had more than $300,000, and nine of them possessed more than half a million. Lobbyists scornfully call these "retirement funds," even as they write additional checks. All unspent campaign money should revert to political parties or charities after each election, an ethical reform that would also help promote electoral competition.

The personal financial reports of lawmakers should be subject to review and random audits by the General Accounting Office, a congressional agency. Presently members are for all practical purposes on the honor system, and can too easily hide embarrassing financial dealings from the voters. Lawmakers should be required to disclose their federal income-tax returns each year, both to deter unsavory deals and to show whether they are avoiding taxes. The upright won't object to this. Disclosure might deter some from seeking public office, but only those with something to hide.

Finally, House and Senate members should be brought under the special prosecutor provision of the Ethics in Government Act, from which they are currently exempt. The House and Senate ethics committees have shown themselves to be entirely too lenient when judging colleagues. Given the collegial nature of Congress, it is hard to imagine that such committees of fellow members could ever act differently. But House and Senate members, if suspected of any wrongdoing, should be investigated just as thoroughly and, if warranted, prosecuted just as vigorously as a member of the executive branch.

Washington insiders will find these suggestions hopelessly utopian and doomed to instant rejection. They aren't trifling, to be sure. And they aren't designed to appeal to the

narrow self-interest of the legislators who have the authority to enact them.

Still, no less will be required to cure the malady, which
victimizes nearly everyone. It freezes Republicans into
permanent minority status in the House, where they grow
increasingly bitter and isolated. It propels Democrats to
consort with commercial interests in ways that don't
square with the traditions of the party of working people.
It makes lobbyists into bagmen for lawmakers, rather
than advocates for the merits of their causes. Tony Coelho,
as much as he exploited the system to advance himself in
the House, is also a victim; his talent, energy, and priestly
urge to help the handicapped and downtrodden were redi-
rected into an unhealthy quest for special-interest money.
Perhaps when the afflicted perceive the ravages the illness is causing them, they will agree to swallow the medi-
cine. Indeed, Coelho himself has drafted a bill jointly with
Common Cause and has promised, to the delight of the reform group's leadership, to push for passage if the Senate
acts.

The Coelho–Common Cause measure has a partisan fla-
vor and relies mainly on unenforceable spending limits. It
would decree that House candidates spend no more than
$400,000 per campaign, including a maximum of $125,000
from PACs. It does nothing to strengthen the FEC. It provides federal subsidies to candidates, but doesn't bolster
parties. In fact, it would reimpose limits on all party spending that attacks candidates by name, reversing Coelho's
court defeat in the St Germain case. It has only two Republican supporters among the first ninety-four sponsors.

Still, Coelho's plan does contain some real, though modest, reforms. It would force disclosure of soft money and
outlaw Valley Education Fund and other PACs controlled
by candidates. It would require candidates to raise at least
$32,000 in small donations (under $250) from residents of
their home state in order to qualify for federal subsidies—a
tiny step toward returning power to constituents. And Co-

elho's rebirth as a campaign-law reformer is itself an encouraging sign.

David Boren's modest PAC-limit amendment in 1986 showed that few members of the Senate are willing to defend the present system and that bipartisan support can be mustered for a reform plan. But it failed in part because it was too weak; it was seen by both parties as threatening their own interests without accomplishing fundamental reform. Common Cause's 1987 proposals for spending limits stalled, not because Congress was unwilling to enact reform, but because the bills were far too partisan and not good policy. The Senate bill attracted more support than it deserved from newspaper editorialists, who correctly sensed the severity of Washington's money fixation but failed to consider whether the plan really made sense.

Reformers have fallen into a trap. In their desire to act in the name of progress, they have been too timid and made tactical compromises that robbed their proposals of moral and intellectual strength. The 1987 Common Cause Senate bill originally included a large amount of public financing for candidates, but that feature repelled some potential supporters. Seeing that Democratic incumbents were mainly interested in putting ceilings on the spending of their opponents, the bill's sponsors redrafted it to strip out nearly all the public-financing features. This picked up a few wavering Democrats but only seemed to stiffen Republican resolve.

Success isn't likely to come from watering down an ill-conceived proposal. It more probably will emerge from rethinking failed solutions and seeking bipartisan support for new ones. This was illustrated when the House in 1986 approved a laudable 100 percent tax credit for small political gifts, a measure sponsored originally by New Yorkers Matthew McHugh, a liberal Democrat, and Barber Conable, a moderate Republican. One reason it later died in the Senate is that Common Cause leaders saw the tax-credit plan as a competitor to their own PAC-limit bill and claimed that a credit would amount to a new "perquisite" for incumbents. Such a "not invented here" mentality breeds only failure.

The common lore in Washington is that a new scandal of Watergate proportions must occur before Congress will agree to further changes. Perhaps that is so. Yet the scandal already seems to be happening, openly, as special-interest groups pour ever-larger sums into the campaign committees and personal bank accounts of incumbent lawmakers. Laws are going unenforced, millions in soft money are being raised and spent in secret, and Congress is letting the nation settle into an economic morass as it tends to hundreds of moneyed patrons. This time there have been no congressional hearings to dramatize the scandal or give it a name, because Congress itself is the center of it. But at the rate things are going, there will eventually be enough prosecutions and exposés to raise a public outcry.

Congress is already embarrassed by the current mess. Old positions are softening, and a breakthrough is possible if reformers dare to think big. Perhaps a challenger like D. G. Martin will win by making special-interest ties an issue, causing other incumbents to feel suddenly that their PAC money has changed from an asset to a liability. Perhaps a new President will make campaign-finance reform a top priority the way Ronald Reagan unexpectedly seized and promoted tax reform. Perhaps Common Cause will reconsider its quest for spending limits and try for a bolder plan with wider support, or perhaps some new reform group will take up the torch.

Until then, matters will surely grow worse.

Acknowledgments

This book is based largely on information provided by Tony Coelho, who risked perhaps more than he knew to show me the inner workings of American politics. By allowing me free access to DCCC meetings, by providing hundreds of pages of internal memoranda, and by speaking frankly in hours of tape-recorded interviews and informal conversations, he came very close to fulfilling his promise to open everything, withholding in the end only a full accounting of the soft money he raised and such particularly sensitive reports as those from his comptroller and the manager of the Speaker's Club. He displayed in the months of our unusual association a candor that could only flow from a conviction that he had nothing to hide. I found him to be a man of enormous warmth, talent, and energy. I view it as a tragic waste that our political process has channeled so much of his drive, and that of other gifted lawmakers, into perverse directions. Tony Coelho and his colleagues deserve a better system.

Phyllis Coelho opened her home and her heart, submitting to scores of personal questions with engaging grace. Martin Franks, Mark Johnson, Terence McAuliffe, Peggy Connolly, Tom King, Tom O'Donnell, Bob Chlopak, Tom Nides, Andy Spahn, Bill Combs, Kathryn Smiley, Michael Fraioli, and the other staff members of the DCCC always made me feel welcome and seldom failed to provide answers to my unending queries. My stimulating talks with Robert Bauer, the committee's general counsel, showed me the legal rationale behind the DCCC's use of union and corporate funds. I gained historical perspective on the DCCC and Tony Coelho's career from Jim Corman, Andy

Jacobs, Bill Sweeney, Marta David, Archie Nahigian, and Mike Berman. Details of Coelho's early career I gleaned from B. F. Sisk, both through conversation and by reading his book, *The Memoir of Bernie Sisk,* an oral-history project by A. I. Dickman published in 1980 by the University of California, Davis.

For allowing me to sit in on regular staff meetings at the National Republican Congressional Committee, I thank its chairman, Guy Vander Jagt, who also made his time available for many hours of interviews. Wyatt Stewart, the NRCC's finance chairman, and Rodney Smith, his counterpart at the National Republican Senatorial Committee, opened their ledgers for me and showed how the NRCC and NRSC had amassed their colossal small-donor base. Joseph Gaylord gave me access to the NRCC's expensive and sensitive tracking-poll data and much more. His staff, especially Barbara Pardue, Ed Goeas, Chris Bowman, Ben Ginsberg, Randy Moorhead, Steve Lotterer, and Dale Weiss, were unfailingly responsive, as was Jan Baran, its general counsel, and Mark Braden, general counsel to the Republican National Committee. Historical information, including Vander Jagt's early exhortations to Dow Chemical executives, I found in *The Orator: Guy Vander Jagt on the Hustings,* by Paul Reid, published by Green Hill Publishers in 1984.

The Federal Election Commission, for all its failings as an enforcement agency, nevertheless employs some of the most dedicated and public-spirited civil servants to be found anywhere in government. Kent Cooper, who presides over the FEC's public records division, has been my guide for many years through the millions of pages of reports filed by candidates, PACs, and parties. Robert Biersack, the FEC's supervising statistician, helped me see the order in that jungle of numbers. It is from his work, embodied in a series of reports issued with the help of Sharon Snyder of the FEC's press office, that I drew many aggregate figures on campaign spending. I owe special thanks also to Fred Eiland, the commission's patient spokesman, for sharing his comprehensive understanding of the FEC's sometimes bewildering actions, or lack of them. But none of the FEC's staff should be held accountable for my own harsh judgment of the commission itself, which I base upon the public record the FEC has written in its own enforcement actions.

For much specific data on campaign donations I relied upon the FEC's innovative Direct Access Project, an on-line computer database instituted by staff director John Surina. It allowed me to fetch reports on candidates' spending and PAC receipts through my own desktop computer. I have also drawn information from a commercial database, *Washington On-line,* through which I could track an individual's donations of $200 or more to any federal candidate or political committee.

Peter Lauer of the American Medical Association PAC, Bob Bannister of the National Association of Home Builders, Albert Abrahams of the National Association of Realtors, Tom Nemet of the Auto Dealers and Drivers for Free Trade, and Wayne LaPierre of the National Rifle Association shared information about their political activities. Ellen Miller and her staff at the Center for Responsive Politics provided additional illumination through their extensive interviews with PAC managers, in which many described candidly—and anonymously—the pressures applied to them. These I drew from the center's treatise *PACs on PACs: The View from the Inside,* which it issued in 1988.

Documentation of Fernand St Germain's financial activities was provided in voluminous detail by the House Committee on Standards of Official Conduct (better known by its informal name, the ethics committee), in its report *Investigation of Financial Transactions Participated in and Gifts of Transportation Accepted by Representative Fernand J. St Germain* (100th Congress, 1st Session, Report 100-46). The committee's investigation was triggered by a story I wrote with the help of my *Wall Street Journal* colleague Tim Carrington. Additional details on St Germain came from persons who do not wish to be identified, and I thank them.

I have also drawn details from ethics committee reports on William Boner, Mario Biaggi, Dan Daniel, George Hansen, Austin Murphy, James Weaver, Charles Wilson of California (not to be confused with the Texas congressman of the same name), and the Koreagate affair. The committee staff's ability to unearth facts, though exercised too seldom and too narrowly confined as to subject matter even when used, has always exceeded by a large margin the ability of the twelve committee members to draw proper conclusions or impose appropriate remedies.

For granting me an inside view of their political campaigns, I thank D. G. Martin, Alex McMillan, and John Holmes, and their campaign aides, especially Martin's campaign manager Henry Doss and staff man Todd Gorelick, McMillan's campaign manager Chris Henick and press spokesman Jay Timmons, and Holmes's press aide Laurie White. All generously shared personal observations, polling data, and internal memoranda not usually given to reporters. I relied heavily on the day-to-day campaign reporting of the Providence *Journal,* especially that of its political sage Charles Bakst, and the Charlotte *Observer,* whose reporter Jim Morrill turned out an analysis of the financing of the Martin–McMillan race that ought to be imitated by other local newspapers.

My information on the rocky fate of David Boren's amendment came largely from the *Congressional Record,* from interviews with Boren himself, and from interviews and countless conversations with his dedicated and patient legislative aide Greg Kubiak. Additional help came from John Chafee, Rudy Boschwitz, the National Republican Senatorial Committee's PAC director John Sheehan, Fred Wertheimer of Common Cause, and from Republican aides who, while most helpful, prefer to remain unacknowledged publicly.

The savings-and-loan fiasco has been covered in a variety of publications, congressional hearings, and court records too numerous to cite exhaustively here. My account is based in part on interviews with Coelho, Tom Gaubert, Edwin

Gray, and George Mallick, among others; on statements issued by Jim Wright and his staff; and on a report by Aubrey Harwell to the chairman of the Federal Home Loan Bank Board.

The influence of big money on American politics is nothing new, as I was reminded by Louise Overacker's classic volume *Money in Elections,* published in 1932 by Macmillan. Fifty-six years ago she concluded that spending limits were futile and only encouraged concealment, that efforts to raise enough money in small donations usually didn't work, and that public financing was the best solution. The good sense and durability of her work helped convince me to embrace party-based public financing of House and Senate races, although I had earlier opposed it and argued instead only for full disclosure, fewer regulations, and strict enforcement. I also found support for party-based public funding in the work of Herbert Alexander of the Citizens Research Foundation, from whom I have learned much in nearly fifteen years of reporting on money and politics.

For his cogent insights I am obliged to Gary Jacobson's works, particularly his *Politics of Congressional Elections,* first published by Little, Brown, in 1983. An extensively revised second edition was issued in 1987. In Mancur Olson's work I found a theoretical explanation for what I had observed to be the perverse effects of special-interest groups. I drew especially on his book *The Rise and Decline of Nations,* published in 1982 by Yale University Press.

Indispensable to me as I worked were the 1986 and 1988 editions of the *Almanac of Federal PACs* by Ed Zuckerman, published by Amward Publications, and various volumes of *The Almanac of American Politics,* by Michael Barone and Grant Ujifusa, published every two years by the National Journal. Other helpful reference works were *Vital Statistics on Congress 1987–1988,* by Norman Ornstein, Thomas Mann, and Michael Malbin, published in 1987 by the American Enterprise Institute; and *Politics in America: The 100th*

Congress, edited by Alan Ehrenhalt and published in 1987 by Congressional Quarterly.

Above all I was inspired, entertained, and informed by the work of a fellow journalist from another era, William Riordon of the New York *Evening Post.* At the turn of the century he captured on paper the political philosophy that George Washington Plunkitt propounded at Graziano's bootblack stand in what was then the New York County Courthouse. Riordon printed Plunkitt's words first in his newspaper and later as a book, *Series of Very Plain Talks on Very Practical Politics,* published by McClure, Phillips, in 1905. The book was re-issued in 1948, and published again as a paperback in 1963 by E. P. Dutton under the title *Plunkitt of Tammany Hall.*

My employer, *The Wall Street Journal,* tolerated my erratic schedule during the 1986 elections, granted me generous leave afterward, and allowed me use of the Washington bureau's files and research facilities. Albert Hunt, the bureau chief, and Norman Pearlstine, the managing editor, gave me freedom to work and think, never suggesting what result I should reach. I am deeply grateful. I also drew encouragement from the example of my colleagues Jeffrey Birnbaum and Alan Murray. I gained both from their newspaper reports and their book *Showdown at Gucci Gulch,* a superb account of the passage of the tax-reform bill, published by Random House in 1987. I owe thanks also to my *Wall Street Journal* colleagues John Yang and Len Apcar, for their reporting of the Texas S&L mess and their willingness to share unpublished material from their efforts.

My literary agent, Raphael Sagalyn, patiently explained to me the difference between writing a book and stapling together all my old newspaper stories. My editor, Ashbel Green, made me look like a better writer than I am. He either rehabilitated or excised lame metaphors, murky phrasings, awkward constructions, and incorrect facts. Thomas Mann of the Brookings Institution, a former executive director of the American Political Science Association, reviewed a draft of the manuscript and offered helpful criticism. However, I absolve all but myself of blame for any surviving mistakes or errors of judgment.

Finally, I thank my family for putting up with me. The cost of writing a book, for them, was measured in softballs unpitched, Saturday morning pancakes uncooked, dinner parties unattended, and vacation trips untaken. To Beverly, Courtney, and Mark I promise better days.

Index

A Note About the Author

Brooks Jackson grew up in Hartford City, Indiana,
and graduated from the Medill School of Journalism
at Northwestern University. As a member of the
investigative team of the Associated Press, he
produced a series of stories in 1974 on illegal
contributions by the dairy-farmer lobby to Richard
Nixon, Hubert Humphrey, and Wilbur Mills, and
the bribery indictments of John Connally. This
series won the Raymond Clapper Award for
Washington reporting in 1975. He covered the White
House for the Associated Press during the Carter
years, and in 1980 joined *The Wall Street Journal,*
where he writes extensively on campaign finance
and the use of money in lobbying. His reports on the
financing of the 1984 elections, including details of
Walter Mondale's legally questionable "delegate
committees," made him co-winner of the Worth
Bingham prize for investigative reporting in 1985.

A Note on the Type

This book was set in a face called Primer, designed by Rudolph Ruzicka (1883–1978). Mr. Ruzicka was earlier responsible for the design of Fairfield and Fairfield Medium, Linotype faces whose virtues have for some time been accorded wide recognition.

The complete range of sizes of Primer was first made available in 1954, although the pilot size of 12-point was ready as early as 1951. The design of the face makes general reference to Linotype Century—long a serviceable type, totally lacking in manner or frills of any kind—but brilliantly corrects its characterless quality.

Composed by ComCom,
Allentown, Pennsylvania

Printed and bound by R.R. Donnelley & Sons,
Harrisonburg, Virginia

DESIGNED BY MARYSARAH QUINN